The Pigs That Ate the Garden

The Pigs That Ate the Garden

A Human Ecology from Papua New Guinea

Peter D. Dwyer

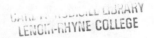
THE UNIVERSITY OF MICHIGAN PRESS

Ann Arbor

Library of Congress Cataloging-in-Publication Data

Dwyer, Peter D., 1937–
    The pigs that ate the garden : a human ecology from Papua New
Guinea / Peter D. Dwyer.
      p.   cm.
    Includes bibliographical references.
    ISBN 0-472-10157-9
    1. Etoro (Papua New Guinea people)—Food.   2. Etoro (Papua New
Guinea people)—Economic conditions.   I. Title.
DU740.42.D89   1990
338.1′9′0899912—dc20

90-32835
CIP

Acknowledgments

To abandon one's own life-style and live with another, where there may be nothing familiar except the humanity of people, is to ask that your hosts be exceptionally caring. If, at the same time, you want to understand a little of the unfamiliar—to record this, that and the other thing using tape measure, compass, vernier calipers, and balances—then your caring hosts need to be tolerant as well. At the very least they need a keen sense of humor. In 1979–80 my friends and I tramped across the gardens of all the people who lived at Bobole in the mountains of the southwest corner of the Southern Highlands Province, Papua New Guinea. We measured their gardens and peered at their crops, but our boots were not gentle and I do not know what or how much we may have spoiled. Like all curious travelers, adrift on new experiences, we were dependent on our hosts. "Which water is for drinking and which for washing?" "Where should we go to urinate and where to defecate?" "What foods are available and from whom is it proper to purchase?" "I have carried an ax but lack the skills to keep myself in firewood." "May I have the skeletal remains from animals you have eaten?" I had gone to Papua New Guinea to collect other people's food scraps! And all these needs and wants had to be met without the ability to speak the language of our hosts.

At Bobole and the neighboring community of Namosado everyone was caring and tolerant and laughed a lot. For the privilege of allowing us to live among them, I thank them all, young and old, women and men. Many are named in the pages that follow, but those who are not also gave practical assistance, taught us, or helped in less tangible ways. Efala's importance in our lives and to this book was huge. He was friend, mentor, and, when necessary, go-between; a patient teacher with slow learners, who, after fifteen months, advanced our language skills from not very adequate pidgin to, perhaps, tourist-standard Etolo. In describing the connections—the relationships—among Etolo people, and between them and their environment, I intend that this book be a *human* ecology of the people with whom we lived. My gratitude for all that they gave is contained in that intention.

Other people and some institutions also assisted. My friends Kristine Plowman and Bruce Dwyer shared life at Bobole, helped in countless ways, and had much better ears than I did for the language. Ray Kelly, who had lived among Etolo a decade earlier, gave useful advice and shared information both before and after our stay. Greg Gordon, Kay Solar, and Jeffrey Willmer each visited for a few weeks, enlivened our home, and did not ask that we explain too much of what we did not yet understand. One day's walk to the northeast, David and Elizabeth Richards and Alf and Wilma Norman of the Asia Pacific Christian Mission at Gangalu looked after many practical details—relaying mail and supplies and hosting us and our friends on trips to and from Bobole. I was granted periods of leave by the University of Queensland, was affiliated to the Biology Department of the University of Papua New Guinea, and was awarded research visas by the government of Papua New Guinea. And, of course, I needed more help while writing this book. Ken Aplin, Tim Flannery, and James Menzies gave advice about identification and nomenclature of mammals. Ray Kelly, Monica Minnegal, Peter Ogilvie, Kristine Plowman, Edward Schieffelin, Jeffrey Willmer, and the late Ralph Bulmer read and commented on parts or all of what I have written. Others helped by asking questions or disagreeing when I gave talks. Robyn Brand, Fay Marsack, Evadne Miller, and Sandra Nielson did the typing and the retyping! Peter Gofton and Lynn Pryor completed the figures. For the warmth, willingness, and needed critical content of their assistance, I thank them all.

Contents

Tables

Figures

A Note on Pronunciation and Spelling of Etolo Words

a:　as *a* in f*a*ther

e:　as *e* in b*e*t

i:　as *ee* in b*ee*

o:　as *au* in c*au*ght; sometimes as *oa* in c*oa*t, especially when at the end of a word

u:　as *oo* in sh*oo*t; sometimes *oo* as in b*oo*k

ai:　as *eye*

au:　as *ow* in c*ow*

ei:　as *ay* in s*ay* but including a variety of sounds that I found difficult to separate. Efala, who was literate and self-trained in writing the language, was inconsistent when representing these sounds.

The following consonant pairs were either difficult to separate or, to my ears, appeared to be used interchangeably: *b* and *p*, *d* and *t*, *f* and *v*, *g* and *k*, *l* and *n*, *l* and *r*. I have used the consonant as I heard it most often. My spelling differs from the system being developed by Efala; for example, I heard Etolo saying *tono* "man" but Efala consistently spelled the word as *dolo*. He regularly used *d* and *l* where I heard *t* and *n*, respectively.

I have adopted one practice that Etolo used as a rule of spelling. They did not use the letter *k* in any words, preferring instead the letter *g*. They did this even with borrowed Huli names that they knew to be conventionally spelled with a *k* (e.g., the personal name Gamia in Etolo from the Huli Kamia) and that I heard pronounced with an initial *k*. Some people would alter my notes when they considered my spelling to be at fault.

An Etolo Text

Sale gosalo ado.

Gaheo i sulo amo. Gaheo naha madeseda sale gosamolo asigila halea sale gosalo. Amala asigila halea gaheo i busa negesegida ha sale fadala digilo.

Gaheo i ado.

Aube ndisembagi gaheo i migawila nulo. Aube ndisembagila naha nea aube Aibologi naha madelo.

Wida gelo ado.

Gaheo negesebe galu bugao sole dagi i gaga negeseda amogi widaea molo mulo. Na masigi fadamaea gelo. I gaga fisosigi ha wida gei amo fadala digilo.

Sagai sagalo ado.

Siabulu odoa memala sagalo odoa gaheo bala moloie asigila halea sagalo.

Elebo sagalo ado.

Elebo gelegi moloie sagalo. Gele elo mogogi nea sagalo. Gele sulubadagi nulo.

Nauge amalamu sagalo.

Nau odoada gelegi nulo odoada gaheo ia nulo. Mida sagasebe amogadola nulo.

Wahalo ado.

Gaheo ia gaheo bala moloie wahalo abelo. Gelegi salea oheo bala moloie wahalo abelo. Sugua foi nufulo neage ha wahalo abelo. Elo nudigi molo asigisigi nudigi abahalea abelo. Elo molo sida bagosigi ha wahalo abelo.

Efala Babe
Bobole
February-March, 1980

Free Translation

The Etolo text was written by Efala in response to my request that he describe what people did to get food and when they did it. He revised several drafts after I had typed them. In his initial text he did not include the comments on sago; these were added only after some encouragement from me. Translation was via pidgin with Efala's guidance. Here, and elsewhere in the book, translations have been edited for style.

About setting deadfall traps.

First there is the red pandanus season. When red pandanus is no longer eaten, then it is time to set deadfall traps. The trapping season finishes at the onset of the next pandanus season.

About the red pandanus season.

In December the red pandanus season is underway. It is available for eating from December until April.

About cassowary snaring.

At the time when red pandanus commence to set small fruit, three kinds of wild pandanus and certain forest trees drop fruit that are eaten by cassowaries. Snares are set here, and cassowaries are caught when they come to feed on the fallen fruit. When the fall is over, the time for snaring cassowaries is finished.

About planting gardens.

Sweet potato may be planted at any time; but if it is desired to eat sweet potato with red pandanus, then the former must be planted at an appropriate time. ["An appropriate time" would be the cloud season.]

About planting yams.

Yams are both planted and eaten in the cloud season. Those planted in the middle of one cloud season will yield throughout the next cloud season.

Taro may be similarly planted.

It is eaten in both cloud and pandanus seasons. It is the case that taro planted in one season will be eaten in the same season of the next year.

About sago.

If one wishes to eat sago with red pandanus during the pandanus season, then sago should be processed in advance. If one wishes to eat sago with game mammals in the cloud season, then sago should be processed in advance. If domestic pigs are to be killed, then sago should be processed. If one is thinking of eating sago grubs, then palms should be cut to incubate grubs and to have sago ready. Or, if other foods are scarce, then sago should be processed.

CHAPTER 1

Introduction

On June 29, 1979, Fuago stopped me as I returned from baiting rat traps. He was a very concerned man. "The pigs," he said, "have got into the garden. They have ruined it. What will everyone eat, for everything has gone?" They were Gago's pigs, and Gago had left the village to trade for sago.

It soon transpired that Gago had released his pigs into the garden. No one removed them. Instead, other people emulated Gago by placing their own pigs into the garden. In doing so they were all careful to protect patches of taro, and banana trees that had not yet fruited, with small fences. Two other gardens were treated in the same way, and the frequency of complaints increased. *Sugua mai*, "pigs ate," was the usual and sufficient statement of the crisis. This conventional message could be read immediately as: "The pigs have ruined the garden; there is no food; we shall all be hungry."

There was no crisis. Pigs rooted with pleasure in three large sweet potato gardens, and there they grew fat. For people, much sweet potato remained in other gardens that did not have pigs; at worst, in four months' time there would be a shortage of these tubers. But there would not be a shortage of food because in those months people would eat yams, taro, sago, and increased quantities of choko and pumpkin.

The pigs that ate the gardens were soon killed and eaten, yet, even after this, the complaints continued. "What will we eat?" people asked at the outset, but gradually this became "We are hungry" and, finally, when sweet potato was genuinely scarce, "We are sick of sago." The dramatics of the early *sugua mai* days gave way to real concern until, equally suddenly, new sweet potato gardens yielded, and it was all over.

I call this suite of events—pigs in gardens, complaints of no food, and associated feasts—Sugua Mai, and the question addressed in this book concerns its meaning. Why did Etolo people lie to themselves? Why did they put pigs into gardens and say those pigs got there themselves? Why did they say there was no food when there seemed to be plenty? I shall argue that Sugua Mai was a message that could be read at several levels. In literal translation it was not true, but no one, unless tainted by an excess of empiricism, would read the message in this way. At a different level Sugua Mai rationalized major pig feasts at which the people, who were modest and never greedy, ate more than was usual. More importantly, Sugua Mai acted to synchronize or, more precisely, to resynchronize the activities of a community of 109 people as they went about their major food-producing tasks. In this it gave tangible form to the valued ethos of communality; it affirmed people's relationships to one another and to the environment within which they lived.

Mt. Haliago is an extinct volcano, reaching 2,689 meters in altitude, at the southeastern extremity of the Karius Range in the Southern Highlands Province of Papua New Guinea (fig. 1).[1] To the northeast the mountains face rolling hills of grassland, dotted with groves of casuarina trees and the numerous gardens and hamlets of Huli highlanders. To the south and west the land falls away steeply, cut by deep gorges and intersected by faults and scarps, to the Great Papuan Plateau at altitudes of 600 to 700 meters. From the summit of Haliago torrential streams fan outward to the plateau, where they gather as rivers—Sioa, Wamagula, Giwa, Rentoul, etc.—flowing west and south to join the huge Strickland River. The land is densely forested.

At the northern edge of the plateau and along the southern slopes of Haliago live the Etolo. In 1979 they numbered 500 people who gardened the slopes of the largest torrents at the places where these were released from the mountain onto the plateau. They lived as scattered communities of 20 to 100 people who regarded Haliago as their own and looked south, across the plateau, to the vast slopes and broad summit of an extinct volcano, Mt. Bosavi. Their neighbors to the west were Bedamini; to the immediate south and in hills to the southeast lived Onabasulu; and across the plateau, on the lower slopes of Bosavi, were Kaluli and Harado people. In total these groups were a few thousand people who spoke five languages and were bound by proximity, trade, intermarriage, and the ecological dictates of the plateau's weather. To them, only the Huli, the thousands of grasslanders living beyond the mountains to the northeast, were truly different. In their turn the Huli named all the plateau people as Duguba.

The lower slopes of Haliago are separated from the plateau by a high scarp running east to west at altitudes between 800 and 900 meters. Most Etolo lived at the rim of this scarp or on gentler slopes immediately beneath it. But to the east, at higher altitudes, was a place where the pitch of the land was reduced and a basin had formed as the torrent Sioa swung through an unusual course. From the confluence of this torrent with another, Bobolegi, a long ridge climbed easily northward toward the summit of the mountain. Here, at an altitude of 1,100 meters, lived 109 people at the village of Bobole.

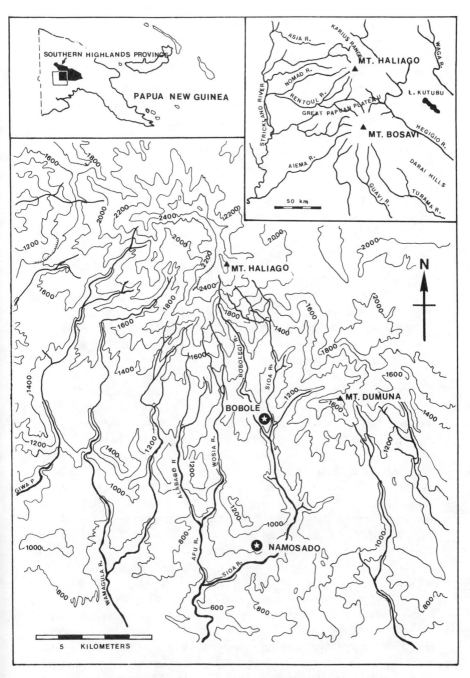

Fig. 1. Locality map. Contour intervals are 200 meters.

The village was spread out along 1 kilometer of ridge. Its central feature was a small iron-roofed church with walls of woven bamboo and a slat floor 1 meter above the damp earth. A low partition separated the places where men and women should sit; a rough table served as altar; and a blackboard with the day's lesson was nailed to the wall. At one end of the building a narrow room was the dispensary; outside a small tank collected rainwater; and the rusted hub of a car wheel was the church bell.

The church, a house and cookhouse for the pastor, two small buildings for visitors, and a few pit lavatories formed the central domain of the village. The ground was scraped and trodden bare with the clearing lined by chili bushes and other ornamentals. On either side of the ridge crest were small gardens for the pastor's family and, on the west, a carefully drained flat was used as a sports field. Nearby, one building was intended as a school, some were family houses, and another was where youthful bachelors sometimes lived.

Four longhouses were the primary dwellings of the people. They were like broad, shallow-hulled ships inverted on the ground. They were substantial, 15 to 20 meters long, their low walls windproofed with fibrous planks made from palm trunks and their arching roofs thatched with sago fronds. At one end a verandah sheltered one or two fire pits. Cooking stones were heaped or strewn nearby, and string bags swung from rafters out of reach of dogs. A doorway from the verandah led into the windowless interior, and a central corridor ran to a single square of light—a doorway for men—at the far end of the house. Each longhouse was divided in the same way. The main door opened into a broad space, with large hearths on either side and with sleeping mats for women, girls, and small children. A young pig might be tethered inside, and a dog could be nosing among the coals. In this part of the house everyone socialized. At its rear a high partition separated this communal zone from a domain for men and boys. The central corridor led to their private portion of the house, where, on both sides, raised platforms allowed them to sit talking or to lie back on comfortable beds. Breaks in the platforms were for personal fire pits and each man's quarters were bounded by flimsy partitions. Against the walls, along both sides of the house, were low, cramped corridors whose only access was through narrow openings in the darkest corners of the communal area. In these poor spaces married women slept, close to where their husbands lay.[2]

Two of the longhouses straddled the ridge, one south and the other north of the central clearing. A third was to the west of the ridge crest, and a path crossed several stiles to the fourth and northernmost longhouse. The people who lived there often referred to these houses by the name of a senior male resident—Ololo, Sabaiya, Saliya, and Awabi—or of an ancestor of the group (or the group itself) that founded the longhouse—Melesane, Waisado fefi,

Sigo, and Habalo. In this book they will be designated more simply, from south to north or—as I preferred to think—when looking from Bosavi toward Haliago, as Houses I to IV.

From each longhouse old and new trails led to family houses or, through rank grass that hid uncatchable rails, to gardens and orchards on the slopes and banks of Sioa and Bobolegi. Northward were the steep forested slopes of Haliago, often hidden in cloud. Immediately to the east, across Sioa, the sheer face of the Mt. Dumuna Range encircled the watershed of Woromo and, to the west, beyond Bobolegi, was a patchwork of regenerating forest, orchards, occasional sago palms, gardens, and the small houses built within them. Below the village Sioa cut southward through a narrow gorge and, across the plateau, when the day was clear, Mt. Bosavi was visible. A broad track led to lower altitudes, to the torrents Wosia and Afu, to groves of sago belonging to Bobole people and to other Etolo living to the southwest—to kin, friends, and possible marriage partners. The other Etolo . . . there was ambiguity here because the western Etolo were often referred to as *the* Etolo by those who lived at Bobole and, in turn, the latter were often named Bobolefi by the other Etolo. There had been a drift of languages that was curtailed in the mid-1970s. At a meeting called for the purpose, the western Etolo taught the Bobolefi how some words the latter used had digressed from correct speech, and in this way the people of Bobole were returned to the fold, willingly, as Etolo.

The people who lived at Bobole claimed approximately 50 square kilometers of land as their own. Crude population density was thus about two people to the square kilometer, but effective density was much higher since not all land was used and some parts were used more intensively than others. The village domain, together with current gardens, recently abandoned ones, and numerous small orchards, amounted to 5 square kilometers. Another 15 square kilometers comprised early and advanced regrowth on old gardening sites. These secondary forests were up to twenty-five years old and never located above altitudes of 1,200 meters. The rest of the land was covered in primary rain forest that the people used only for trapping and hunting animals and for collecting various plant products as food or for making material items. Higher reaches of the mountain and some precipitous gorges were rarely or never visited.

In February, 1979, there were 109 Etolo residents at Bobole; a Huli pastor and his family added three more to the population. During the following fifteen months one infant died when a whooping cough epidemic swept briefly across the plateau, two births occurred, and there were two marriages. One of the young women who married left the village to live with her husband at another Etolo community, Namosado, about 5 kilometers to the south. A third of the population were children younger than ten years while five men and one or two women were older than fifty-five years. The sex ratio was biased toward males (sixty-six males, forty-five females), particularly among people in the ten-to-thirty-years age class; there were, for example, seven bachelors of twenty-five to forty years and nine youths between fifteen and twenty-four years but, by May, 1980, there were no young women eligible for marriage and only two girls who would reach marriageable age within the next five years. At Namosado, with thirty-three residents, the disproportion was even more striking with eight unmarried males between fifteen and thirty-five years and only one girl approaching marriageable age. People said this pattern prevailed across the Great Papuan Plateau.[3]

All people at Bobole were affiliated to one of two Etolo lineages, Gaibi and Waisado, though, by birthright, two married men were Onabasulu and Huli, respectively. Gaibi were represented by four named groups, Melesane, Gago, Sigo, and Habalo; and Waisado by two, Waisado fefi and Waisado daiefi. Historically, people of Melesane and Sigo arrived earlier and had more substantial claim to land near Bobole than other groups. Longhouse residential groupings cross-cut this classification. This occurred because older bachelors had moved to the longhouse where a sister had gone in marriage, because sons-in-law had moved to the longhouse of their fathers-in-law, and as an outcome of past conflict that had divided groups. Less serious disputes were sometimes also resolved by one participant living elsewhere for a period. Within a longhouse people addressed each other either by one of several personal names or, irrespective of consanguinity, by kinship terms.

Eligibility as marriage partners required that people had not shared the one longhouse for a lengthy period and were not of the same group. Waisado and Gaibi could intermarry but, with the exception of Gago, groupings within these lineages could not. The anomalous position of Gago related to their historically late arrival at Bobole from western Etolo territory. Their subsequent alignment as coresidents with Melesane effectively debarred marriage between these groups; Gago could, however, intermarry with Sigo and Habalo. Polygynous marriages had been commonplace in the past but by 1979 were out of favor. At Bobole there were four elderly men who were married to more than one woman; one with three wives and the others each with two wives.

Because the recent history of the people who lived at Bobole had been deeply influenced by disease, interregional movement, and realignment of groups, patterns of residential and lineage affiliation were not sharp. At House I residential affiliation centered around two Gaibi brothers (one had died in 1978) who had married two sisters; at House II all but one married man were Waisado fefi; at House III the founding Gaibi group had disbanded following accusations of witchcraft; and at House IV a senior Gaibi man was actively inviting his sons-in-law and others with Waisado affinity to join his household. The surface expressions of the social alignments of people seemed to be based in pragmatic rights to land where they gardened and hunted and to the places where their sago grew. They were also reflected in choices of marriage partners and the extended economic rights these could confer. A rather resolute individualism countered emergence of hierarchical social forms or inherited authority, made the family (nuclear or extended) an autonomous economic unit, and cemented relations between siblings and age mates. (A detailed statement of Etolo social arrangements is available in Ray Kelly's book *Etoro Social Structure: A Study in Social Contradiction.* Kelly lived with Etolo-speaking people at Gabulusado, a lower-altitude western community, from April, 1968, to July, 1969.[4])

Bobole was not an isolated community. Visitors were common, and because the village was a staging post between the plateau and the highlands, trading parties were routine. The villagers themselves were regularly on the move—on church business, trading expeditions, or visits to kin at other communities. During 1979 one young man was away for six months at Bible school, and a boy, in his early teens, attended a Huli primary school for a few months. With all these travelers there was a flow of goods through Bobole. Packages of sago, thigh-rolled string, gourds filled with tree oil, palm wood for bows and ax handles, sometimes a young cassowary trembling in its cage, or the pelt of a spotted cuscus (*Spilocuscus maculatus*), were all carried from the plateau to the markets of Huli. Axes and bush knives came the other way. So did salt, matches, cotton clothing, a few nails, metal billies, spoons to eat pandanus sauce, a prized potato peeler, always soap, and the inevitable books—*Matyu, Mak, Luk, Jon*—translated into Huli, bringing the *tok bilong bikpela Jisas Krais,* at the close of the second millennium, to its last destination on earth.

From February, 1979, to May, 1980, I was one of three Europeans living at Bobole Village. I had come as a biologist, interested in people, planning to undertake three related studies. First, to study small terrestrial rats in vegetation that ranged from newly prepared gardens to undisturbed rain forest. I wanted to explore the ecological idea that the diversity of animal species was linked to the phase of forest succession or the intensity of disturbance. Second, I wanted to learn from the Etolo something of the way in which they viewed the natural world and, to this end, planned to study the classificatory frame within which they situated animals in general and mammals in particular. My third aim was to learn how the people used wildlife and, here, my primary focus was to be on hunting. I had chosen Bobole as a base because the combination of available altitudinal span and low human population density held the promises of a rich variety of mammalian species and of people interested in eating them.

Research has the frequent habit of taking its own direction; it teases with unexpected questions tempting one to follow. I do not resist, which perhaps indicates a lack of discipline. In Papua New Guinea the weakness may be justifiable. Suddenly—it may happen in a week—you are transported from familiar city to isolated village. It perches on a muddy ridge above a torrent where, half an hour earlier, you had faltered and accepted a guiding hand. The ridge is dwarfed by seemingly limitless mountains, shrouded in an evening mist and enveloped in rain forest. You are out of breath, as much from the new language filling each moment as from the rigors of the day's walk. Nothing is familiar. The people, terrain, evening storms, plants, animals, and food jostle for attention in thoughts, already so crowded, that you have commenced to filter. You see and hear only as much as can be comfortably savored at any moment. Projects abound, but the initial need is to confine attention to a few possible tasks and avoid the temptations of the dilettante. And the first obligation is to adapt to the prevailing social milieu, to discover projects or strategies for work that will not affront your hosts. Under these influences early research plans may be overwhelmed by new experiences or by a wealth of unexpected data.

At Bobole men, women, and children were skilled hunters, trappers, and collectors of wildlife and, with little hesitation, soon provided much information relating directly to the three research tasks I had in mind. Before long I was being deluged with the skulls of mammals—the memories of other people's meals—and under this impact my interest in hunting grew. I now wanted to position hunting within a larger frame by examining all the food-getting activities of the people. The result is this book. Two of the initial aims, the studies of rats and of Etolo classification, will intrude only occasionally. It is the modified third aim that is central, and here my intentions are twofold—descriptive and explanatory.

The descriptive material—the ethnographic orientation—concerns the food-getting activities of the people who lived at Bobole. These were varied. The people were gardeners who used different techniques for growing their staple root crops of sweet potato, taro, and yams. They processed starch from sago palms by employing a technology that was surely small and beautiful. At orchards they tended fruit pandanus and near the village kept domestic pigs. The larvae of beetles were incubated in specially felled and prepared palms; eggs of jungle fowl were harvested from litter mounds where they had been laid; and small fish were captured by poisoning at dams. In the forest hundreds of traps were used to capture game mammals; snares were set for cassowaries; and people hunted with axes and sometimes with dogs. At many different locations, and while engaged in a variety of tasks, they collected crayfish, spiders, insects, frogs, lizards, and fledgling birds. These activities and their associated technologies form the descriptive core of this book.

Chapter 2 depicts the setting within which people operated; it treats several imperatives, or givens, of Etolo existence—time, place, rain, and the world of spirits. It depicts the moment that was 1979 within a mood of past and present change. Chapters 3 and 4 concern gardening; chapter 5 treats pigs, pandanus, and sago; and chapters 6 and 7 are about hunting, trapping, and the collection of wildlife. In each of these chapters I show what the activities concerned look like, describe associated technology, depict seasonal and annual patterns and ways in which people—male and female, old and young—shared the necessary tasks. Chapter 8 considers awkward problems of technique and interpretation that I imposed by using cash payments to obtain data about the capture of game animals; it has something to say also about strategies of research, about what could and could not be done, and about ways in which local conventions influenced propriety. In chapter 9 the focus shifts from getting animals to eating them. I describe patterns of sharing and giving meat, the contribution of animals to diet, and the celebrations that were marked by feasts.

In the three closing chapters of the book I adopt an explanatory stance. Chapters 10 and 11 draw earlier themes together. They are concerned with ecological patterns—the shape of Etolo ecology—and with possible explanations of the timing, sequence, and synchrony of events. They show that different sorts of food-getting activities were emphasized at different times; that different families and longhouse communities were closely synchronized in these successive activities; and that the synchrony observed cannot be sufficiently explained as a necessary response to environment. These two chapters, taken together, are the link between preceding descriptions and concluding explanation. They lead to, though fail to defend, the proposition that ecological action was, ultimately, legislated through social action and, in this, return us to Sugua Mai.

Chapter 12 elaborates and defends my case that Sugua Mai—as a collocation of culturally based messages that passed from the people to themselves—acted to resynchronize the diverse food-getting activities of the families who lived at Bobole. This response served to offset a future shortfall in the availability of sweet potato and had impacts upon both ecological and social spheres of people's lives. Sugua Mai was a communicatory device that, through theater, recreated a sense of community among people who lived in one place. It gave order to the system, social and ecological, of which the people were a part. This chapter, then, is concerned with processes of communication in open systems and draws upon the writings of Gregory Bateson and Anthony Wilden, whose ecosystemic perspective I find attractive.[5] The perspective escapes the impasse of stasis that has been too common in ecological writing and, thus, is crucial to my reading of Sugua Mai. While my primary purpose is to understand and give expression to the form of Etolo ecology as it was during 1979–80, it remains true that that form was contained within a frame of change. Sugua Mai was new; ten years earlier it had not been part of Etolo experience. The separate events I bring together as Sugua Mai were themselves part of a continuum of change. To do justice to the people and their historic experience, one must recognize that form, though resilient, is inherently vulnerable and accommodate form within the dynamic process through which it is forever dissolved and reconstituted. To achieve this, one must consider the process of change itself.

Why, though, the insistent attempt to separate description from explanation? At one level I want to free the facts for possible accommodation to the theories of others. Not everyone will be sympathetic to my theoretical predilections, and I myself cannot know them to be correct. Of course, this rationalization of the separation is influenced by my training within science where, so often, the pretense is made that results and discussion of results are entities of different kinds. I do not subscribe to this view. The descriptive material of this book must fail to meet that ideal. First, it will be incomplete since I have selected activities to record and measure and cannot easily assess any resulting bias. Nor can I know what may have been filtered out because there was too much to see and, unconsciously, I drew some blinds. Second, much of the descriptive material is hung on a peg of annual periodicity, but since the study lasted only fifteen months, the level of repeatability sometimes assumed cannot be guaranteed. More serious, because this impinges on the theoretical tenets used, is the fact that I have punctuated the description of Etolo ecology. In describing the ebb and flow of various activities, in exhibiting traces to capture Etolo ecology, I must unavoidably impose form. I will "write in" a grammar of their ecological acts and hence be entangled by the central problem of methodology—that what was seen was no more than a reflection of the mind that saw.

My second reason for separating description from explanation is more personal. It has to do with attitudes concerning responsibility. I write about people of a culture other than my own and attempt to position them within some global perspective. But I wish not to abuse the immense privilege experienced in living with them. Although Sugua Mai is the story I want to tell—this is intentionally transparent in the opening words of this chapter—I also want the ethnographic reporting to be true, to the Etolo collectively and the individual men, women, and children whose lives are depicted. I have tried not to write anonymously, either of the people or myself.

CHAPTER 2

Sege: *That Which Was Given*

In the beginning, when we were all the same, we lived together at a place that is now spoken of as *wafule molulu fi salia,* "the place where the earthworm was eaten." At this time there were no trees, there were no sago palms, there were no taro or yams, there were no stinging wasps, and there were none of those large ants that have enormous jaws and a savage sting. Nor were there any of those small stingless bees that lap human sweat and the sap of trees. There were just humans, all living together in one house.

Each day the older people would leave the house to go to their gardens. The small children would stay behind and play. But often with the old people away a child would vanish. It was always inexplicable. Had the child wandered away and perhaps died? Had someone carried it off? The older people became anxious.

One morning the parents of some of the children remained behind when the others departed. They hid among the grass and the bushes near the house. They were armed with axes and with bows and arrows, and they watched the children playing to see what might happen.

In the afternoon they saw movement beneath the ground. A mound of earth was forming and was moving closer to the house. Something was crawling beneath the earth toward the area where the children were playing. It was very large and very long; and when it reached the children, it poked its head up from the ground. It was a bald man named Dabaia. It was he who had been killing and eating the children.

The older people who were hiding in the grass rushed out, and they killed Dabaia with arrows and with their axes. They prepared his body for cooking, and they called to other people, who had gone to their gardens, to come and share the meat and to join the singing that would accompany the feast.

These other people started to arrive. Those who were close came first, and those at a distance came later. As each group arrived, they would sing and be given a portion of Dabaia. Some groups were given portions of the body, another group received the head, and so forth. Today descendants of these groups live at different places, and they are sometimes named according to the portion of Dabaia that their ancestors

11

received. For example, the Onabasulu people who live at Api are known as Guni-gamo—they are the people who ate the head.

Finally, Dabaia was entirely eaten, but groups of people continued to arrive. The first of these latecomers were given fronds of tree fern to eat; these had been cooked with Dabaia in the same manner that tree ferns are nowadays cooked with pig, and they were soaked in grease. The descendants of these people are spoken of as "those who received greens."

Next to come were the Nebali people. They were small people, and when they arrived, all the food was finished. They received only the cooking stones and they licked the grease from these. Later they became stingless bees [called *nebali*]. They continue to arrive late at pig feasts and to lick the cooking stones. Or they come to singed carcasses of game mammals that are hung on racks in the forest and they lick the grease that seeps out of these.

Then the I people came, but now everything was gone. They were cross and said they would go away and become trees. Then came the Waharo people, and they, too, decided to leave the community of humans, to change their skin and become sago palms. You can still identify different kinds of palms as old men, married women, young women, and so forth. After the Waharo people had left, some women known as Nau and men known as Elebo arrived. They, too, abandoned the community. The Nau women went to live near water in damp places down below. They became taro, each of whom, to this day, still wears a remnant of a woman's skirt. And the Elebo men went to live on the slopes of hills, where they became yams and still have beards.

The Auwi and Sesani peoples were the last to come. They were very angry, complaining that everyone had eaten Dabaia, leaving nothing for them. They, too, changed their skins. The Auwi people became stinging wasps while the Sesani became large ants that inflict painful bites and stings. "In the future, when you walk about in forest or in your gardens, we shall bite and sting you," they told the people, and then they departed.

This is what happened in the beginning at the place where the earthworm was eaten. And today you must not be angry with or laugh at trees, sago, taro, or yams or at ants or bees or wasps because all of them are really people.[1]

The Etolo word for place was *sege*. It had various connotations. *Segeligi,* "place exists," was one of three names for wild pigs. Another was *iliba,* "of the forest," and the third, which was part of a language of metaphors used in propitiation of forest spirits, was *ibo hawa aligilo,* "beneath the leaves it is." *Sege sane* were deadfall traps built within the forest to capture mammals. In these cases *sege* connoted somewhere else, not here. It conjured a distinction between nondomesticated and domesticated realms and took the former as its referent. *Sege* was out there; it was the forest, streams, mountains, and the forces that motivated them. It was other than cultural. Yet equally *ne sege* was "my place," *tie sege* was "your place," and, here, the mood of *sege* was affective. It embodied the sentiment of belonging—to the village, the gardens, the pandanus orchards, the sago groves, the forest, the streams, and the mountains—of being in and of the landscape, of being, and hence of culture. Again, *sege* could be neutral in value as in *sege hedabi* for a "good place," *sege nafade* for a "bad place," *sege falai* for a "dry place" and thus good for yams, or *segebi* for "mountain."

Sege was also the Etolo word for rain. *Sege yafi digasabe,* "a huge rain is coming." In the forests you would hear it racing across the tree tops, chasing a scatter of birds into temporary cover, easing its first cool drops through the canopy to delight clammy skin till suddenly it shattered the forest ceiling with an exuberance that obliged humility. Rivulets poured from trunks, buttresses, and vines, and fresh streams tumbled in ever-changing anastomoses across the ground. Then it would be gone, racing across a further ridge, leaving the world transformed as a twilight of flickering green, an atmosphere lush with decomposition, the timid explorations of thicket flycatchers and the abrupt screech of a white cockatoo heralding one more new, though familiar, beginning.

Sege was also the word for time. *Sege afate,* "once upon a time," were the words that commenced so many stories. The seasons themselves could be described as *sege gene,* "the time of cloud," and *sege gaheo,* "the time of fruit pandanus." And the word *sege* had been taken for both the newfound notion of ordered hours and the peculiarly powerful clocks that contained it. *Sege afate*—once upon a time—no one lived at Bobole, the people were numerous, they were decimated, they fled, they regrouped. The stories went on, blending the mythological with the historical.

Time, place, and rain: these givens of Etolo existence were subsumed by a single word—*sege.* They were the innate, the root imperatives of the ecological and social conditions within which people acted out their lives. They were the stuff of which the people *were,* the springboard of their intellectual explorations, aspirations, and motivations. Nor was this all. The *segesado,* the "people of time, place, and rain"—the forest spirits—were till recently just as concrete.

In the past when men went hunting on Haliago, they would carry sweet potato to eat. At a certain place each hunter would contribute a large sweet potato to a pile placed to one side of the forest trail. When this was done, one of the hunters would call loudly to the *segesado* saying sweet potato had been left for them and asking for game mammals in return. The hunters then continued to their forest camp where they would heap the remaining sweet potato beneath the beam of their shelter. They would not eat sweet potato at midday or through the afternoon. They would eat it only in the morning, holding it over the fire before they did so, and addressing the *segesado,* "Give us game mammals, show us game mammals." Then they would go hunting. In the afternoon they would return to their camp. They would arrive one at a time with the catch. But they would not eat game nor even singe the animals they had obtained.

They would wait until evening when everyone had returned. One man would take all the animals by their tails and would hold them together toward the flames of the fire. Again he would speak to *segesado:* "We came and we got game mammals; we did not eat sweet potato." Now the fur could be singed off the animals and their carcasses placed on a rack in the forest. They could not be stored in the shelter. Unless these things were done, the *segesado* would not release game mammals to the hunters.[2]

It had been necessary also that appropriate language was used within the forest domain of the *segesado.* In particular it was important not to refer directly to many products of gardens or to women and sago, all of which were associated with moist places at lower altitudes. The usual names for crayfish, fish, and some mammals from low altitudes were also avoided. For all these things, and for many others, metaphorical names were used. String bags were "hair," and hair became "moss" while women were denoted by the term for the string belt to which they fastened their skirts. Stones became "cooking"; fish became "beneath the cooking"; and crayfish became "grasshoppers." Highland pitpit was "wild ginger"; garden ginger was the "mother of wild ginger"; green vegetables were "tree leaves"; and sweet potato became "its name is ground." Nor was this system of metaphors universal across Haliago. Within the territories of different lineages, and hence of different *segesado,* there were different codes. The *segesado* were angered whenever language was spoken in the wrong place.

To the Etolo the spirit world had been as actual as the forest itself. In the act of being, each person had participated in that world; people were an extension of it just as it was an extension of them. Each living person had a dual spiritual essence, *hame* and *ausufani,* of which the latter part could separate from the body and wander alone when the person slept. There were *gesame,* the spirits of the dead, that were manifest in numerous birds and certain fish. There were witches, *mugabe,* that occupied the bodies of particular individuals and preyed upon the *ausufani* of others. There were *segesado* of the forest that invisibly mirrored the society of people, and a class of heinous *segesebe* that once had been young unmarried men, that imitated *segesado* but behaved as vicious witches. Each class of spirits could, in different ways, assume the form or voice, or occupy the body, of plants or animals. Through seances conducted by experienced mediums, it had been possible for people to communicate with some of these spirits and enlist their assistance, advice, or permission in treating illness, diagnosing witchcraft, identifying those who harbored witches, planting crops, and taking game. Through seance and ceremony the worlds of people and spirits had communicated a mutual dependence.

The sensory world of vision, touch, and hearing had been, for people, as much an experience of spirits as it was an experience of plants, animals, and rocks. A pale, soft-skinned cricket—recently molted—attracted to the fire, could have been a child's *ausufani*. Raggiana birds of paradise with full plumage had been the *gesame* of widows while drabber birds of the same species had been *gesame* of younger women. The *gesame* of men or women killed by people appeared as hornbills; at the base of the bird's beak a stain of blood showed. But hornbills and birds of paradise could themselves die or be killed by people, and then the spirits of the dead that lived within them descended to rivers and occupied the bodies of catfish and eels. In the late evening or at night the strident calls of certain crickets, cicadas, young bandicoots, and koels had been the cries of patrolling witches and, by day, earthworms and repugnant leeches sometimes had been witches in other forms. Striped possums had been the hunting dogs of *segesado,* and they called in the darkness as they pursued their quarry. Thunder and lightning had been caused when *segesado* held ceremonies and danced or sang—when the spirits were beating on the walls of their houses then thunder rumbled around the mountains. The *segesado* themselves could be invisible, appear as huge people, or occupy the bodies of wild animals. Cassowaries and wild pigs, pythons, certain frogs, and even invertebrate animals such as large insects, centipedes, fleas, and bedbugs once may have been transformed *segesado*. So it was also with bananas, taro, edible hibiscus that had grown tall, or highland pitpit. And *segesebe,* who originated as young men, who had quarrelled with the married people, broken the house, and taken their portion away, had been able to assume the same forms as *segesado*. These spirits could not always be distinguished, though the *segesebe* should always be avoided. At the junction of Sioa and Afu, huge rocks that arched across the water were the portion of a longhouse the *segesebe* had claimed. They resided there when they were not wandering as wild pigs or cassowaries. Not until recently had people dared to visit the place. And in the past the *segesado* died as people did and their essence joined the *gesame* of dead people within the largest rivers.

It was *segesado* that had implanted each person's *hame,* the breath of being, when that person was growing in the mother's womb and *segesado* that gave a person's *ausufani*. Each person's *hame* and *ausufani* were reunited as *gesame* when the body died and, throughout life, it was the *ausufani* wandering at night that was vulnerable to attack from witches. By consuming portions of the *ausufani,* a witch could injure the body of the person concerned, causing illness and even death. At seances a medium, or his *ausufani,* could cross to the spirit world and seek intervention from *gesame* or *segesado* on behalf of a sick person. Through the medium it had been possible to discover the physical location of the witch responsible and, if the victim of witchcraft had died, to demand compensation or initiate cannibalistic revenge. Even without witchcraft the fate of men was sealed. Each heterosexual or homosexual act deprived them of *hame,* causing progressive debilitation and aging. Yet those acts were necessary to ensure both the existence and the vitality of another generation. Death was the inevitable consequence of the sacrifices that granted life. The evil of witches could hasten this process, but, as witches were evil, so *segesado* were potentially fair. The latter were the guardians of the animals in the forest; they maintained watchful guidance over the yield of crops or of starch from sago palms. They were powerful forces that could grant or withhold sustenance from people; their strictures were numerous, and their wrath could be severe. It was not politic to scorn plants and animals that might harbor *segesado;* it was proper that certain foods were eaten at a prescribed time of day; it was necessary to seek the advice of *segesado* before setting cassowary snares and to placate them with offerings if an animal was caught. When behavior was inappropriate, gardens could fail or the game sought by hunters might remain hidden. Coughs, headaches, and breathlessness were penalties for minor transgressions and death for those of greater moment. At worst *segesado* had the ability to entomb entire groups of people by changing a longhouse to stone. Though, when they seemed bent on such violence, was it perhaps *segesebe* instead? After all, it was *segesebe* who had sworn enmity to people.[3]

Sege afate—once upon a time—Waisado were a numerous people. They lived at low altitudes, below the confluence of the torrent Wosia and that called Alababo, where there was much sago. Fighting broke out and, except for two young boys named Amasulu and Mahia, everyone was killed. The boys ran away and wandered naked with the pigs, eating worms and fungi as pigs did. The place where they lived was the slopes of Wosia.

    Far to the west, at Galima on the torrent Hesau, lived an elderly man and woman. They were without children of their own and when they heard the tale of Amasulu and Mahia, they were saddened and set out to find them. They searched till they found the boys with the pigs, but the latter ran off and the boys went with them. It was night before the old people came to where the pigs slept. They frightened the animals away and took the boys to Galima. They gave them clothing and proper food and treated them as their own children.

    When the boys had grown to be young men, their foster parents told them about the past. Amasulu and Mahia went to see their true place at Wosia. It was good, there were many game mammals and much sago, and they decided to stay. They married, and their wives had many children so that, once again, Waisado became numerous. Indeed, there were so many people that they split into six or more groups. Each group lived in a different place that became its own. There was a group who lived at Bogalibo on the banks of Wosia because at this place many game mammals could be trapped. Another group lived at lower altitudes near the torrent Afu where edible hibiscus grew strongly. There were some who traveled southwest to Gemisado; others went southeast to Namosado; and another group abandoned the territory of Etolo and realigned with Onabasulu. All this happened long ago. Waisado people who are alive today know that these were the places where their fathers were born.[4]

In 1935 two European explorers, Jack Hides and Jim O'Malley, with a party of police and carriers crossed the Great Papuan Plateau from west to east. They skirted the southern border of Etolo territory, leaving behind the first chips of wood cut by steel axes as well as two dead men. The two men had been shot. Within a decade axes and bush knives reached the Etolo from the south, and there were rumors of other strangers who had ventured to the plateau. The bush knives and the strange people were named *helepe*, the name learned, apparently, from Kaluli who themselves said that these wonders appeared from south of Bosavi, from a place named Helebe. Years earlier *helepe naga*, the "ground of Helebe," had come by the same route; this was the plant *Bixa orellana*, the seedpods of which yielded a bright red pigment used to decorate string bags, pubic aprons that men wore, and the bodies of people. Bush knives remained *helepe* to Etolo speakers, but Europeans did not. When the latter returned in the mid-1960s they were renamed Heligei in reference to their tanned, light brown skin. These Europeans represented the government and, until the early 1970s, they usually came once a year to control the people and encourage change. In their wake came missionaries and, eventually, anthropologists and biologists.

During the late 1940s and through the decade of the 1950s, new diseases had played havoc with the people of the plateau. Influenza and measles reduced the Etolo population to about one half of its former numbers. Entire longhouse communities vanished, at others the few survivors dispersed and reassembled as new combinations of people. It was a time of fear, of accusations and counteraccusations of sorcery, and of the killing of people thought to harbor witches. One legacy was to reduce the proportion of females within the surviving population; females, it seemed, had the misfortune that they were more likely to harbor witches. Not then, nor even later, was it understood that the epidemics were merely the advance guard of the Europeans. The plagues had abated before the Heligei returned in person.

I do not know when people first lived at Bobole. The myths did not answer this though they placed the origins of people "down below" where the sago was. People of Gaibi were the first to settle at Bobole. They came from near Afu, retreating to the mountains during periods of strife, and returning to lower altitudes in more peaceful years. By the 1950s, probably earlier, they claimed both places as their own, gardening for about three years near Afu where their sago grew, then drawn for another three to Bobole and the hunting grounds of Haliago. There were periods when people from Gaibi lived with Waisado and others when they lived apart. There were rearrangements that occurred among Gaibi themselves when different groups built separate longhouses or temporarily aligned with other Etolo people. Efala, who is Gaibi, was born near Afu in the mid-1950s. Within ten years he had transferred three times between his birthplace and different longhouse sites near Bobole. Thereafter he remained at Bobole and, late in the 1960s, at an age when he would undertake his first personal garden plot, his father, Babe, and his uncle, Ololo, combined with some Waisado people to build and share a longhouse on the ridge between Bobolegi and Sioa. That longhouse was still standing in 1979 though one end had broken and blown away in a wild storm of 1977.

Through the late 1950s and the 1960s Waisado came in piecemeal fashion to live at Bobole. They came from the west, from the watershed of Wosia, where they had been shattered by disease and a wave of witchcraft killings necessitated by the deaths that resulted. They came seeking land for gardens and, in exchange for this and for access to game mammals on Haliago, they gave the rights to some of their own abundant sago. Some came to join sisters who had married Gaibi men; others married Gaibi women and lived with their fathers-in-law. One group held itself apart as a distinctive Waisado household in which Sabaiya was the senior man.

Diseases and Europeans are powerful forces. The village of Bobole consolidated as people fled from the consequences of incomprehensible epidemics; it grew and stabilized by government decree and gained heart and fresh expectations from the words of fundamentalist Christian missionaries. At Bobole people turned away from their knowledge of forest spirits, looked cynically but warily upon their witches, abandoned their sad, beautiful theater of song though not their nostalgia for it, held their last seance, and hung their bows and arrows on the longhouse wall. And it was at Bobole, in 1979, that people were still silenced and anxious when thunder grumbled and broke overhead, were nervous if a koel called at night, and were left bewildered, seemingly without past or future as support, if a child died. The recent history of the people who lived at Bobole had been of frequent realignments and gradual consolidation of the ridgetop village itself. Its latest phase, in the late 1960s, was encouraged by Europeans who required greater stability of residential sites for the purposes of conducting censuses, dispensing medicines, and curtailing traditional antagonisms. The location was administratively useful in being just one day's walk from the nearest government patrol post and on a direct, though rugged, route between the highlands and the plateau. The bond between Gaibi and Waisado was reinforced when four men were sent to Mt. Hagen jail as penalty for killing an Etolo woman who harbored a witch. Their continued peaceful coexistence grew out of the new truths taught by missionaries.

The first missionaries to live among the Etolo were Huli men trained as pastors under the auspices of the then Unevangelized Fields Mission, which later became the Asia Pacific Christian Mission. Two men arrived in 1969, and from that time the people were guided by one pastor living among the western Etolo and another resident at Bobole. In style the pastors were ardent evangelists. They taught the "good word" of *Jisas Krais* and interpreted it as a prescription for conduct; they announced that the second coming was nigh and promised that material goods and immortality would arrive simultaneously; they sprinkled their sermons with tales that had been gleaned, with some distortion, from the Old Testament; and they warned of the awesome powers of *Mugabe*—Satan.

The pastors also brought a small medical kit containing penicillin and made possible access to well-informed medical care. They discouraged traditional religious practices as being non-Christian and, with the government, outlawed child marriages that had been economically based and never consummated in childhood. They opposed polygynous marriages but were successful with only the young; and they opposed homosexuality, which, in Etolo belief, had been crucial to physical and intellectual growth of young males. They taught that bare breasts led to lust and that smoking was a sin. The pastors successfully encouraged longhouse communities to draw closer with the church as centerpiece of a new village. They taught the rigorous hygiene that high-density living requires, promoted conversational fluency and literacy in the Huli language and sport as healthy recreation, and introduced new vegetables. They fostered the growth of a loose organization of church deacons and lay preachers that might consolidate their own status within Etolo society and made it possible for young men to attend Bible school or train as pastors in the highlands. Their impact was considerable but was not always what they intended nor always as it might have seemed.

The pastors who lived at Bobole did not generalize their power. They had influence but not authority in secular affairs. The installation of deacons and lay preachers had democratizing effects in that it dispersed the new powers throughout the community. The Etolo reacted as though once they had mastered the new and puzzling forms of religious observance then they themselves would be in control. It seemed they were creating their own Christian order while they imagined they were learning a preordained system. For example, within the hierarchy of the mission there was concern that pastors devoted too much effort to ensuring a large congregation and that few people were being prepared for baptism. But at Bobole the symbolic purpose of baptism was, at the least, obscure to the pastors and unknown or irrelevant to the people. The Etolo symbols took more concrete forms. Church attendance *was* admission to the body of the church; participation *was* purifying. Only one man dissociated himself entirely from church functions. All others came regularly, three times on Sundays and frequently through the week.

They came to murmur prayers, hear the good word, and copy the blackboard lesson into their books, to learn to read and write, improve their Huli, and sing hymns in that language, to discuss forthcoming church events, air grievances, and socialize. Awabi would sit on the floor on the east side of the church, his three wives to the west. Suieme and Matali with their husband, Ololo, and Aboiya and Torome with their husband, Sabaiya, were seldom missing. At Bobole no one behaved as though polygyny were a barrier to purification. The pastor sat with the people and heard but did not always understand a service spoken in Etolo; nor did he often travel to preach at outlying communities; the young men he and his predecessor had trained did this.

In transferring allegiance to a new religion, the Etolo were still adapting the old. The process of change was far from complete. The terror of witches and their name, Mugabe, had become the awful power of Satan. The omnipotent capacities of God were once those of the forest spirits. The seeming imminence of Jesus was an innovation, but the status of the spirits of the dead hung in the balance. The old and the new were being blended subtly, of necessity and not of planning. In years past the capture of a cassowary would have been followed by a seance to communicate with and placate the forest spirits. In 1979 the first cassowary snared was eaten communally; people had gathered at an impromptu church service and sung hymns for two hours while the cassowary had steamed in a special oven. Once, the forest spirits had had power over the well-being of crops, but now people expressed thanks to God before they ate, even before snacks in the garden or along forest trails. He was thanked, too, for the rain and sun and for the forest products that people ate or used.

Much remained to be resolved. Were the late night calls of koels the cries of witches as they had been a decade before? Were they perhaps made by Satan himself as he walked through the night, or could they be neither? How were births, marriages, and deaths to be celebrated or otherwise marked since, in the past, they had been surrounded by ritual and theater but not governed by forest spirits? In 1979 these events were no more than superficially touched by Etolo Christianity; they were hurried and businesslike and performed with an air of uncertainty. Sometimes, indeed, past forms gave greater security as the following incident suggests. Sagolia was with his parents processing sago when he collapsed in a coma. "His eyes are dead, but he breathes," people said. He was beyond the reach of Bobole medicines and, by fatalistic decision, too distant from life to be carried all day to the nearest hospital. Mugabe had taken over his body and was gnawing his insides. The wake for the dying boy was two days of hymns and visitors. Mugabe was slowly contained, confined to the heart at first, then forced by the power of hymns into the boy's throat until, at last, Sagolia's eyes lived and Mugabe had been driven from his body. The exorcism was a success.

Within the secular sphere there had been many changes that people who remembered the past felt with deep pleasure. The bows and arrows that hung on the walls of longhouses were a warm private joke, and people were forgetting the fear of being killed or eaten. These changes were attributed to the impact of the mission and not that of the government. The latter required new modes of conformity but was not seen either to be helping people achieve them or to be articulating a future purpose. The people at Bobole regarded themselves as members of the newly emerged Evangelized Church of Papua; they thought of the mission as guiding that church to independence. The mission sustained a tangible interest in the people in ways that the government did not. The Christian model was more visible than that of nationalism and, inadvertently, fostered the integrity of Etolo as a people. To them it was an important day when Efala, as one of their own, became their pastor.

After 1975 the word *heligei* underwent another change of meaning. This change was symbolic of Papua New Guinea's shift to independence and of an Etolo perception of government. *Heligei* had once named a color and had been used as a personal name for some light-skinned Etolo men. Later it was used as a class term for all Europeans irrespective of their particular and varied hues. After independence the government officers who patrolled the plateau were no longer Europeans; they were Papua New Guineans of many shades—some, the blackest men ever to walk on Haliago. They wore boots, were alarmed by snakes, and visited once a year. They erected tables, flew the national flag, and traveled with an interpreter who sometimes changed the words. They gave crisp orders; conducted the census; asked about local problems and desires; and, upon hearing the ever-repeated requests for a schoolteacher, a doctor, and an airstrip, said these were matters for other departments. It was Kafkaesque. The flag was lowered, the table was folded, and they departed for another year not aware of the keen frustration they left behind. They had the authority, the tasks, and certainly the style of the Europeans who used to come but who had returned to Australia. They became Heligei—those with authority.[5]

In the past game mammals, dogs, and people lived together in the same longhouse. They ate the same food and spoke the same language. The tree kangaroo, *gageleso,* was the most respected of the game mammals.

One day, early in the morning, everyone left the longhouse to find food—everyone, that is, except a small dog who was so young that he had no hair. This small dog hid himself in a dark corner of the house. During the afternoon the game mammals were caught in heavy rain. They were wet and cold and returned to the house. They did not see the little dog in the corner and while they warmed themselves, they derided the dogs. They said "When it rains, the dogs remain close to the fire licking their fur; they don't go anywhere." And they said some very bad things, too. When the little dog heard these things, he jumped up and ran down the corridor out of the longhouse. He ran to the path that followed the garden fence. He was looking for the other dogs. When he found them, he reported what he had heard, that the game mammals were at the house mocking all the dogs. Then he said, "I will grab and hold *gageleso,* and you should grab the other game mammals, and we will kill them." And he instructed the other dogs thus: "You must not eat the game mammals when you kill them. You must bring them to the house, and we will cook them in the evening and eat them together."

So all the dogs returned to the longhouse and attacked the game mammals. The small dog attacked and killed *gageleso* while the other dogs attacked the rest of the game mammals. The mammals were afraid and ran away. Some ran into holes in the ground, some into holes in rock. Others escaped into streams. Some hid among roots at the bases of trees while others fled up trees and hid in hollows or among epiphytic ferns. Each kind chose its own hiding place and still uses it today. One dog captured *gauso,* the forest wallaby, before it could hide. *Gauso* said to its captor, "You will kill me now but you may not eat my head. Remember we are cross-cousins and have laughed and played together." So the dog killed *gauso* but did not eat its head. This is what dogs still do; they eat the body of forest wallabies, but they never eat the head because they remember that wallabies are their cross-cousins.

By evening not all the dogs had returned to the longhouse. Some had killed game mammals and brought them to the house while others had killed mammals but had not returned. The small dog called to the latecomers, but they did not appear. Instead they ate the animals they had caught without cooking them and without sharing.

That is how it came to pass that dogs eat game mammals. Nowadays, instead of everyone living in one longhouse and speaking the same language, there are three groups. Two of the groups, people and dogs, still live together. The third group is the game mammals, and each kind lives in its own house.[6]

There was no dry season at Bobole; there were merely different expressions of wet weather. At one extreme, persistent drizzle fell from a dismal mist; at the other, startlingly clear skies gave way to torrential afternoon storms. Exceptionally, three, perhaps four, consecutive days were free from rain and the forest understory wilted as though stricken by drought. At the height of storms minor streams became impassable.

From October to April the days were clear and warm. At dawn, mist would hang over the plateau and within the deep valleys of Sioa and Bobolegi but would disperse quickly. As the day warmed, the ground dried and hardened; wisps of cloud would form overhead, draw together, and by early afternoon be piled as columns against the slopes of Haliago. Brief showers might scud across the mountain or turn south, trapped in gorges, and race toward the plateau. A storm usually broke late in the day and persisted for an hour or more or, perhaps, long into the night. It might commence high on the mountain and spread gently across the land, or the entire sky might open in an instant.

Through April and into May the weather changed. Prevailing winds swung gradually from northeast to southeast. The dawn mists persisted longer and swirled across the ridges that separated major torrents. Through the afternoon the clouds were low; showers were more frequent, and their chill was more penetrating. Temperatures crept downward, and the ground no longer dried; within a month there was mud everywhere. By July the air was saturated, endlessly dripping; and, each evening, mist would slip from the mountain to envelope Bobole through the night and beyond dawn. Only rarely did a storm shatter the mood and, for a day or less, clear the sky. But the promise of those storms was that the winds would turn again to drive the cloud from Haliago. The change came slowly; the ground was a little drier, the walking easier; the clouds were higher, and the morning mists softer and sooner gone. By October the worst was over. It was warmer, and soon biting march flies appeared and, after them, the stingless bees that lap sweat. On distant ridges new leaves reddened the forest canopy while nearer at hand the fruit pandanus ripened. An occasional mist-filled day seemed like a careless relapse because the storms had returned to the mountain.

Figure 2 shows some meteorological records from Bobole. In twelve months, from March, 1979, nearly 5,000 millimeters of rain fell. At higher altitudes the total would have been greater, and it may be, as the figure hints, that March and April consistently had somewhat higher falls than other months. Days and nights were nearly always mild, although, to people who have acclimatized to temperatures of more than 20°C, a once-only sudden drop to 13°C was bracing. From the middle of April to September daytime temperatures were low, and the daily range was reduced relative to other months. Both effects were the result of low clouds persisting through this period. Abnormally low minimums occurred when a full moon coincided with a clear night.

The shift in temperature regimes allows me to divide the year into two seasons: the cloud season, from mid-April to September, and the pandanus season, from October to mid-April. This nomenclatural plagiarism does a disservice to Etolo perceptions. They also named two seasons—*genegi*, "cloud exists," and *gaheoi*, "fruit pandanus exists"—but their distinctions lacked the calendar-bound rigidity of mine. To them the existence of cloud or fruit pandanus specified the season. Only when the latter were bearing well and their red sauce was being eaten regularly was it *gaheoi*. And only when pandanus ceased to provide much fruit and the cloud hung in the air throughout the day was it *genegi*. Through this season, too, hundreds of

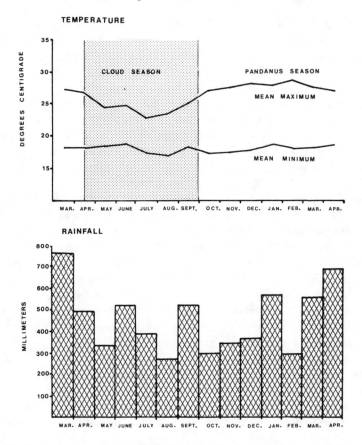

Fig. 2. Temperature and rainfall at Bobole, March, 1979, to April, 1980.

mountain pigeons abandoned the high forest at first light, sped noisily to their fruit tree gardens on the plateau, and returned as high, lazy, well-fled flocks before evening.[7] Etolo nomenclatural distinctions allowed for many variations between years but were ambivalent about weather patterns late in each year. The clouds could blow away and the number of pigeons decrease before October to leave *genegi made,* "not the cloud season," but the fruit pandanus and thus *gaheoi* might not flourish before December. The people did not name this intervening period that I have included within the pandanus season.[8]

The daily routine of the people was shaped by prevailing weather. In the cool hours before dawn, fires were stirred to life. Smoke would seep through glistening thatch and, for a while, hang in the air above longhouses. A breakfast of sweet potato would be readied by burying it in hot ash, and there was murmured conversation as people relinquished sleep. From tall trees near pandanus orchards came the harsh calls of Raggiana birds of paradise. A man would stretch himself awake, step outside, and yodel a chorus in reply. The night's gossip or the day's plans might be shouted between long-houses or across the valley to someone who had slept at a garden house.

Through the pandanus season work started early. By seven o'clock a few families would be moving to their gardens; before eight the village might be almost empty, left to a man curled up in mild fever at his fire or to a few small children in the care of an elderly relative. The day would be warm and clear; plumes of smoke would trail above gardens where people were plant-ing; and from several directions came the sounds of trees being felled. Be-tween 3:00 P.M. and 4:00 P.M. people commenced returning to their houses though they came earlier if a violent storm interrupted the day's work. The remaining hours were for talking, sharpening axes, weaving string bags, cooking, and eating the leisurely evening meal.

The cloud season was less conducive to a prompt start. People loitered within the longhouse or clustered beneath the verandah, postponing the inevi-table moment. It might be 9:00 A.M. before diminished mist, increased warmth, or the necessary tasks induced departure, but, with the decision made, the day was often long. As late as 5:00 P.M. people would return laden with food and firewood through the settling mist. The meal would be hurried because darkness came abruptly after 6:30 P.M.

Just as the weather shaped the routine of the people so their activity at different times shaped the distinctions they made within each day. *Yosei, esowa, diadi, gasigi* translate readily as "early morning," "middle of day," "late afternoon and evening," and "night." But to people who had set out early for their gardens it was already *esowa;* to their tardier coresidents, waiting another hour at the longhouse, it remained *yosei.* In the same way the transition from *esowa* to *diadi* was marked by the end of the day's work and the return home; storms or weariness from hard labor might encourage that transition. Christianity and the notion of a seven-day week imposed another rhythm. The church declared that Sunday was for the celebration of God; neither work, which was intrinsically good, nor monetary transactions should take place on this day. With rare exceptions people asserted strong adherence to these principles, and on Saturday evenings most families carried in sufficient food for the next day's meals. On Sundays, between church services, they rested or visited pandanus orchards or lines of traps in the forest. These two food-getting activities, which were themselves overt mark-ers of the rhythm of people's lives, were not perceived as work, and God's law therefore was not undermined. On many Friday afternoons men and youths played football; the women often watched.

The people of Haliago had been shaped by time, place, rain, and a world of spirits that resided there. They had been shaped by their notion of *sege* and in this process had shaped that notion. Neither they nor *sege* had ever been still. In the brief moment that was 1979 the mood of their lives was change. It sometimes appeared they had abandoned one world of spirits for another. This was not so. They had embarked upon an extraordinary, puzzling, but never absolute, transformation of the old. They were adapting ancient concepts to new forms. They had stepped across the boundaries of their own place into a larger world and were optimistically waiting for the reciprocal step. They had discovered literacy and through this were committed to a different concept of time. They had merged with history. To the Etolo nothing would ever be the same though in truth nothing ever had been; nothing, that is, except the rain falling on Haliago.

CHAPTER 3

The Making of Gardens

Sailo commenced his garden early in July. Along the crest of a ridge, where moderately advanced secondary forest abutted a well-used walking track, he built a robust picket fence 37 meters long. It was 1.5 meters high. North and south of the fence Sailo cut swathes through the forest, arching them westward and downhill toward steep gullies that dropped to the mountain torrent Bobolegi. The swathes were from 5 to 10 meters wide and, as they turned parallel, were nearly 200 meters apart. When completed the garden would exceed 5 hectares. It was an ambitious undertaking; no other garden approached these dimensions. But it misfired; ten months later it was still not finished.

Sailo concentrated his work to the north. The southern swath ran downhill for 200 meters to a gully and was left unattended. Sailo built a fence through the middle of the northern swath. This comprised logs stacked one on top of the other and held in place by irregularly spaced pairs of poles that were thrust into the ground on either side of the stack and tightly bound above it. Trees had been felled so they dropped along the intended fence line. The trunks of larger trees were not shifted; where they fell, the fence was built. After 150 meters the fence reached the edge of a steep, rocky stream that tumbled downhill, cutting to the southwest, to join Bobolegi. Here Sailo turned the fence to follow the southern bank of the stream, dropping trees on either side of the gully so they fell as a tangle into it. Where the bank was very steep, he did not need to build any fence.

The fence twisted and turned downhill a distance of 250 meters. By now August had passed, and Sailo's mood was of restrained panic. He and his wife, Sebele, had done two months' work but had planted almost nothing. Sebele had managed a narrow band of sweet potato, aibika, some pumpkins, and cucumbers along the lower reaches of the fence, and two youths, Bauwa and Wosia, from Sailo's longhouse, had each been encouraged to plant a minute plot. But there would be no security from pigs till the entire fence was finished. The yield from older gardens was falling drastically, and Sailo and Sebele had not processed sago since late June. Relative to other people, they were far behind schedule. Then they were interrupted for two weeks. Their younger son, Malai, became sick—he was malnourished—and they left Bobole for a time to take him to a hospital. Sailo's project had failed because others had not joined in. He had planned to be the initiator of a magnificent garden, to consolidate others about him by his enthusiasm, and to invite even more, appointing them plots within his garden. They had worked elsewhere, commencing different projects. Five unfenced hectares were not attractive. Yet Sailo could hardly foreclose. He was a proud man. His efforts earned him the nickname Segebi—Mountain.

In September Sailo and Sebele changed tactics. They took the risk that pigs would reach their garden and commenced clearing and planting on the northern side. They worked up the slope, Sebele clearing undergrowth and Sailo felling trees, opening a strip 20 meters wide that expanded to 45 meters as it continued up hill. Where practical, Sailo felled trees like dominoes, weakening those that were down slope with a few blows from his ax and collapsing these to the ground under the weight of a larger tree up the slope. Most logs lay where they fell but saplings, limbs, and brush were cleared away and heaped to the south of the growing plot. Here at least they might afford token protection from pigs.

As the land was cleared, Sebele planted, following Sailo's vigorous axmanship up the hill. He was beautiful to watch. And sometimes nerve-racking, as he perched high in a tree cutting away limbs that might jeopardize the direction of fall he had calculated. The theme of the garden was sweet potato. With a digging stick Sebele thrust holes into the ground and inserted one or two runners, spacing them about 1 meter apart. Between these she planted greens—highland pitpit, acanth spinach, and some aibika. Scattered sugarcane and lowland pitpit, a few bananas, and the dry adapted tannia were included. Along fences and near brush heaps there was more aibika, together with pumpkins, cucumbers, choko, and climbing yam vines. Compared to many other gardens, this was not a diverse assemblage. By the end of October Sebele had planted one quarter of a hectare; the tiny plots that had been planted earlier, another 0.13 hectare, were being weeded. For Sailo and Sebele life was now vastly more relaxed. On September 8 three men from Sailo's longhouse had started work on the southern fence line. They completed this within a few weeks. On October 1 Sebele gave birth to a daughter, Habasiome. Within the next two weeks she captured two bandicoots that were disturbed as she cleared undergrowth. The following week she was beating and washing sago. At the end of October Sailo found time to go hunting.

After October work continued at a less frenetic pace. There was more clearing and planting with Sailo and Sebele always working up the slope. Two to three months after they had planted one section, they would thoroughly weed it. In late November Sailo spent two weeks finishing his grand fence, extending it 45 meters across a flat on the northern side to end at a cliff, and building about 40 meters in bits and pieces wherever pigs might gain a foothold on the steep edge of the southern gully. He converted the frame of a shelter that had been started months before into a small, comfortable, garden house. By late December he could at last take up an option on a plot in a second garden—the very one he had competed with—and here, through January, he and Sebele planted more sweet potato and a patch of yams. At this time, too, other people joined his venture though the portions they planted were all small. They had already attended to most of their needs. Sebele's mother, Uali, and Uali's husband, Awabi, were first, choosing 0.1 hectare on the lowest portion of the block where a seepage was ideal for a tiny plot of taro and for watercress.[1] Away from the seepage they planted sweet potato and a mix of vegetables. In February Awabi's sons, Bauwa and Wosia, who had planted small areas early in the life of the garden, took up additional plots. Four others also commenced work. In early March the lower reaches of the garden included small patches that had just been weeded, others soon to be weeded, newly planted sweet potato beneath uncut trees, and areas where the undergrowth had been pulled and piled but where planting had not yet occurred. All but one couple who worked in the garden were related directly or through marriage to Awabi; the extra couple shared a plot with the husband's brother, who was married to a daughter of Awabi. As Sailo's garden began to take on the form he had envisaged, its focus shifted from him to his stepfather-in-law.

On April 10 I saw Sailo's garden from high on the opposite ridge. The enclosure was impressive; 700 meters of fence on very steep slopes was a considerable achievement. On the northern boundary a long strip of garden clung to the fence and swung out across the flat above Bobolegi. To the south, patches of garden were dotted down the lower part of the slope. At the top and through the middle a great area of forest remained uncut. In ten months Sailo's 5 hectare dream had produced less than 1 hectare of crops; almost half was his own. The track at the top of the ridge still ran beside the picket fence he had built, but now that fence was overgrown with weeds. Behind it Sailo's garden was unseen; cultivation had not spilled over the crest.

Sailo's garden was atypical in its size, the spread of effort through time, and the fact that it took so long to complete. Despite this, its form—its essence—was typical. It was a Bobole garden in slow motion. More accurately, it was a sweet potato garden in slow motion because, at Bobole, different sorts of gardens were made for sweet potato, taro, and yams. Most were for sweet potato, fewest for yams. The sites chosen for these and the strategies of felling and planting differed. Topography, drainage, ease of access, fencing requirements, age of the regrowth to be felled, and the scale of the project, individual or communal, all influenced choice of a garden site. For some people there were also aesthetic considerations—would the garden be visible? Superimposed upon these factors were constraints of history, residence, and marriage that governed rights of access to land. They might place some families at a disadvantage or could be manipulated to advantage.

The dispersion of sweet potato gardens established near Bobole in the year following May, 1979, is depicted in figure 3. The gardens are coded according to primary affiliation with particular longhouses. Areas utilized by the residents of one longhouse showed little overlap with areas utilized by residents of other houses. Sites used in the previous year did not disrupt this pattern. The four gardens that are not assigned to a longhouse in figure 3 comprise one, situated centrally within the village, that was a continuing community service for the pastor and his family and three others that were shared equally by residents from three longhouses. At two of those three gardens the primary participants were two sisters and a brother with their respective families; at the third there were no strong kinship ties among the participants.

To the north of the map, at Walibe, two gardens are attributed to House III and two others to House IV. The last two were joint projects undertaken by the families of Gawani, from House IV, and Ilabu, from House I, with Gawani, whose family was larger, taking the greater share. Gawani and Ilabu are brothers. Historically their residential affiliations were with an older brother, Sagobea, of House III, but both had changed residence; Ilabu to live in the longhouse of his wife, Didia, and Gawani to House IV, where neither he, nor his two wives, had relatives. Thus, at Walibe, both men were gardening on land where they held customary rights. Gawani's family did not, in fact, have garden plots in areas used by other residents from House IV. His change of residence had occurred many years earlier; it was motivated by a dispute that arose when his older brother's wife was killed in response to witchcraft accusations. His new association with House IV was at the invitation of the senior resident, Awabi. One of Gawani's wives had strong claims to land in the now abandoned upper reaches of the watershed of Wosia, west of Bobole. Awabi appeared to be establishing rights over this land by inviting the customary owners to reside at his longhouse and then promoting minor ventures on the land.

For House II, much of the gardening effort in 1979 and in the previous year was at Walataia. Most of the gardens clustered there belonged to Sabaiya and members of his large family. Much of the area felled to make these gardens had been relatively young regrowth; perhaps less than ten years since tree ferns were a conspicuous component. The land had therefore been fal-

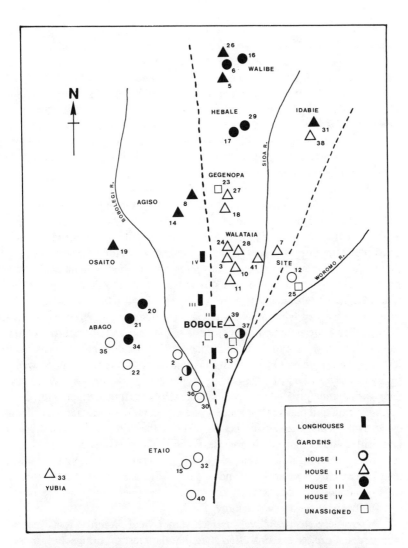

Fig. 3. Dispersion of sweet potato gardens near Bobole. Numbered symbols represent gardens and are coded according to the longhouse at which most participants lived. Gardens 4 and 37 were shared equally by residents from Houses I and III; gardens 9, 23, and 25 were shared equally by residents from at least three longhouses; and garden 1 was a communal project on behalf of the pastor. The gardens are numbered in the order that they were prepared.

lowed for a shorter period than was usual—perhaps a shorter period than was desirable. Sabaiya's customary rights were centered in the middle reaches of the Wosia watershed. He was a relative latecomer to Bobole and, for him and his family, this meant dependence upon others for access to gardening land. In 1979 the area available to him seemed limited and, with many sons but a shortage of marriageable women, there was no easy resolution to the difficulty. The importance of marriage in this connection is that both husband and wife acquire rights to make gardens on the other's land. At Bobole these options were regularly taken up, though, for most couples, residence was the more important consideration.

With the exceptions of the gardens at Walataia nearly all others were cut in regrowth forest that was from fifteen to twenty-five years old. The older regrowth, dominated by oak trees up to 25 meters in height, was preferred. A few small gardens near longhouses or on river flats were made in grassy areas; there sweet potato was grown in mounds, and fallow periods were less than a year. One garden was cut into forest that no one remembered having been gardened before (fig. 3: no. 40) and another, at Yubia, represented a return by two Waisado men to the land of their past (fig. 3: no. 33). The location of the last two gardens hints at a shortage of suitable land near the village. The eastern and western slopes of Bobolegi and at least the western slopes of Sioa were either under garden in 1979 or dominated by regrowth less than fifteen years old. Few areas remained with forest as old as twenty-five years. Ten years of high-density living and gardening—by Etolo standards—had transformed the vegetation near Bobole. It had affected the distribution of fauna in that several species of game mammal were no longer found close to the village and two species of bird, the willie wagtail and sacred kingfisher, had colonized cleared areas within the previous decade. In 1979 few sweet potato gardens were beyond a one-hour walk from the village; none was more than an hour and a half away. The most distant gardens usually included a comfortable, sometimes elaborate, house where people sometimes lived for a week or more.

Moderately steep and well-drained slopes were preferred for sweet potato gardens. Larger gardens often started at the crest of a ridge and, in their lower portions, spilled onto a flat. On the flat sweet potato was grown on dry ground and taro where there were seepages. Many gardens spanned the zone between two gullies. The gullies provided obvious topographical boundaries, often reduced effort in fence building, and might have reduced the amount of tree felling immediately outside the fence where this was needed to prevent shading at the edges of the garden. Gullies also served as convenient dumps for much of the rubbish that accumulated during felling and clearing.

Felling trees on either side of the selected fence line and building the fence itself were the initial tasks in a gardening project. The rationale for fencing gardens was the exclusion of pigs. Because the torrent Sioa was considered a barrier to domestic pigs and because wild pigs were rare near Bobole, very few gardens east of Sioa were fenced. Most fences were of stacked logs, but short lengths of picket fence were often built where the ground was level. Fences incorporated the trunks of larger trees and took in steep embankments or cliffs, where this saved work. Nearly all gardens that were less than .25 hectares were fenced in their entirety by one man even though he might later invite a second family to share the area. Larger gardens were usually initiated by two families, rarely by more. The men commenced work on the fence while their wives cleared undergrowth from the zone adjoining the fence. Men worked with axes and women with bush knives though neither partner was averse to using the other's tools if this was more convenient. As the enclosure started to take shape, the initiators might seek assistance with fence building, inviting their helpers to participate in the garden at the same time. Other people might offer help without being asked but by way of indicating interest in a plot should this be available. Sometimes, if the undertaking was large and had been delayed, the owners might coerce a party of volunteers for a major effort and then reward the workers with a small afternoon feast. Working bees of this sort also arose in other circumstances. Volunteers were usually forthcoming if fences had been badly damaged by landslides or by pigs, and a day's assistance with fence building or tree felling could be used to offset some social tension. People from Houses III and IV, for example, had a burst of reciprocal gardening help after a man from one of those houses had won heavy compensation from the other household for a claim that some of his coresidents regarded as dubious.

Felling, clearing, and planting followed fence building though some planting usually occurred before the fence was completed. In sweet potato gardens there were two strategies for clearing and planting. In one method undergrowth was removed, large trees were felled if they were present, and sweet potato runners were planted beneath the canopy of the regrowth forest. Most people refrained from planting much else at this stage though some interspersed acanth spinach with the sweet potato. Two to six weeks later, though usually within a month, the remaining trees were felled over the sweet potato and the rest of the crop was then planted. In the second method trees were felled in advance of clearing and planting, and a diversity of crops was planted synchronously. Both methods might be used in one garden, but there was a clear preference for felling trees after planting at gardens that were made late in the year when daytime temperatures were higher. In these months shading may have been important to the establishment of sweet potato runners. People said that they cut large trees before they planted to avoid damaging the crop, but, in fact, in some gardens, small trees were also felled before planting. In any case the art of tree felling was so finely honed that the crop went unscathed; the trees only *seemed* to fall on the crop. I think that by planting first and felling later people gained one month's grace before the onerous task of weeding was upon them. By felling first and planting later they could control the pattern of the yield, skimming off greens, beans, and corn before the garden was choked in knee-deep sweet potato runners. Gardens that were felled before they were planted usually had a greater diversity of crops. Sailo's tardy giant was an exception in this regard.

In tiny gardens trees might be removed before fencing occurred, their crowns dropped beyond the garden boundary. Small portions of larger gardens were sometimes treated in the same way. The usual technique was to work up the slope felling trees in domino fashion. With particularly large trees flimsy chopping platforms were built, and the worker perched nonchalantly several meters above the ground. At the center of a garden, especially if this was felled late, trees were dropped in a radial pattern, inward from the outside of the plot. This procedure avoided damage to flourishing portions of the garden and simplified the task of cleaning. Trees were also routinely felled so that the greater part of their trunks floated above the ground—across dips where they served as bridges, perched in the limbs of other standing trees, or balanced precisely upon larger stumps. Perching trees in these ways was common when planting had preceded felling. It called for fine axmanship but was abetted by the practice of cutting trees at shoulder height. By cutting trees well above ground level, people probably also avoided potential injuries to legs and feet since all remnant stakes remained clearly visible above the tangle of plants. In addition, felled trees that came to rest above the ground did not become waterlogged; they dried out and were then used as the primary source of firewood. Trees with bark that was valued for making string or rain capes were stripped before being felled, and most gardens included some standing trees when they were finished. Fishtail palms were regularly left, their crown of fronds battered and torn by trees that had fallen around them. Useful trees were left and others, too, simply because it was not necessary to remove everything. Many of the others were ringbarked and eventually died; they towered skeletally above regrowth for years afterward.

Most fencing and tree felling were done by men while women contributed most to clearing undergrowth from beneath trees. Men and women shared the task of cleaning after trees had been felled. This entailed cutting saplings, tree ferns, tree crowns, and branches and throwing them out of the garden, into minor gullies or onto scattered rubbish piles. Potential firewood was stacked or propped, and some was cut in advance to portable lengths. These tasks were followed by planting, and, at least in early phases, women did most of this work. Established and failing gardens were robbed of sweet potato runners. Cuttings of anything that could be grown vegetatively—even pumpkin and choko—were collected. Treasured seed stock of beans and corn appeared, and gravid cucumbers were planted whole. The inedible and bulbous aerial nodules of certain yams and low-grade tubers from others were retrieved from storage in garden houses. The tops of recently eaten tannia corms were saved, and young banana suckers were uprooted and transported to the new site.

Women arrived at their new gardens bowed by string bags that overflowed with sweet potato runners. They laid these out in ones or twos across the area to be planted and, with a digging stick made for the occasion, put the cut stems into a hole and casually scooped soil over them. Different varieties of sweet potato were interplanted. The runners lay limp for a few days and then took. Between them cuttings of acanth spinach and highland pitpit were planted with minor concentrations of the former where soil moisture was higher than usual. Aibika, lowland pitpit, sugarcane, and tannia were scattered through the garden, and yams were provided with crude trestles of sticks to climb. Corn and beans, often planted together, with climbing poles for the latter, were seeded into small beds of ash, and for the few people who experimented with it, Chinese spinach was planted with them. Ash beds were occasionally used for other crops—cucumbers, some aibika, or small patches of acanth spinach in the burned-out undercut of a stump. There was no general burn; the vegetation was too sodden for this. Most planting was directly into the natural mulch of leaf litter that covered the ground. The small columns of smoke that hovered above gardens nearly always indicated that beans and corn were about to be planted. Many crops were clumped or grown in special situations. Sugarcane and bananas, both long to mature, were often planted together. When *marita* pandans were planted among sweet potato, then lowland pitpit was usually present also. Flats were favored for small plots of cassava, and concentrations of highland pitpit, aibika, and tannia or a line of bananas were placed at fence lines, near logs, at stumps, or near rubbish heaps. Pumpkins, gourds, chokos, cucumbers, and more yams were allowed to run wild over fences, rubbish-filled gullies, and rubbish heaps. Pumpkins and chokos provided greens as well as fruit. A few yams climbed high into standing trees. Rare inclusions in gardens were pineapples and peanuts.[2]

Different plots in the one garden included different mixes of crops. This reflected individual preferences. Different participants to a garden were often out of phase, and individuals who had more than one plot might be harvesting and planting in the one garden at the same time. Nor was all planting in a particular plot necessarily synchronous. When trees were felled after sweet potato had been planted, then ancillary crops were added later. And, at the time of weeding, people often planted more sugarcane, lowland pitpit, and bananas. A finished garden always suggested disorder. By the time it yielded it looked to be in disarray. But these impressions were false. Logs strewn through the garden delayed erosion. They, together with fences and rubbish heaps, captured and held litter as this was washed from slopes. Except for the hardiest crops, sweet potato and acanth spinach, planting was concentrated in places where mulch would accumulate. When seeds, rather than cuttings, were used, then soil fertility was promoted with a patch burn. Climbers were given room to maneuver. The mosaic of crops was carefully conceived.

Weeding commenced two to three months after initial planting—two months when trees were felled before planting and three months when they were felled afterward. Rarely was weeding postponed to the fourth month. The task was onerous, but it was critical. It was shared by men, women, and older children though most was done by women, the elderly, and the incapacitated. People jollied the work along by turning it into a family affair or a social outing. Women in particular, offered each other much help. A multitude of herbaceous rubbish and grass threatened to choke the crop. This had to be pulled by hand, working patiently from one fragment of garden to another while further uphill other weeds seemed visibly to be growing. In some gardens hundreds of seedlings of a wild cucurbit appeared. Nearly all of these had to be removed; a few were allowed to trail over rubbish heaps, where they produced large edible fruit. Weeds could not be dropped where they were plucked. They took root too easily. Near the fence they were tossed out of the garden. Elsewhere, they were carried to rubbish heaps or draped to dry across a convenient log. Within a week or two of weeding the sweet potato seemed to gallop across open ground and in a month it carpeted the garden. But the weeds were insidious, and, although there was no other concerted assault upon them, incidental weeding continued for several months. People harvesting sweet potato combined their probing search for good tubers with desultory, necessary, weeding. Contact with the ways of the Western world and the creation of a growing grassland in rain forest have not lessened the burden. A few species of attractive birds have entered the modified environment, but, in addition, new species of weed (Compositae) and previously unknown grasses have appeared to challenge the gardens themselves.[3]

Taro gardens varied in size from half a dozen plants clumped at a seepage on the bank of a stream to communal gardens over a hectare in size. Some taro plots were within sweet potato gardens; others were areas dominated by taro. In larger taro gardens planting was usually beneath the canopy of regrowth after the ground had been cleared. Trees were felled over the crop about one month after planting, and only a limited amount of cleaning was done. Weeding followed three to four months later and, at large gardens, was even more of an event than at sweet potato gardens, with all workers and their families camping at a garden house for several days. There was little need for subsequent weeding because as the plants grew their broad leaves overlapped to shade the ground. A few greens were grown among the taro; some acanth spinach; the delicate leafed, parsley-like dropwort; and always aibika. Banana trees were usually planted throughout the garden and often served as markers to separate plots owned by different families.

While many yams were scattered singly at suitable places in sweet potato gardens, most were included in special plots. In 1979 one large yam garden was a separate entity; others were on very steep slopes within areas enclosed for sweet potato. All the larger yam gardens were communal ventures. They epitomized disorder—there was minimal clearing before planting; trees were felled down the slope over the crop; and there was no cleaning other than to lop the few saplings that had been missed in the holocaust. The crop was then left to its own devices. It was not weeded. Only banana palms and tannia were likely to be planted with the yams.

In addition to the sweet potato, taro, and yam gardens, people made small gardens near longhouses and family houses. They used these as a small supply of handy food for occasions when they had been caught short. The garden areas were rotated on an approximately nine-month cycle and were richly fertilized with debris from fires and earth ovens. Sweet potato or tannia was the dominant crop with the former grown in mounds that had been mulched for about two weeks before being dug in and planted. Mounded sweet potato yielded at about four months—a month in advance of the usual growing technique. Bananas and bamboo were planted near all houses, and there was usually some aibika. Small cordyline palms whose leaves were used as clothing by men and as wrapping for food were scattered throughout household gardens, and the recently introduced pineapples and pawpaws were seldom found away from the village area. One last crop deserves mention. This is tobacco. It was uncommon at Bobole because mission influence had reduced the number of smokers to two men who grew for their own needs and for limited trade with neighboring Onabasulu. The plants grew beneath the eaves of longhouses and beside garden houses. Small portions of green leaf were dried over the fire, rolled, and inserted into a hole near the end of a bamboo pipe. The tobacco was smoldered with hot coals and the rather bitter smoke inhaled deeply and held in the lungs. It was a powerful, rough brew.[4]

At Bobole girls were responsible for their own garden plot from the age of about eleven or twelve years. Their training commenced early. From birth they wore skirts. As toddlers they carried string bags slung from their foreheads and helped carry some of the harvest from garden to house. As they grew older, they were expected to share in cleaning undergrowth, planting and weeding or, perhaps, to care for younger children while their mothers worked. By the time they menstruated, they had acquired basic gardening skills and, with their father to fell trees and their mother to guide and assist, embarked on their own garden plot. Boys were seemingly less constrained. Not till they were three or four years old were they encouraged to dress, and if they showed little interest in clothing, there was seldom much insistence. Small boys led a free and easy life, sometimes helping in gardens, sometimes sent to check traps but left, for the most part, to go swimming or practice hunting or mud fighting with their age mates. By the age of ten they would have received instruction about hunting, gone camping in the forest with groups of men, and started experimenting with their father's or older brother's ax. This leisurely introduction to life ceased abruptly when boys were fifteen or sixteen. It was an awkward age for them; they were growing rapidly, were listless and potbellied, but were required to start their first garden plot. They did not always enjoy the new responsibility and, in Huia's case, for example, needed some encouragement to complete the task. Gago had invited Huia to take up a small plot in a garden that Gago was making with his wife, Heaga, and his elderly, widowed, sister-in-law, Wade. Huia was related to Gago by residence and as a son of Gago's aunt by marriage. With Gago's help Huia felled the plot and, assisted by Heaga and Wade, planted it. When it was time to weed the plot, Huia left the village and spent one month at Namosado. No one tended the plot in his absence. When he returned, people remarked to him, always lightly but very frequently, that his weed patch had no visible sweet potato. No one offered help. It was not till he himself had weeded a fragment that Heaga assisted and finished the now awful job with him. His immediate family observed with amused interest but did not intrude. For boys, learning to be responsible was treated with some tolerance, but subsequent irresponsibility was not accepted. People said, "If a man does not work a garden"—the tone was emphatic—"then no one else will feed his children."

Earlier in this chapter I commented on the association between residential affiliation and the choice of gardening sites. Within this broad pattern there were many subtleties that concerned relationships between those who initiated a project, their relationships with those who participated in the garden at a later time, and relationships between gardeners and others who assisted with various tasks. At each garden, or at each plot within a communal garden, the usual association was between one male and one female. A man and his wife were thus the ideal working combination, and, at Bobole, the family was a conspicuous unit in the recurring round of making, maintaining, and harvesting gardens. They departed together in the morning, worked alongside each other through the day—sometimes at different tasks, sometimes at the same task—and often returned together in the afternoon, the woman carrying the day's harvest, the man with firewood.

Some gardens were operated entirely by the members of one family;

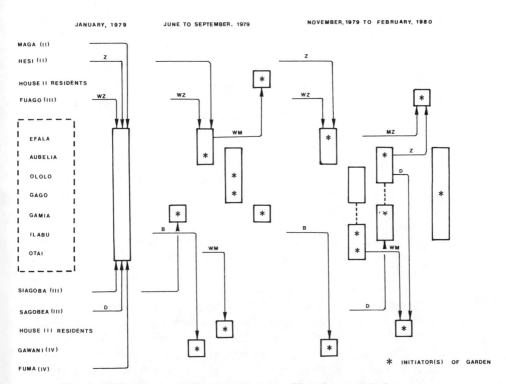

JANUARY, 1979   JUNE TO SEPTEMBER, 1979   NOVEMBER, 1979 TO FEBRUARY, 1980

MAGA (II)

HESI (II)

HOUSE II RESIDENTS

FUAGO (III)

EFALA

AUBELIA

OLOLO

GAGO

GAMIA

ILABU

OTAI

SIAGOBA (III)

SAGOBEA (III)

HOUSE III RESIDENTS

GAWANI (IV)

FUMA (IV)

* INITIATOR(S) OF GARDEN

Fig. 4. Affiliations at gardens: House I patterns. The primary gardening affiliations of families resident at House I are summarized for the period January, 1979, to February, 1980. Names of the senior member of each of these families are enclosed in a box; Aubelia was a widow; other named persons were male. Families from other longhouses who participated in House I gardens are indicated (again, by the name of the senior male), as are six cases in which House I families participated in communal gardens initiated by residents from Houses II, III, and IV. Codes show the strongest relationship between the senior member of a family from one longhouse and a participant at a garden initiated by residents of a different longhouse: B = brother, D = daughter, M = mother, W = wife, Z = sister, WZ = wife's sister, etc. Gardens are not drawn to scale.

others were shared by all families within a longhouse; and, at other times, families who resided apart but had close kinship worked together. The network of associations was ever changing. Figure 4 shows part of this network as it concerned the families who resided at House I. All of them held plots in a large garden that was commenced in January, 1979. Two families from House II, three from House III, and two from House IV participated in this garden. The wave of gardens established between June and September separated the activities of House I families. The few intrahousehold links were now between a recently married man and his widowed mother (Efala with Aubelia) and a widow and her husband's brother (Aubelia with Ololo). There were more associations with brothers or sisters who lived at other longhouses (e.g., Hesi and Fuago participating in Aubelia's garden and Ilabu sharing in Gawani's garden) or with the communal projects initiated by longhouse groupings from which a recent marriage partner had come (e.g., Efala and Otai, with their wives, sharing in ventures of Houses II and III, respectively). In the later waves of gardens, between November, 1979, and February, 1980, these patterns recurred, but, increasingly, the families of House I combined in single projects. During this period the last garden initiated by residents of House I was shared by all families except those of two recently married men (i.e., Efala and Otai); there were no participants from other longhouses.

Departures from the sorts of arrangements depicted in figure 4 arose as youngsters were introduced to their future responsibilities, when elderly widows remained dependent upon men to fence and fell garden plots and when older bachelors, unable to find assistants whom they could easily reciprocate, simply did all necessary gardening tasks themselves. It is possible that the predominance of males at Bobole, the moderately large number of older bachelors, and the lack of eligible young women as future wives had necessitated changes in the distribution of different gardening tasks between the sexes. If this had occurred, then the changes were of a quantitative sort. People were not performing tasks that ran counter to their perception of proper conduct. There was never a suggestion of ambivalence.

CHAPTER 4

Amogadola: *The Gardening Cycle*

The previous chapter portrayed the mood of gardening. By describing the sequence of tasks and their form, the sorts of gardens and the array of crops, by saying something of relationships between the people who worked together, its focus was upon what gardens and gardening looked like. At Bobole, the different activities—fencing, felling, planting, weeding—that followed one after another when each garden was made were not spread evenly through the year. There were periods of sustained effort and other times when the work load was light. This was true for families, for residential groups, and for the village as a whole. New gardens appeared in waves, and this synchrony imparted a seasonality to both inputs of labor and yield of crops. The present chapter is about these temporal patterns.[1]

Fencing and felling trees were the most conspicuous phases of garden preparation. They were the most visible, the most audible, and the easiest to measure. Figure 5 shows the temporal distribution of these activities through twelve months commencing in the middle of May, 1979. It records the length of new garden fence built and the area of trees felled during each of thirteen consecutive four-week periods. It also shows the planting regime of sweet potato gardens and, as a kite, an approximation of the felling regime of taro and yam gardens. The information summarized in the figure represents an overview for the entire community. All activities occurred throughout the year, but each showed periods of intense and reduced effort. Fencing was the most synchronized activity. There was a major peak from late June to the middle of August and a secondary peak through November. From December to April there was little fencing. Because it was usually necessary to enclose entirely a new garden area before it was safe to plant, felling followed fencing with a major peak in August and September, a minor peak in December, and a gradual decline in effort thereafter. The regime of work for felling was more regular than that for fencing. There were two reasons for this. First, felling could be a more leisurely activity than fencing because, with

41

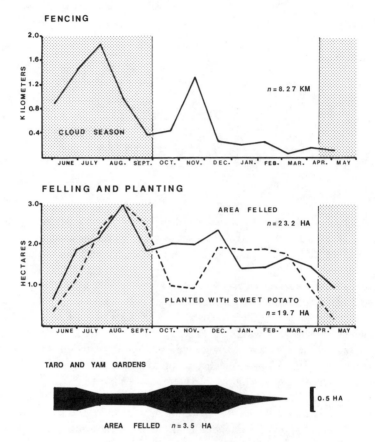

Fig. 5. Fencing, tree felling, and planting: the village pattern. Data points on figures 5 and 6 are from thirteen four-week periods, commencing on May 20, 1979, distributed across twelve months. Throughout the figures the cloud season is indicated by shading.

the garden secure from pigs, there was little urgency. Second, because felling could either precede or follow planting, the work was spread over a longer period. With sweet potato gardens planting showed an early high peak and a later, though lower, sustained peak. From October to December the total area felled exceeded the area of sweet potato gardens that was planted; in these months many people made taro and yam gardens.[2]

Figure 5 shows two waves of garden preparation. The first commenced rather abruptly soon after the onset of the cloud season and faded as that season ended; the second commenced in November and trailed away gradually through the pandanus season. The first wave appears, from the figure, to have been more intense but this requires qualification. Although two-thirds of the 8.27 kilometers of new fence line was built by early October, only 41 percent of the 23.2 hectares of new garden area was felled in this period. With sweet potato gardens 47 percent of 19.7 hectares was planted by early October. The discrepancy between the distribution of fencing and felling effort arose for several reasons. The first wave of gardens included many small areas that were felled in their entirety soon after they were fenced together with some larger gardens, portions of which were not felled until the second wave was underway. Thus, seventeen gardens prepared in the first wave, and felled without much delay, averaged 0.45 hectares with a range from 0.11 to 1.35 hectares. Another five gardens initiated at this time, but including areas felled later in the year, averaged 1.04 hectares. Their range was 0.58 to 2.15 hectares. Gardens prepared in the second wave were larger on average than those of the first wave that were felled quickly. Sixteen averaged 0.67 hectares, with a range from 0.10 to 1.75 hectares. The larger of this last set of gardens were planted progressively.

The smaller average size of most gardens prepared in the first wave, combined with the enclosure of areas that would be felled much later, helps account for the disproportionate emphasis upon fence building early in the cloud season. There was, as well, a difference between the two periods in the length of fence line that did not have to be built. There were many ways to save on fence building. Old fences could be repaired; new gardens that commenced as separate ventures could be combined; steep gullies and cliffs could be incorporated into the fence line; or gardens placed where they were inaccessible to pigs. At the series of gardens made before early October saving was well distributed among these categories and amounted to 1 kilometer of fence line. At gardens made after early October people avoided building about 2.5 kilometers of fence; nearly 1.5 kilometers of this were saved in gardens made east of Sioa beyond the range of pigs.

Figure 5 does not account for all the garden area at Bobole. Village gardens and two small gardens near mountain torrents added another hectare although only one-third of this area was productive at any time. In these gardens sweet potato was usually grown in mounds; fallow periods were short; and there were no trees to fell. There were also many tiny plots of taro, some of which did not require felling, others which did. A few larger taro plots were present in the upper reaches of Sioa watershed and, rumor had it, Awabi's large family, from House IV, tended a relatively large taro garden at lower altitudes where the family's sago was. The total area used for gardens in twelve months probably approached 25 hectares, or 0.23 hectares for each of the 109 people. For 16 hectares I obtained information concerning the sequence in which felling and planting occurred. In the first wave of gardens, felling preceded planting in 54 percent of about 5 hectares; in the

second wave in only 37 percent of about 11 hectares. At gardens prepared
after December the lag between planting and felling is shown in figure 5.

The patterns described here refer to the entire community of Bobole.
Differences of emphasis between longhouses are shown in figure 6 and merit
some comment. For House I the second wave of gardens was more intense
than the first with only 43 percent of fencing, 28 percent of felling, and 34
percent of planting in sweet potato gardens completed in the latter period.
About 0.24 hectares of yams were planted in December, but taro plantings
were spread through the year as many small plots both within and away from
sweet potato gardens. Some fence building in March and April, 1980, was
needed after a pig wreaked havoc in part of an old garden. For House II the
first wave of gardening was the more intense with 66 percent of fencing, 49
percent of felling, and 66 percent of planting in sweet potato gardens completed. Taro and yam gardens were made from October to December. One
taro garden was of 0.72 hectares, and a large yam garden, initiated by people
from House II but including participants from other longhouses, was 0.45
hectares. For House III there was a relatively close fit with the pattern
described for the village as a whole. Seventy-two percent of fencing, 50
percent of felling, and 48 percent of planting in sweet potato gardens occurred in the first wave of effort. The high value for fencing arose because a
1.15 hectare taro garden was initiated in May, 1979. A few small taro plots
were made from September to November, and a 0.13 hectare yam garden
was made in January. Finally, for House IV, the picture was dominated by
Sailo's grand miscalculation. Here, 81 percent of fencing, 50 percent of
felling, and 46 percent of planting in sweet potato gardens occurred in the
first wave of gardening. There was no clear second phase of fencing because
Sailo had already done more than enough to accommodate everyone's needs.
Indeed, the area of 4 hectares, enclosed but not felled by May, 1980,
approximated the 4.3 hectares of sweet potato garden planted by all House
IV people through the preceding year. Presumably Sailo's garden alleviated
much fence building in the year after we departed. People from House IV
made several small taro and yam gardens in October and November.

Available information was not sufficient to separate household patterns
into those of families. In most cases families who lived together at a longhouse gardened to the same pattern, though, at large communal gardens,
they were often somewhat out of phase. Families from Houses I and III
combined in gardening ventures more often than did families from other
combinations of houses, and this accounted for the similar overall patterns
shown by these longhouses (fig. 6). Gawani's family, from House IV, often
worked with Gawani's brother's family from House I; if their gardening
activities were considered separately, they would resemble patterns for
House I.

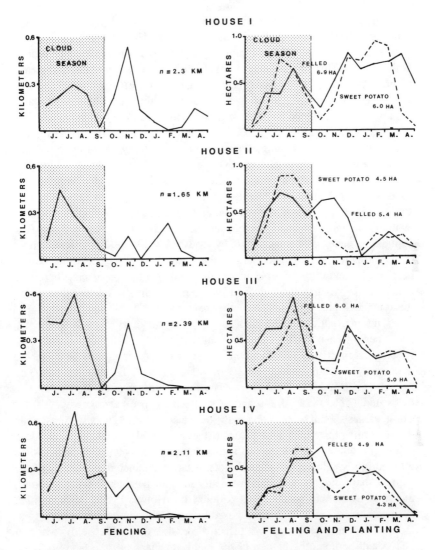

Fig. 6. Fencing, tree felling, and planting: longhouse patterns

The gardening cycle at Bobole may be characterized as follows. Between June and September many small sweet potato gardens were made. These were felled and planted in their entirety shortly after they had been fenced. In October and November emphasis shifted to planting taro and, to a lesser extent, yams. At this time additional areas, larger than those made in the cloud season, were enclosed for sweet potato gardens. These areas were gradually planted and felled through the months December to April; some of them included plots of yams. In the earlier gardening phase some people chose to enclose areas large enough to meet their planting needs in both phases. This meant more work building fences early on but greatly reduced labor later in the year (e.g., House II, fig. 6). For the village as a whole the first wave of gardening occupied more time than the second wave. This was because fence building was concentrated in the first wave and was the most arduous and sustained of the gardening tasks. Three final matters are important. First, fencing, felling, and, particularly, planting could and did occur at any time of the year. The bias for planting before felling that occurred in the pandanus season, and perhaps the planting of yams, may have been determined by climate. Otherwise, there appeared to be few constraints requiring strict adherence to a particular regime. Second, the options available to families or to longhouse communities were considerable. The contrasting patterns of work shown by Houses I and II and the different times that Houses II and III planted large areas of taro reflect these options. Third, despite the flexibility possible in timing major gardening events, there was considerable synchrony within and between households. Factors motivating the synchrony are discussed in a later chapter.

The areas cultivated by each longhouse community were different. On a per-person basis Houses I to IV cultivated 0.24, 0.19, 0.31, and 0.15 hectares, respectively. Known commitments to taro and yams near Bobole amounted to about one hectare each for Houses I, II, and III and 0.60 hectares for House IV. Thus, for sweet potato gardens only, Houses I to IV cultivated 0.21, 0.15, 0.27, and 0.13 hectares per person, respectively. These values should be regarded with some caution. First, they underestimate the commitment to taro and yams in that nearly all sweet potato gardens included scattered yam vines and some included tiny patches of taro that are ignored in my calculations. Small plots of taro were included in many of the gardens that residents of House I made through the pandanus season. Second, they miss some taro gardens that people from Houses II and III made high in the watershed of Sioa and the possible lower-altitude garden belonging to House IV. These problems will affect discussion of garden yields. My emphasis will be upon the pattern of the yield, its shape in time, and not upon actual quantities. Indeed, I have no information concerning quantities beyond the general statement that, at sweet potato gardens at least, yields must have been low. In densely populated regions of the New Guinea Highlands where garden produce is not supplemented by sago starch, the amount of land required per person for one year is often less than one-half the average value at Bobole.[3]

Knowledge of the planting regime of sweet potato gardens provided a guide to subsequent yield of sweet potato from those gardens. Figure 7

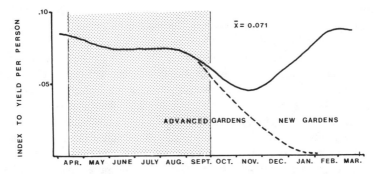

Fig. 7. Availability of sweet potato: the village pattern. Data points on figures 7, 8, and 9 are from thirteen four-week periods distributed across twelve months.

depicts the pattern of sweet potato availability through one year. Because there are no direct measures of yield, estimates in the figure incorporate two assumptions. First, it is assumed that the yield commenced in the fifth month after planting, was sustained at a high level to late in the eighth month, and declined steadily through the next two months.[4] This assumption permitted calculation of the area of garden expected to be yielding sweet potato in each four-week period; the estimate was adjusted to allow for lower rates of production early and late in the life of each garden. The assumption was supported by casual observations from several gardens. It was contradicted in three known cases; once when a small plot was harvested rapidly and was left to grow weeds in its ninth month and twice when portions of large gardens were searched for poor-grade tubers into their twelfth months. The larger gardens had been established in mid-1978 and are not relevant to the figure. No adjustments have been made for the rapidly harvested smaller garden or for others that may have been treated similarly. Nor have I adjusted for the fairly frequent observation that people delayed the harvest until the sixth month, giving early tubers the opportunity to increase in size. Although several options were available regarding the harvesting of sweet potato, these were not unlimited. Figure 7 depicts the shape of the potential yield and, I think, represents actual availability fairly well. The second assumption incorporated in the figure could be more serious. Available information is from gardens that began yielding in October, 1979, and would finish in January, 1981. We left Bobole in May, 1980! To illustrate the likely pattern during one twelve-month period, mid-March to mid-March, I have summed the estimates from the months October to January that are repeated twice. In truth the early part of the figure follows rather than precedes the tail end. The assumption I have written in is one of annual periodicity; that yields from one set of gardens in the months March to December, 1979, matched the pattern from a later set in March to December, 1980. This is not a timid assumption. I shall defend it later.

Figure 7 shows that availability of sweet potato dropped slightly from a peak in late March and April to hold at a high level from the middle of May to early September. It then dropped to a low in November. This drop was associated with a relatively steep decline in yields from old gardens. It was not until December that new gardens produced much sweet potato. Thereafter, availability increased rapidly to March. The lowest estimates of availability are half the highest estimates. Because there was no evidence that people grew large surpluses of tubers, the figure demonstrates that from at least October to December they were unable to meet starch requirements from sweet potato alone. This preliminary conclusion refers to the village community as a whole. It will be modified in reference to longhouse communities.

Information from the four longhouse communities is separated in figure 8. For each longhouse the shift from old gardens to new ones was initiated in October or November and became significant in December. There were differences between longhouses in the pattern of availability of sweet potato. For Houses III and IV the availability of sweet potato was low from October to December and higher in other months; this was the pattern observed for the village as a whole. For House I availability of sweet potato was highest through the latter half of the cloud season, dropped to low levels in November, rose steadily thereafter, and increased rapidly after June. For House II availability of sweet potato was highest in March, fell to a sustained low between late June and October and then steadily increased.[5]

The numerical values implied or stated on figures 7 and 8 are indices to sweet potato availability; they are transformations of the area that was yielding sweet potato in a given period corrected for times of low yield and adjusted as per-person availability. They have nothing to say concerning actual yields per day or per hectare. If yields per hectare did not differ greatly across all gardens, then comparison of the values assigned to longhouses is instructive. Average availability was highest per four-week period for House III. The average estimated for House III was approximately twice that estimated for Houses II and IV. There were only minor differences in the composition of longhouse communities by age. Thus, people from House III did not grow more sweet potato per person to feed a disproportionately large adult population. Since people did not grow a great excess of tubers, the trace shown for House III can be interpreted to mean that starch requirements may have been satisfied from sweet potato alone when the index to availability exceeded 0.09. On this argument people from House III required starch supplements from at least late September to the end of December. If an index value of 0.09 is accepted as meeting minimal needs of starch for people from

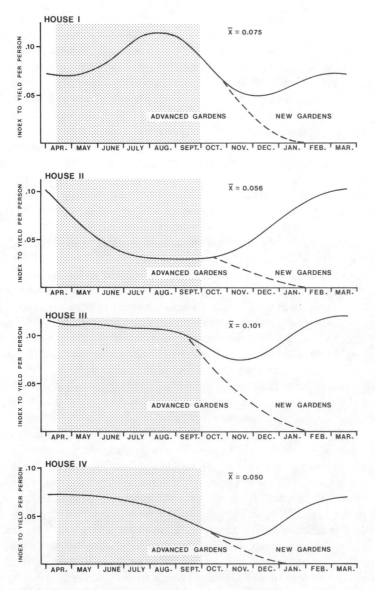

Fig. 8. Availability of sweet potato: longhouse patterns

House III, then it must be accepted as the value that met minimal needs for other people. Thus, sweet potato gardens may have satisfied starch requirements for people of House I from late June to mid-October, for people of House II in February, March, and April and for people of House IV not in

any month. The quantity of sweet potato produced per person by House I
was 75 percent of that produced by House III. The quantities produced per
person by Houses II and IV were only 56 percent and 50 percent, respectively, of the amount grown by House III. The implication is clear. Even
House III did not meet all starch requirements from sweet potato gardens.
At House I, more than 25 percent of starch must have been derived from
supplementary sources, and at Houses II and IV this supplement must have
exceeded 44 percent and 50 percent, respectively.

Sago, taro, and yams were the major starch supplements. The importance of sago will be considered in the next chapter. Here I comment on the
role of taro and yams. It was not possible to specify a yield profile for these
crops because, first, available information concerning planting was too im-
precise and, second, harvesting options, particularly for taro, were flexible.
Most yams required nine or ten months before they were ready to harvest and
the planting regime at the larger yam plots suggested that in 1980 most of the
crop would have been harvested from about late July to October or November. In 1979 yams were most visible as food in July and August and as stored
seed stock from September to November. Taro was most visible as food, and
as young sprouts held for planting, from September to December. Taro was
ready for harvesting about twelve months after planting. These few observations suggest that yams and taro did provide important supplements when the
supply of sweet potato was at its lowest ebb. How important is difficult to
assess. The areas under cultivation were small relative to the area of sweet
potato garden. But precise details are lacking. My conclusion is merely that
the availability of yams and taro was geared to the lull in sweet potato
production. It was neither as precisely tuned to that lull nor as important as
sago starch was. Two other crops were also significant in filling the sweet
potato gap. Both were introductions. They were pumpkin and choko, and,
together with sago, they were highly visible and frequently mentioned when
people complained that sweet potato was scarce. Bananas did not provide a
major starch supplement. They were not sufficiently abundant, and the supply appeared to be fairly uniform through the year.

At this juncture I must return to the assumption of annual periodicity
and defend the form in which figures 7 and 8 are presented. In those figures
I tore my estimates in half and took the tail to be the head. For House I an
approximate pattern of sweet potato availability was derived for the latter
half of 1979. Late in June of that year pigs were placed into a garden of about
1 hectare even though it was still supplying sweet potato. From that time
until new gardens began to yield in October the people of House I relied
upon four gardens. Details for these gardens are less precise than for later
gardens but allow calculation of tentative indices to sweet potato availability
from gardens harvested after June, 1979. The outcome is shown in figure 9

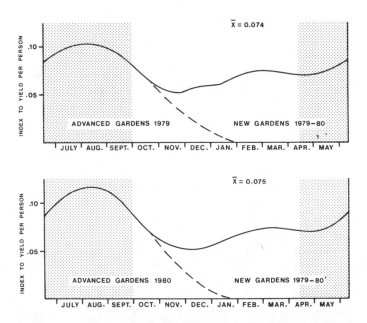

Fig. 9. Availability of sweet potato: House I patterns, 1979–80. The lower panel of this figure repeats information about House I contained on figure 8.

and is compared with the equivalent trace from figure 8. The two traces are of similar shape. Average sweet potato availability was essentially the same during corresponding periods of both years. For House III a large communal garden was sacrificed to pigs early in July, 1979. Thereafter, these people relied upon one moderately large garden that was turned over to pigs late in November together with plots held in two of the gardens used by House I. Sweet potato yields from these gardens would have declined after September. For people from House IV, other than Gawani's family, the situation was poor, or worse, after July, 1979. Sometime in July pigs were granted temporary access to a moderately large garden. After they were removed in the middle of August, people continued to take pumpkin, choko, and poor quality sweet potato from the garden. The pigs, in rather devastating fashion, had weeded the garden and either given remnant sweet potato a brief growing spurt or rendered meager takings accessible to the people. After July a garden of about .25 hectares was the primary source of sweet potato for people from House IV. This ceased to yield in January, 1980, and was given to pigs in February. The implied pattern of sweet potato availability for House IV residents in the latter half of 1979 differs somewhat from the trace shown in figure 8. The shift from relatively high to low availability was probably more abrupt in 1979 than in 1980. Sailo's garden was presumably the cause of the difference. I cannot comment usefully on the 1979 gardens of House II. These people did not sacrifice a garden to pigs in the middle of the year and contributed little to our larder from July to November; they were short of garden food during this period. In broad outline, though not necessarily in detail, patterns of sweet potato availability at Bobole through 1979 were similar to those predicted for 1980.

In this chapter I have described the preparation of gardens and the pattern of yield in terms of a repeated annual cycle. I am sure there was a lot of truth in this. I am equally sure that this framework for description did not reflect Etolo perceptions. For them, gardens did not follow neatly one upon another as a sequence that was tidily accommodated within a year. Their interest was with yields, and, of course, different crops operated on different time scales. Cucumbers yielded at the time people weeded their new gardens. Corn, leafy greens, and then beans followed. The corn and beans may have been entirely harvested before sweet potato was ready while some greens continued through the life of a garden. Ten months after planting, when returns of sweet potato had fallen drastically, the garden might still be important for pumpkin, choko, tannia, and taro. At fifteen months, with the garden smothered in grass, regenerating shrubs, and sprouting tree stumps, banana trees and sugarcane might have started to yield. It was these interlocking time scales that concerned the people. Within one year each family might initiate four, five, or even six garden plots. With some crops the yield shifted from one plot to another; with other crops it overlapped. Some plots that had ceased to produce sweet potato remained important for tannia, bananas, or sugarcane while elsewhere lowland pitpit might be gathered from what was no more, though never any less, than the memory of a former garden. There was not just one cycle; that was my abstraction. There was a constellation of overlapping, mutually containing cycles that progressively expanded the temporal dimension within which people moved. This dimension shifted from the immediacy, the abruptness, of corn and beans to the diffuseness of lowland pitpit and the pandan orchards in which it grew.

There was a sense in which time accumulated about the site of an old garden. A vine, used to make fish poison, would remind Gamia that this patch of regrowth was once his father's garden, that his father had planted the vine. Or, in tall regrowth, on the banks of Wosia Stream, Sailo would recall the taro garden that his long-dead parents had harvested two or three decades earlier. A family moved through this time each day. In one place they might be planting a newly cleared plot. From a garden they had made, perhaps six months earlier, they would harvest greens and sweet potato. On their way home they might divert to collect tannia, to tie tall sugarcane, or check the progress of young pigs at another site that was a year old. In an earlier garden there might be bunches of bananas to gather or to wrap as protection from fruit bats. And, in the pandanus season, both lowland pitpit and pandanus would return them to even earlier experiences.

Annual repetition was not the perception of the people. History itself was repeated—they were clothed in it—as they moved through each day. *Amogadola* was the word Efala wrote when describing how taro, which was planted in one season, would be ready to eat "in the next season of the same kind." The word hints at an unambiguous notion of annual periodicity. But, if I risk an interpretation of its etymology, my argument may be undiminished. *Amogadola* appears to be a composite term, its two parts having literal meanings that approximate "concluding" and "connecting," respectively. For the Etolo the cycle seems to enfold; any implied trajectory was hardly linear.

CHAPTER 5

Pigs, Pandans, and Sago

Pigs

Cross words were not unknown at Bobole. Anger erupted in response to intrusions—or presumed intrusions—upon pride or property. A nagging mother-in-law, demanding co-wife, irritating child, or lapse of diplomacy on my part could all at times raise temperatures. So could the feeling that someone had contributed less than expected to a garden, a village project, church matters, and so forth. There were also times of carefully controlled anger when a skilled protagonist might win compensation for a doubtful injury. Nearly always the mood was restrained. Words exchanged or speeches made were loud and vigorous but rarely spilled over as physical conflict. A lone hunting trip could dissipate a tense mood, or, when compensation was at stake, there was recourse to public negotiation before a village court. Ilabu bore this burden. Appointed years before as village policeman and granted a token monetary reward, Ilabu, by village consensus, was to hear and delicately to resolve or deflect such cases. It was also his duty, by government decree, to act as intermediary, messenger, and organizer of labor for the few demands imposed from outside; to clear weeds from the village, repair the guest house, build new lavatories, or upgrade the walking track. Often, it seemed, these tasks arose only in the few months before government officers would arrive. Ilabu did it all well and with dignity. There was no rancor.

In fifteen months violence came near the surface on only one occasion. A man's dog had killed one piglet and had injured another. The piglets were litter mates. They were three months old, and their owner had arrived to take revenge. He carried his ax and confronted the owner of the dog. The dog was prized as a hunter; it would not be relinquished easily. The men shouted at each other, threatening with their axes. They had to be held by others until their fury had subsided into a quarrelsome search for resolution. The harangue invoked the dog's murderous temperament, the worthlessness of people who could not care for livestock, the exceptional health of these particular piglets, their runtiness, the money they would have earned as adults, the fact that only one was dead. The dog's owner paid twenty kina and both men declared their satisfaction with the outcome.

Domestic pigs were important to the Etolo both as food and for exchange. They were exchanged either directly for money or as bride wealth and in return for hospitality or favors received. Most of the exchange was internal, some with neighboring Onabasulu and a very little with Huli people. The barrier that separated Etolo from Huli was less formidable as topography than it was in economic terms. There was little direct trade in pigs; the high prices charged by Huli ensured this. A few piglets were purchased from Huli or exchanged for sago, and some cooked meat reached Huli people as repayment for debts. In 1979, five to seven pigs together with seventy to one hundred fifty kina and perhaps a bush knife or ax was the recently inflated price for a bride, and there were strong moves to reduce this price.[1] Among the Huli the price for a bride was four or five times greater. Yet despite the different economic values Huli people sometimes fostered pigs with Etolo and had done so before Europeans arrived. To the Etolo who cared for the pigs the return might be money or a share of the carcass or of piglets produced. To the Huli owners the advantages included reduced work loads, the possibility of deception within their own community, and exploitation of Etolo. The last was accomplished through demands for compensation if a fostered pig died or, more seriously, if a Huli connected in some way to the pig's owner fell ill and died. By playing upon Etolo beliefs concerning witches, Huli people could sometimes win high compensation. At Bobole the feeling was strong that they were always the losers in these dealings with Huli; because "civilization" lay over the hill, it was always Etolo, and never Huli, who were bound to the other's hospitality.

Etolo pig husbandry seemed lackadaisical but was, in fact, a serious concern occupying much time and discussion. Pigs were not conspicuous in the village. Their presence and importance were manifest in less direct ways. The major commitment to building garden fences was necessary to prevent pigs from destroying crops. Many of the fences were maintained for a year or more after a garden had ceased yielding and the old garden was used as an enclosure for pigs. The village itself was ringed by a fence—sometimes hugging the ridge top, sometimes trailing inconspicuously along the edge of a steep gully in tall regrowth—designed to banish pigs from the central domain of people. At higher altitudes trails leading to primary forest were barred by other fences that reduced the chances that domestic pigs might run wild. The network of barriers was ever changing as gardens shifted and more recent fences replaced older ones. Maintenance was ongoing, but the responsibilities were diffuse; there was seldom a conspicuous work party for this purpose alone.

In the evenings, in that brief pause of the tropical day before dark, pigs were again always present. Penetrating, nasal, calls—*na, na, na,* "me, me, me"—came from several directions as people called their pigs for a portion of sweet potato, a vigorous scratch, to say goodnight, and to reinforce bonding. Grown pigs did not sleep in the village. At more distant gardens where family houses had been built off the ground they might sleep beneath the house.

Shortly before a female pig gave birth, she was housed either in a pen beneath a garden house or in a small, robust shelter built near a garden. This protected piglets from other people's dogs and, more importantly, was intended to capture and hold the litter. There was anxiety that the sow would give birth in the forest and that her piglets would become wild animals. The essence of Etolo pig husbandry was to tame the piglets before giving them free range. From the day of the birth, itself a time of keen excitement, the sow was released to forage alone. She had to return to the pen to nurse her litter. Later, with the pen clearly established as a nighttime retreat, the piglets would wander with the sow. But as soon as weaning was practical, the sow and her piglets were separated, and the piglets were cared for by people, nearly always women or older girls. The piglets would ride in string bags, wander in gardens, or be hurried along tracks with a rope tied to one leg. They slept in the longhouse, were pampered with good food, and became regular members of the congregation. For six weeks they were constantly with people to whom, inevitably, they became bonded. It was during this period that they might be sold and that they received personal names. There was a fatalistic streak to the Etolo. When I conducted a pig census, there were seven young pigs that had not yet received names. I asked why and was told: "When we are certain it will live, that will be time enough to name it." If the time came, then the pigs were named according to their color or pattern, after place names or in commemoration of their Huli origins. Two were named with economy as *Na,* "me," while two others whose early prospects had been doubtful were named Small. There were Moon, String, Raincoat, Tree Leaf, Marsupial Cat, and many others I could not translate.

Piglets grew rapidly during the weeks of domestication. Then it was time to release them while holding them close. People who had other pigs, well-trained animals that came when called, might introduce the youngster to the mob. Other people were more cautious. They placed the youngster in a securely fenced old garden where forage was reliable but roaming was confined. They might do this gradually, at first leaving the pig through the day and retrieving it at evening and only later abandoning it at night. For several months it might be carefully controlled in this way. Eventually it would have greater freedom and forage widely through areas of regrowth; at times it might be unrestrained by fences.

After the period of taming there was little need to feed pigs. Old gardens and regrowth provided ample food and recently abandoned gardens were fit for gluttony. The pith from sago and other palms was an irregular supplement to the diet. But all pigs were kept on a strong though invisible leash. The evening call to a small snack and a scratch was commonplace. More distant pigs were expected to answer a daytime call and be similarly rewarded. Woe betide a suspected renegade pig; its inevitable fate was sealed that much earlier.

Censusing the pig population was tricky; the animals were widely scattered and were often moved, and some were fostered away from Bobole. I could not count them directly. Instead I asked people to list their pigs by name, sex, and size. Different members of the one family usually claimed all pigs held by that family as their own, and the details I recorded allowed cross-referencing of pigs that might otherwise be counted twice. Privacy was needed before asking the questions, and it was necessary, as well, to penetrate modesty. People with few pigs usually told me they had none, so, pretending to misunderstand, I would ask for the pigs' names and learn of a couple. Some people were proud of their herds, giving details of litters that failed and others that were expected, and a few would gossip quite freely about other people's pigs. Finally, because the census was late in our stay, from mid-February to early April, it was stopped before completion; hinting that pork be included in one's own farewell feast is hardly well mannered.

The census accounted for eighty-three pigs owned by ninety-three people. Five pigs were fostered at other Etolo communities, and it is possible that details of a few others were withheld from me. The sex ratio for seventy-three animals was even, though females were more numerous than males among larger animals. Large sows, of course, were important for breeding whereas large boars could prove troublesome. At Bobole most male pigs were castrated while young; only a few—vividly portrayed by clenched fists, inverted and pressed together, or by a curled index finger placed in the mouth to evert the cheek—were needed to serve females. Thirty-three of the pigs were described as suckling or as small. They were probably less than about 25 kilograms. These balanced the twenty-nine animals killed by Bobole people during twelve months, suggesting that the pig population was relatively steady through that period. The distribution of pigs was very uneven between both families and longhouse communities, and there was no relationship between the number owned at census time and the number killed by a household during the year (table 1). The 18 residents of House III had more pigs per person than did people from any other longhouse. They had benefited from bride wealth payments of five pigs in May and seven in December. The 32 residents of House IV had contributed generously to feasts and may have depleted their herd on this account.

TABLE 1.   The Distribution of Pigs Among Longhouses

	Longhouse				
	I	II	III	IV	Total
No. of people in house	29	29	18	32	108
No. of owners in pig census[a]	29	25	18	21	93
No. of pigs reported	26	21	25	11	83
Pigs per person at census	0.90	0.84	1.39	0.52	0.89
Pigs per person killed in 12 months	0.21	0.17	0.39	0.34	0.27

[a]Owners include all members of a family.

At Bobole the motives for killing and eating pigs varied. Kills occurred irregularly; the information on figure 10 covers sixty-four weeks but may miss some small pigs that died of natural causes and were eaten in private by their owners. Two feasts, in July and August, accounted for seventeen pigs. One of these feasts was to honor the departure of Damule, a Huli pastor who had lived at Bobole for four years; the second was said to be because the pigs concerned had damaged gardens and were likely to damage others if they were not killed. Six large pigs were killed for distributions in connection with weddings, two for each of three weddings. Another two were killed to celebrate a visit from Huli religious instructors. The remainder were from a variety of causes; one to cover a debt to Huli, four youngsters that died of natural causes, another killed by a dog, one because it was said she was an inadequate mother, three that were renegade pigs, and one wild boar.

Renegade status could sometimes be attributed to pigs when this was convenient. One huge boar was a true escapee that had been missing for four years until it was found within 1 kilometer of the village by dogs that belonged to visiting Huli people. The pig was killed by a highly excited group of men and youths. It was Ilabu's pig, and he confounded everyone that day by making no effort to cook and share it. Even residents of his own household were confused and upset by his failure to issue the expected invitation; some of them slept elsewhere or waited till after dark before they returned home. Next morning—it must have been planned coincidence—one of Gago's pigs appeared in a garden. Gago was Ilabu's brother-in-law. The pig was declared a renegade and, with Gago's blessing, was dispatched after a chase with bows and arrows. Death in this manner reinforced its status as a renegade because domestic pigs were killed by a blow to the head. By adding this

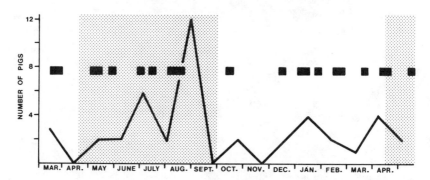

Fig. 10. Pig kills during sixty-four weeks. The figure shows the number of pigs eaten in each of sixteen four-week periods, commencing February 25, 1979. The broken bar records the actual weeks during which at least one pig was eaten.

animal to the unexpected capture of the previous day, Ilabu's honor remained untarnished. The amount Bobole people received appeared worthy while the irritating necessity to share generously and ostentatiously with the Huli visitors was satisfied.

On some occasions entire pigs or parts of pigs were sold. These included animals owned by Huli that had been fostered at Bobole, pigs brought from more distant Etolo communities, two owned by the pastor Damule, and five contributed by residents of Bobole. The pigs were sold after they had been cooked, and the practice was a relatively recent innovation. It was apparently borrowed from Huli and may well have been encouraged or introduced by pastors. At two levels the practice seemed to create tension and ambivalence. This was not apparent when the pig came from outside Bobole or had been reared locally but was not an Etolo pig. Ambivalence occurred when pigs were sold by residents of Bobole to other residents of Bobole. In more traditional practice residents could have presumed a free distribution of pork. Indeed, the kill for Damule's farewell feast may have been smaller than expected because some people were hesitant to contribute an animal for nothing. Certainly within three weeks of the feast two men each killed and sold a pig. The motives of one of these men were suspect because, it was said, he had offered a pig for the feast but then complained that the animal in question had escaped to the forest on the very day it was required. Pig markets were tense affairs. The owner of the pig did not negotiate. He appointed an agent and hovered nearby, nervously observing the proceedings. Transactions were rapid and curt; the money was concealed as it changed hands; and those who made purchases abandoned the marketplace at once. The atmosphere generated was of discomfort, of a veil torn from secrecy and of an event vaguely obscene. To sellers and purchasers alike, the transactions they had entered were the antithesis of sharing, and it was in this, I presume, that ambiguity was manifest.[2]

Pandans

The ripe fruit of *marita* pandanus grow to 90 centimeters in length. They are cylindrical, taper to the tip, and consist of hundreds of seeds arranged in whorls about a central fibrous core. Each seed is enclosed by a thin layer of bright red or yellowish flesh that abounds in oil. This oil was highly desired by people and was also eaten by Raggiana birds of paradise, small and large rats, and a multitude of insect pests.

The fruit was prepared by splitting it longitudinally and scraping out the core with a bush knife or cassowary bone dagger. The two long flaps of seeds, embedded in mats of spongy pith, were steamed in earth ovens. Cooked portions were placed in bowls—enamel if available or specially prepared from the base of a palm frond—mixed with water, and squeezed by hand to separate seeds from pith and the softened flesh from the seeds. The result was a bright red, thick sauce riddled with unwanted seeds. Decorous eating was an acquired knack. The mixture was scooped into the mouth, perhaps by hand in a private group but with a leaf spoon or a purchased one for communal eating. It was then sucked, the sauce was swallowed, and the seeds were spat on the ground to be licked clean by dogs. Young children, who might choke on seeds, were given the sauce after it had been squeezed or spat on sweet potato or taro. This was also done to save part of an evening meal for a flavorsome breakfast.

Pandan trees have a garish appearance. They perch on low trailing stilt roots, and their twisted gray trunks, with a scatter of spines, divide as half a dozen branches, each terminating as a tight head of long and narrow, jagged-edged fronds. The trees grow 4 meters tall, budding new heads as they age or throwing adventitious heads from the trunk. At Bobole *marita* pandanus were grown in orchards. These occurred near longhouses, at old longhouse sites, beside gardens, on the banks of large streams, hidden away in re-growth, or much further afield in places where people had lived fifteen or more years earlier. Sometimes one or two breadfruit trees towered awkwardly above the pandans; more often, in young orchards where the crowns of the trees did not touch, there was lowland pitpit.

All the orchards were below 1,200 meters altitude, and most were on moist slopes with good exposure to the sun. Very well-drained slopes were avoided. In some places there might be two or three trees only, either the remnant of an old orchard, an experimental planting, or as marks that signaled ownership of nearby resources. Elsewhere orchards of ten to twenty trees were common. The few orchards with hundreds of trees were the result of planting progressively over many years on areas that had proved very productive. In the vicinity of Bobole I obtained a rough estimate of four thousand to five thousand trees occupying about 10 hectares. People were actively expanding orchards, and at least three hundred cuttings, perhaps as many as five hundred, were planted during our stay. Most sweet potato gardens included a few transplants, and some gardens, which abutted flourishing orchards, had sixty or more young trees spread through the crop. A few people cleared parts of failing gardens and replanted with pandanus.

When they are four or five years old, pandans begin to bear fruit. Each head can produce one fruit each year, but in fact many fail and others are ruined by pests. At Bobole the care of orchards and of fruit was an ongoing though relatively inconspicuous affair. Men and women shared the tasks. Grass that grew beneath the trees was cut, and encroaching shrubs were slashed back. Pruning occurred frequently either to space developing heads, to remove unwanted adventitious growth, or to prepare other heads for transplanting. These last were trimmed so that only a tight sheath of cut fronds, 30 or 40 centimeters long, enclosed the growing tip. The sheath might be tied with vine for added protection. Some adventitious heads were treated in this way as were the heads of trees, planted years before, that had failed to yield well. Eventually these heads were cut from the trees and transplanted to new sites. Fences were not necessary for established trees, but all new plantings were protected from possible disturbance by pigs.

The ripening fruit was always watched with care. Large specimens were propped to prevent breakage, and many were wrapped tightly in dried leaves to discourage pests or to delay ripening. Bandaging in this way was used to spread the supply of fruit toward the close of the season. At this time, however, fruit often rotted before it ripened; it fermented rapidly and was smothered in ants, beetles, and wasps. The fronds of the trees would become spotted and yellowed, and some people associated the unhealthy appearance of trees and fruit with a coincident outbreak of stomach upsets.

The Etolo named at least thirteen varieties of *marita* pandanus. One bore yellowish fruit, the others bore red fruit. Four of the red varieties were early bearing; the other eight yielded later in the season. Eleven of the thirteen named varieties grew near Bobole itself and were mixed together in orchards; the missing two grew best at lower altitudes but were not abundant anywhere in Etolo territory. *Marita* pandanus had been subject to generations of artificial selection to produce varieties suited to different altitudes and, particularly, to spread the yield over as long a period as possible. It was a major cultigen and was propagated solely by vegetative means.

Despite the long program of selection, the fruit of *marita* pandanus was seasonal, more so than any other food except lowland pitpit. The trees commenced to set fruit in the latter half of the cloud season. The fruit matured slowly; it would not be ready to eat until the weather was warmer and the dismal, daylong mist and drizzle had given way to clear days and invigorating afternoon storms. When the march flies announced their irritating, biting presence in November, then, people said, it was time to be eating *marita;* and when, to everyone's relief, the march flies vanished in April, then the *marita* season was nearly over. *Gaheo* was the Etolo name for *marita* pandanus, and the season of its abundance was named *gaheoi.*

From late May to September pandanus was eaten infrequently. On one night a single fruit, small and damaged, might be shared by several people, but then there would be no more for several days, perhaps for a week. Exceptionally, in these months, three or four fruit ripened together, and a small feast would follow. It was difficult to keep track of what was happening. The frequency of eating seemed to decline as the cloud season progressed, but, in parallel, the extent of concealment increased. The new fruit was hidden away in string bags, sometimes wrapped for good measure, and the sauce was eaten within the longhouse. The rare gift was accepted with surprised pleasure.

In mid-October the mood relaxed. There were small feasts with eight or more fruit to celebrate the change of season. Now a few people would return home in the afternoon with a fruit hung jauntily across a shoulder. At each longhouse half a dozen fruit might be cooked every other night. The pace increased, though erratically. By early November we were being offered free helpings perhaps once a week. By early December guests were welcome at the longhouse, and the meal had shifted outdoors. By January pandanus was everywhere. Hands, clothes, feces, children were stained red. The ground was littered with spat seeds, and the treat was nearly every night. It was for breakfast, too. It was eaten at innumerable daytime picnics in gardens or beside streams. It was carried on hunting trips and traded to Huli. Through this period of abundance the entire mood of eating changed. Gardens were flourishing, work loads were low, and the weather was enjoyable. The late afternoon was relaxed with numerous visitors from within and outside Bobole. This continued until March and then gradually declined. An increasing proportion of fruit that remained at orchards was bandaged to stretch out the last of the harvest. By May most of it would be eaten.

Sago

The huge fronds of sago palms spill from the top of an 8 to 12 meter trunk. A grove of them scatters the light so that the air itself seems suffused with green. Beneath the palms is a gentle marsh of reeds and scattered shrubs since they flourish where the ground is saturated—in swamps, on banks of streams that are prone to flooding, in awkward dips of landscape that have become soaks, or in and alongside diversion channels that have been dug for the purpose.

The Etolo grew some sago palms as high as at altitudes of 1,100 meters but were dissatisfied with the yield of starch these plants produced. The palms they spoke highly of were at lower altitudes, at 700 or 800 meters, and to process these people left the village for extended periods. People said the palms had been planted, that they did not grow wild. In fact suckers were common, and these, if not simply cut away, were either transplanted or left to their own devices. Like *marita* pandanus, sago palms were individually owned but treated as a family resource. Adults planted for each of their children, and children, in turn, could inherit through either parent. There were at least sixteen named varieties of the palm. They were distinguished by size, the form and thickness of the trunk, the fall of the fronds, and the color of the starch. Two varieties were exceptionally large; three had reddish starch; and one was rare within Etolo territory. All of them, on their trunks and along the ribs of their fronds, bore vicious, three-centimeter spines. The people named these "sore."

Sago palms take many years to mature, and, at higher altitudes, this period may exceed twenty years. Once mature, they flower, and the accumulated starch in the trunk is redirected to the flowers and fruit. Before this process started, or had proceeded too far, people felled the palm and claimed the starch. A family camped near the sago grove for this purpose. They built a temporary shelter from fronds of the felled palm and might save unused fronds to use as thatch on a later occasion.

After a palm had been felled, it was cleaned of spines; the heart was saved for later eating; and basal sheaths of old fronds were trimmed along the length of the trunk. The trunk was then opened by splitting the tough outer rind and removing a portion to expose the pith. This was now pounded, fragmenting it to help free the contained starch. The back of a steel ax might be used for pounding, but the traditional tool—a shaped stone tightly bound to the short arm of an L-shaped handle—was preferred. Chopping the pith was not enough. To free the starch, one had to pulverize the material, breaking it into small pieces. The shape of the traditional pounder provided a forward blow as the tool struck down upon the pith. As pounding proceeded, the trunk was hollowed, and people sat within it as they continued work. These tasks were usually done by men and youths.

Fragmented pith from the trunk had to be beaten, washed, and filtered. These were done in troughs that were made by men and women. They were built near water from the basal portions of several fronds all of whose spines had been meticulously trimmed away. Two troughs, an upper one for beating and washing and a lower one for settling, formed a set. For the upper trough the bases of two fronds were placed end to end, overlapped, and pegged. They were fitted within the arms of an inclined trestle to form a central bowl, about 60 centimeters wide, that tapered to each end as long spouts. The complete trough was about 2.5 meters long and positioned so that a person standing in front could easily beat material in the bowl or standing beside it could squeeze that material. The lower spout from this trough opened above the settling trough, which was constructed so that its central bowl was narrower and deeper than the bowl of the beating trough. The settling trough rested horizontally on the ground or in a low trestle and was positioned so that it would not inconvenience a person beating pith.

Women collected pulverized pith from the sago trunk in open-mesh string bags and carried it to the beating trough. When the trough was full, a little water was poured over the pith, which was then beaten with long, slender, and flexible rods and a powerful overhead action. Pith that slid down the spout was caught in the close mesh of a string bag pegged at the lower end of the spout. When the pith had been beaten, it was washed and squeezed. The string bag was first repositioned halfway up the spout to act as a filter. Two-thirds of the pith was pushed into the upper spout, and water, scooped up in leaf basins, was poured over the remainder, which was then squeezed and manipulated by hand. This released the starch, which ran down the lower spout and filtered through the bag. When the water had drained away, the bag was twisted and squeezed, forcing starch into the settling trough. Retained pith was returned to the washing bowl, and the process was repeated several times until water running down the spout was relatively clear. The waste pith was then thrown aside onto a growing heap, and half the unwashed pith from the upper spout was moved into the bowl. Washing, squeezing, and filtering continued. The fine sago flour settled in the lower trough, where it was caught by pegged leaves that could be moved to drain off surplus water. After the flour settled, large cakes of it were placed in other closely woven string bags. Flour that was not intended for immediate eating was wrapped in leaf packages weighing as much as 10 kilograms. Some of these were stored temporarily in trees, and others were buried in mud where they remained good for more than a year. Storing indoors was not advised because the flour dried and crumbled and was not suited to cooking.

Pith toward the top of the palm often yielded little starch, and this section was sometimes covered to incubate the larvae of rhinoceros beetles. Some entire palms proved unsatisfactory and were treated in the same way. Failures in this grub-rearing program were frequent because either, at higher altitudes, few adult beetles laid eggs in the pith or, at lower altitudes, other people's pigs—tactfully referred to as wild animals—ruined the yield. People from Bobole processed sago palms in country that was increasingly used by other Etolo for other purposes. The palms they processed were their own, but the status of the land on which these grew was more ambiguous. When seven people returned almost empty-handed from a two-day trip to collect an expected large haul of sago grubs, they could not conceal aggrieved feelings as they shrugged off the depredations of pigs. They said that the proximity of domestic pigs had prevented them from protecting their intended harvest by building deadfall traps. One man, who was not concerned with the venture, indicated his opinion forcefully: if Bobole folk were responsible enough not to build traps, then other people should be equally responsible and control the behavior of their pigs.

Sago palms may be processed at any time of the year. Despite this, commitments to sago processing were not evenly spread through the year. Figure 11 depicts the pattern of activity. It is based on both an index to the number of families who left Bobole for a week to work sago and an estimate of the total number of workdays devoted to this activity. There was an increasing commitment to sago from late May to October and a rapid drop thereafter. The sawtooth shape to the graphs arose because different families synchronized their sago trips. They might share a camp and assist each other with various tasks. Or they would camp relatively close to each other and pay visits. The trace showing the number of workdays should be interpreted cautiously. On the one hand, it underestimates the total in that I was not always aware of what people were doing. On the other hand, it overestimates actual commitment in implying that people who were away spent all their time busily processing sago. Of course they didn't. The hard work got done, but the pace was relaxed, leaving time to socialize. When families processed palms only a few hours' walk from Bobole, then there was often much movement between the camp and the village. The aggregate of 1,536 days summed over all likely workers represents time not available for other major activities. This tally is for ten months, though it included the peak period of processing. It does not include numerous short excursions to retrieve sago from mud. Nor does it include trading activity. Two thousand days committed to sago might still underestimate the annual input.[3]

Seventy-three people at Bobole were older than about ten years and thus likely to contribute to sago work. Their average known contribution was 21 days in ten months. This was not uniform among longhouses. Differences among longhouses related to their respective commitments to sweet potato gardens. Thus, House III planted more sweet potato per person than did any other household; at House III 14 potential sago workers averaged 16.4 days for this activity. By contrast House IV planted the least sweet potato per person and the 21 potential sago workers committed an average of 25.5 days to processing sago. Values for Houses I and II are consistent with this pattern. The former household was much more reliant upon sweet potato than the latter and the average commitments to processing sago were 17.5 days

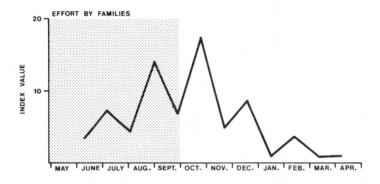

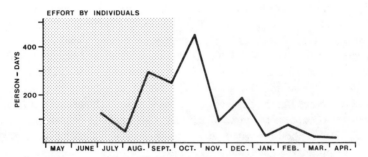

Fig. 11. Allocation of effort to processing sago palms. Data points concerning effort by families are from twelve four-week periods, commencing on May 20, 1979; data points concerning effort by individuals are from eleven four-week periods, commencing on June 17, 1979.

for 21 workers at House I and 24.4 days for 16.5 workers at House II. For twelve palms the average time required to complete processing was 25 person-days of work. Variation was high, however, with two palms processed in 30 person-days and, on another occasion, four palms occupying 152 person-days. The average value suggests that about sixty-one palms were processed by people from Bobole during the ten months I kept records. The annual total was probably a little higher than this.[4]

The frequency with which sago was eaten varied enormously. The annual pattern of eating would match that of processing the palms, provided the curve depicting the latter (fig. 11) was smoothed, dampened out, and shifted slightly in time. That is, although some sago was eaten throughout the year, and sago stored in mud was available to fill out lulls in the availability of root crops, most was eaten soon after it was obtained. In effect, this meant that sago, together with taro and yams, replaced sweet potato as the major source of starch from September to November in the transition phase between old and new gardens. The peak of sago processing in October was not merely preparation for a pending shortage of sweet potato. It also removed people physically from the proximity of failing gardens to an immediately available alternate source of starch. My guess is that, at Bobole, sago flour may have provided more than 30 percent of the calories derived from primary starch foods; for a few families this proportion may have exceeded one half.[5]

At Bobole people both purchased sago from neighbors at lower altitudes and traded it to Huli. Purchases filled two purposes. They offset shortages for immediate local consumption and permitted people from Bobole to act as intermediaries in a broader trading network. There was a scatter of both purchases and trade throughout the year but the peak period of the former was from June to August. Early in July and again in August large quantities of sago were required for feasts, and the limited processing that had preceded these events failed to meet needs. Immediately after the second feast, in mid-August, sago was exceedingly scarce; several groups traveled southwest to make purchases and large-scale processing of palms got under way. Trade in sago showed a clear peak from November through March. This followed a period of intense processing in October and reflected an accumulated surplus at this time. But the period of peak trade also corresponded to generally lighter work loads, pleasant weather, and an abundance of root crops from gardens. It was the time when large trading parties of Bedamini and Kaluli people from the west and south were passing through Bobole on their way to and from the highlands.

CHAPTER 6

Oheo Yafi: *Many Game Mammals*

The rolling hills of the Great Papuan Plateau are at altitudes of 600 to 700 meters. Fifteen kilometers to the north and 2,000 meters higher is the summit of Mt. Haliago. To journey from the plateau to the mountain is to encounter lower temperatures, more cloud cover, and fewer mosquitoes. Every few kilometers the vegetation changes. On the plateau the canopy of the hill forest is uneven; there are large trees supported by buttresses; and the understory is sparse. Between altitudes of 900 and 1,200 meters an oak forest dominates, though there, as at lower altitudes, the abundance of oak trees has been increased through the gardening activities of people. Oaks are easier to fell than are many other species; they provide good firewood and have been encouraged in garden regrowth. At and above 1,200 meters, beyond the zone of gardening, the frequency of oak trees declines. At these altitudes beech trees are present on ridges, and above 1,500 or 1,600 meters beech forest becomes the dominant type of vegetation.

Within the forests the understory, epiphytes, shape of trees, and the form of their bark change with altitude, aspect, drainage, and soil type. At lower altitudes palms, giant stilt-pandans, tree ferns, rattan vines, and a diversity of fig species are abundant. The forest litter includes many large leaves. With increasing altitude palms become less common and pandans are reduced to understory shrubs; the variety and abundance of gingers and ferns increase, and many trees have dense clusters of rotund fruit on their trunks. Pitcher plants disappear while orchids, prickly ant plants and rhododendrons are conspicuous epiphytes. There are fewer large-leafed trees, and the vines are more slender. Higher still, in the beech forest, everything changes again. The forest is less flamboyant. The trees are more regular, palms vanish, and ginger is less abundant. The litter is of small, compact leaves. There is more moss here, but there are fewer fungi. Vine bamboo trails across gaps in the forest, and high on the mountain nut pandans appear.

69

The forest provided plant food for people and for their pigs. It yielded material for building and for craft work. It provided fuel, utensils for cooking and eating, clothing, ornaments, and dyes, and a variety of trade items. Until very recently it was the source of medicinal and magical substances. The bark of some trees was spun into fiber and used to make skirts for women, aprons for men, and string bags for everyone. The fiber was traded to high-landers, who used it for the same purposes. Sheets of bark from some species of fig were beaten until soft and pliable and able to be used as rain capes. Rattan and many different kinds of lianas served as rope or cordage for tying parcels or for binding timber during house construction. Pig ropes were made from the long coarse fibers found within the stilt roots of pandans; containers for cooking or for holding water were made from bamboo; and ax handles and bows were made from certain palms. But the forest yielded more than plant products. It was also the source of animals that could be eaten.

The fauna of Haliago was abundant, and rich in kinds. At 800 meters tiny mounds of earth revealed entrances to burrows of claret-red crabs that lived on the floor of the forest. At 1,200 meters these terrestrial crabs were absent. The variety of ants, butterflies, and edible wood-boring larvae decreased on the journey up the mountain. Fish, frogs, reptiles, and birds behaved similarly. In the larger rivers of the plateau there were catfish weighing a kilogram, and there were large eels. Where the plateau fell away to the west, beyond the territory of Etolo, there were crocodiles and fresh water tortoises. Large varanid lizards and pythons were relatively common to altitudes as high as 800 or 900 meters; at these same altitudes, half a dozen species of small fish occurred in streams, and there were many species of frog, lizard, and snake. Above 1,000 meters only two species of fish were present; varanid lizards were rare; pythons were uncommon; and the variety of smaller reptiles progressively declined.

The largest birds—cassowary and mound-building jungle fowl—lived at high and low altitudes, but many medium-sized species such as magnificent ground pigeon, hornbill, and the bizarre barefaced crow seldom ventured up the mountain. Species of fantail, thicket flycatcher, and honey eater that were common at lower altitudes were replaced by related forms in the higher-altitude forests. Many other species were found where people had modified the landscape. In areas of grass there were wren warblers; in shrubby regrowth graybirds, pitohuis, and peltops with their bright red rumps and dazzling white cheeks, were all common; at pandan orchards Raggiana birds of paradise called loudly, displayed, and raided fruit; and over clearings swallows, swiftlets, and nightjars hawked for insects.[1]

At Bobole people lived and gardened between 1,000 and 1,200 meters. Their faunal environment was very different from that occupied by other Etolo. At the lower altitudes people had ready access to edible animals from many different groups—insects, fish, frogs, reptiles, birds, and mammals. At Bobole, when people thought of eating animals, they thought primarily of mammals. With one notable exception, residence at Bobole was advantageous to the pursuit of mammals. The exception was wild pigs, which were rare above 1,000 meters but because of their size were very attractive game. Wild pig chases that did occur at Bobole were frenetic events—ten or more men and youths shouted instructions as they converged upon the intended victim—but were usually false alarms. The ears of the quarry were clipped; it was a domestic pig in somebody's garden. During fifteen months only one genuine wild pig was taken, and it exacted a great price. Two days before our planned departure from Bobole, in May, 1980, Sigo suffered deep rips to one arm, his groin, and both legs when he ran headlong into a furious and frightened pig. The pig had already been struck in the rear by a well-aimed and well-sharpened ax. Sigo, who had bad cataracts, had arrived late at the chase and blocked the flight path of the pig. If Siagoba had not come at once and flung the boar from Sigo's fallen body, the outcome may have been more horrid. As it was, Siagoba himself received a gaping wound to the thigh. The pig was killed, cooked, and distributed, and our departure was brought forward by one day. It was necessary to carry Sigo across the mountains to a hospital; we traveled with him.

In addition to pigs, the other wild mammals of Haliago comprised two species of echidna, twenty-seven of marsupial, twenty-seven of rodent, two kinds of fruit bat, and an unknown number of small bats. Wild dogs had once occurred high on the mountain, but none had been seen or heard for about eight years. Among the echidnas, marsupials, and rodents the variety of kinds was greater, and there were more species of larger size above 1,000 meters than below. Of mammals heavier than 200 grams, the increment in species number at the higher altitude was produced by species that were arboreal (e.g., ring-tailed possums, cuscuses) or combined arboreal with terrestrial habits (e.g., some giant rats). This is shown on table 2. Strictly terrestrial animals such as bandicoots and wallabies were more evenly distributed across the altitude range although some of the species were more abundant at higher altitudes. The greater variety of mammal species above 1,000 meters contrasted with the pattern found in other groups of animals and contributed to the prominence of mammals in the diet of people who lived at Bobole.[2]

Larger species of echidna, marsupial, and rodent were classed as *Oheo* by Etolo. The category included all species heavier than 200 grams together with a few small species. I shall call them game mammals. They contributed more animal protein to the diet than did other wild fauna or, indeed, than did domestic pigs. During a 52-week period I received the skulls of nearly all game mammals killed by residents of Bobole. Often I saw the carcass before it was eaten and received the skull later. With most of these animals I learned something of the circumstances of capture, how it was obtained, who had obtained it, and so forth. After twelve months the collection comprised 1,802 skulls—probably more than 95 percent of all the game mammals that had been captured—and included thirty-four species. The species varied in numerical representation from a single individual of the diminutive ring-tailed possum *Pseudocheirus mayeri* to more than three hundred of the copper-

TABLE 2. The Distribution of Echidnas, Marsupials, and Rodents at Mt. Haliago

| | Number of Species within Altitudinal Range | | |
Weight Class	Seldom above 1,000 Meters	Above and Below 1,000 Meters	Seldom below 1,000 Meters
<200 g	2	17	4
200–1,000 g	2	9[a]	4
1–5 kg	3	4	7
5–15 kg	2	0	2
Total	9	30	17
Arboreal or Arboreal and Terrestrial Species > 200 g	4	3	10
Terrestrial species > 200 g	3	7	3

[a]Three species are aquatic or semiaquatic in their habits.

TABLE 3. Captures of Game Mammals According to Technique of Capture

Technique	Number of Captures
Trapped by	
Lines of deadfalls	501
Single deadfalls[a]	52
Tree traps	95
Snares	1
Not specified	28
Hunted	653
Casual encounter[b]	331
Stolen from dog	31
Technique not known	110

[a]Number includes some captures from short lines of deadfalls.
[b]Number includes many captures from unspecified hunts.

colored *Pseudocheirops cupreus*. They varied in size from the 100-gram gliding possum *Petaurus breviceps* to a species of tree kangaroo, *Dendrolagus dorianus*, that weighed more than 10 kilograms. They were captured by trapping, hunting, casual encounter, and robbing dogs. Table 3 separates the total catch according to the technique of capture, although, in 110 cases, this was not known. Each method requires some description.

Trapping for mammals was a very serious pursuit that occurred mostly during the cloud season. There were two primary sorts of traps, deadfalls and tree traps, and there were variants on each of these themes. In addition, I knew of one snare being made for mammals. It was built by the Huli pastor and one other man, and it yielded one specimen of the ring-tailed possum *Pseudocheirops cupreus*. Deadfall traps were made in large numbers. They consisted of a heavy log pivoted on one end and arranged to fall neatly between an avenue of stakes if an animal, traveling along the avenue, dislodged a carefully positioned trigger stick.[3]

Most deadfall traps were built into long fence lines. As many as forty traps would be spaced 5 meters apart in a fence of several hundred meters. The lines of traps were built within advanced secondary forest or in primary forest. Fifteen of them were operated during 1979; they amounted to nearly five hundred deadfalls in more than 3 kilometers of fence. Most of the lines were in primary forest between 1,000 and 1,400 meters altitude, but at least five were in advanced regrowth forest. The fence lines, up to 1 meter high, were sloped so that animals running beneath the overhang would pass the openings leading to each deadfall. There was no need to tempt animals into the traps with bait. The fence line was placed to block routes that animals might regularly traverse, and the design of the fence encouraged the animals to run along it. Each set of deadfalls was owned by one or two family groups. The traps were repaired, and the fence line sometimes was extended, early in the cloud season and were kept in operation for four or more months until returns of game seemed too low to warrant the effort of checking for captures and of maintenance.

In addition to the large systems of deadfall traps, people built shorter series of, perhaps, four or five traps. These were usually situated near gardens, where they were handy for checking without the need for a long walk. Single traps were made also in or near gardens where animals had destroyed or damaged crops and in the forest, either where animal tracks had been seen or beside a shelter. These traps did not have a fence to guide the quarry into the avenues of stakes, and thus they were baited. Sweet potato was the usual bait at Bobole though people said that live bait—a grasshopper or a wood grub wrapped in a small leaf package—was more effective. One last variant of the deadfall was intended for a single species of mammal, the cuscus *Strigocuscus gymnotis* that rests by day in terrestrial dens. When a den was located, the deadfall was built directly above the entrance and the entire trap was encased in a solid boxlike frame. No bait was used. The animal could either remain within its den and starve or leave the den and be killed by the log that it triggered to fall. These traps yielded a series of captures since, after one success, they were opened temporarily to let another animal occupy the den.

Tree traps were elaborate devices. They consisted of three nooses about 10 centimeters apart that closed rapidly when a hanging log was triggered to drop. The nooses were arranged above a horizontal limb, either a narrow log lying across a stream or a branch that people had placed above a track. In the latter case, other branches overhanging the track were cut away for some distance on either side of the track. This reduced the number of places where an animal could cross from one side to the other. Vines were used to weave a platform beneath the nooses and to make sidewalls so the animal had to move through the nooses and trigger the trap. Most tree traps were in re-growth forest. Others were in primary forest at places where there were few arboreal routes across a gully or a stream. The majority were made after lines of deadfalls had been repaired at a time when people were preparing new gardens.

Although hunting produced as many game mammals as did trapping, the former activity was characterized by a minimum of paraphernalia. Most men owned bows and arrows, but unless a wild pig was in the offing, the weapons usually remained hidden inside the longhouses. Men or youths who carried the weapons at other times, and this was seldom, were subject to lighthearted teasing. The implication was that the weapons belonged to a recent past when they had been essential for protection of self and family. That time had gone, and the bows and arrows, though not discarded, were an anachronism. For hunting, the essentials were physical endurance and a sharp ax. A good dog was a desirable addition. Virtually all hunting occurred during daylight, and hunting excursions lasted from a few hours to several days. Short trips were often by a solitary hunter, but on longer hunts several people would build a shelter in the forest and travel from it each day. They would depart soon after dawn and remain away for perhaps ten hours. Heavy rain in the afternoon would bring them home early. The basic strategy was to patrol the forest covering a great deal of extremely rugged country while scanning for likely dens of game. Discovery of a den would be followed by a stalk, a chase if the quarry had been flushed, or by climbing or felling a tree. Sometimes two hunters worked together, picking different routes through the forest but remaining sufficiently close so that they could come to each other's assistance if needed. There were occasional hazards. The lunge for a giant rat might be rewarded by a fearful bite; a scramble over rocks might become a tumble full of bruises; or a branch might break, dropping the hunter to the ground.

When Fuma fell toward the close of one day's hunt, he was stunned, spent a lonely and painful night huddled against a tree, and stumbled, badly scratched, into camp the next morning. He had lost his ax, but his bag of game was secure.

The presence of dogs on hunting trips tended to boost the catch and redirect the pursuit to different species. The dogs would patrol with or near the hunters and, to an extent, might direct the route taken. The initial choice of the area of search was the prerogative of the hunter but, thereafter, it was often the hunter who had to keep up with the dog. At the start of a hunt the dog might be carried part way along the route or would be repeatedly called or whistled to heel. Even so the dog could be an unwilling participant, abandoning the hunter and circling back to camp, pursuing wallabies by itself, or returning to the village if a bitch were in heat. There were usually about thirteen dogs at Bobole. They were named after particular species of game mammal or, with thought for their use, as Eye, Bark, Bark-for-Father, or just plain Dog. For the most part they were a motley lot—thin, scrawny, and cringing. Their staple diet was of sweet potato, with meat as an irregular luxury. Young dogs were introduced to their future role by being taken on hunts, preferably in the company of an experienced animal. They might be taught how to kill by being given live animals to shake to death. Older dogs that had proved themselves to be skilled hunters were spoken of with pride, and people always attributed the catch to the dog if the latter had been first to contact the quarry. My insistence upon knowing who had hunted with the dog was an irritating intrusion.

Some hunting occurred throughout the year, but most was in the pandanus season from December onward when people had a break from gardening and processing sago. Nearly all hunting was in forest above the altitude of the village, usually in primary forest above 1,200 meters. This was not influenced merely by the availability of species of game or even by the fact that, south from the mountain, people were entering country where territorial rights were held by other Etolo or Onabasulu. There were deeper reasons. When residents of Bobole traveled to lower altitudes, the forest still seemed vast and there were many animals to eat, but the land felt crowded with other people and their gardens. To go down the mountain was to enter a social domain. It was to turn one's back on Haliago and exclude, for the moment, the peculiarly beautiful and personal encounter with nature that is hunting.

Captures classed as casual encounters were a mixed bag. They included truly fortuitous captures as, for example, a bandicoot flushed from its nest by someone walking to a garden or a small carnivorous marsupial, even a cuscus, presenting itself as reward for the impulse to climb a tree. The category also included half-expected, half-hoped-for captures made while preparing new gardens, together with returns from brief hunts when a man, weary of planting or weeding, took his ax and dog and a long detour home. It was not always possible to know that a person had been intentionally hunting, but unless I knew this for sure the captures were classed as casual. Only a small number of animals were stolen from dogs. This usually happened when a bitch was caring for pups. The latter were held captive in an enclosure built onto the longhouse of the bitch's owner, and thefts occurred when the bitch was seen carrying an animal to her pups. Most of the animals obtained in this way were wallabies, *Dorcopsulus macleayi*.

The capture of an individual of a particular species of game mammal was influenced by many factors. These included attributes of the prey—its relative abundance, altitudinal distribution, habits, and habitat—and others intrinsic to people. The latter included available technology, the places where and the times when it was used, ownership of a dog, the desirability of the species as food or for other reasons, and the day-to-day circumstances that situated people in particular places at particular times. These multiple influences interacted. In aggregate they created a relationship between a person seeking game and the game animal itself. Ecologists call this relationship the "search image." To understand the nature of the annual catch, it is useful to explore some of these influences for the different species. Factors affecting the patterns of capture for species of bandicoot provide an instructive starting place.

Bandicoots are terrestrial and insectivorous or omnivorous marsupials. Four species occurred at Haliago and contributed 19.5 percent of game mammals captured in the year. The species differed in size, altitudinal distribution, and the variety of habitats they occupied. From smallest to largest they were the striped *Microperoryctes longicauda,* the drab brown *Peroryctes raffrayanus,* and the short-tailed, spiny-furred *Echymipera kalubu* and *Echymipera rufescens.* Large adult males of these species grew to 0.5, 1.0, 1.5, and more than 3.0 kilograms, respectively. Adult females of *M. longicauda* and *P. raffrayanus* were of similar size to the males, but females of the *Echymipera* species were only about half the size of the largest males.

The largest bandicoot species, *E. rufescens,* was common below altitudes of about 800 meters; at higher altitudes abundance declined; and none was recorded above 1,000 meters. *E. kalubu* and *P. raffrayanus* were present across the available altitudinal range; both were common, although the latter probably attained higher densities, at higher altitudes. The small *M. longicauda* was very abundant and complemented the altitudinal distribution of *E. rufescens* in being absent below about 900 meters; it made bulky nests beneath thick, relatively dry tangles of undergrowth or under logs. *P. raffrayanus, M. longicauda,* and *E. kalubu* were all present within primary forest. *P. raffrayanus* was largely restricted to this habitat. *M. longicauda* was also common in secondary forest; and *E. kalubu* occurred in all forest types, in recently abandoned gardens, and in areas of grass beside tracks, at pandan orchards, or at the village. The lower altitude species, *E. rufescens,* used secondary and primary forest.

The terrestrial habits of bandicoots made the animals vulnerable to traps, but the altitudinal distribution of *E. rufescens* placed it below the zone where trapping was frequent and quite outside the zone of hunting. Thus few *E. rufescens* were taken. One was from a line of deadfalls at 1,000 meters and three of the remaining four were known to have been obtained when people had left the village and traveled to lower altitudes to process sago. There were numerous captures of the other three species—66 *E. kalubu,* 194 *M. longicauda,* and 99 *P. raffrayanus.* Trapping accounted for 49 percent of *E. kalubu,* 58 percent of *M. longicauda,* and 78 percent of *P. raffrayanus* with the vast majority of trapped animals being taken in lines of unbaited deadfalls. The differing importance of trapping as a means of capturing each species corresponded to differences between them in habitat preferences. Because traplines were built in primary forest and advanced secondary forest, all three species were vulnerable to this mode of capture. The presence of *M. longicauda* and *E. kalubu* within secondary forest resulted in many captures at times when undergrowth was cleared from new garden sites. *E. kalubu* was additionally vulnerable because people disturbed it in grass near the village or at pandan orchards, and *M. longicauda* because it was abundant and its nests were moderately conspicuous. Only a minor proportion of the captures of each species was obtained on hunts. The importance of trapping and the association of many casual encounters with a major period of garden preparation meant that captures of all three species were concentrated in the cloud season. These temporal patterns are shown on figure 12.[4]

Altitudinal distribution and habitat preferences were important factors influencing the likelihood of capture of each species of game mammal. Species restricted to altitudes below about 900 meters were unlikely to be encountered except when people were processing sago, and species restricted to primary forest were unlikely to be taken in casual circumstances. Terrestrial or arboreal feeding habits were also important because, in primary forest, this separation partly corresponded to the chance that a species would be trapped or hunted and, in secondary forest, to the chance that it would be taken in a deadfall or a tree trap. Rarity or abundance added another dimension to the probability that a species would be captured, and, of course, size was important in the sense that small species might sometimes be ignored. Thus, hunters tended to concentrate their search on the largest species available while traps were designed to take all but the tiniest species. There were other peculiarities that influenced the capture of particular species.

In addition to the bandicoot *E. rufescens,* eight species of game mammal were either absent or rare at altitudes above 900 meters. A gliding possum,

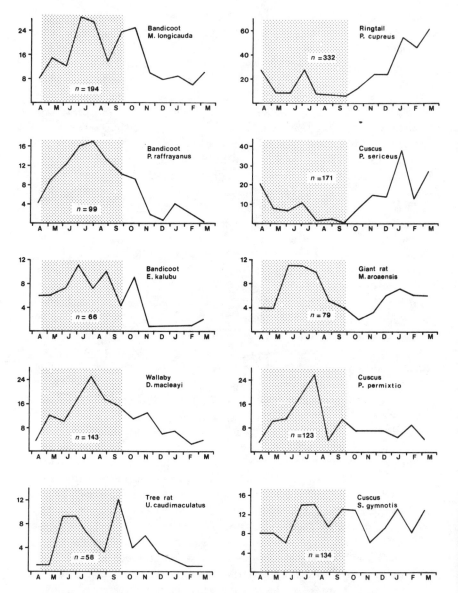

Fig. 12. Captures of ten species of game mammal. Data points on figures 12 and 13 are from thirteen four-week periods, commencing on March 25, 1979, distributed across twelve months.

Petaurus breviceps, and a ring-tailed possum, *Pseudocheirus mayeri,* occurred at higher altitudes, but their rarity and very small size influenced the
extremely low capture rate. Only one of each was taken in twelve months.
The remaining species were confined to lower altitudes. They were an
echidna, *Tachyglossus aculeatus;* two cuscuses, *Phalanger orientalis* and
Spilocuscus maculatus; another ring-tailed possum, *Pseudocheirus canescens;* a tree kangaroo, *Dendrolagus goodfellowi;* and a medium-sized rodent,
Xenuromys barbatus. Except for the tree kangaroo, most of these species
were obtained when people were processing sago. There were thirteen captures, though none were of the echidna or the rodent. Three were tree kangaroos taken in tree traps set at about 900 meters; at Haliago this species was
uncommon and apparently confined to a few small patches of undisturbed
forest on precipitous slopes of the torrent Sioa. One *Spilocuscus maculatus*
was obtained in unusual and unexpected circumstances when it was spotted
by two girls who had excused themselves from a Sunday service. The animal
was a visitor to higher altitudes, and its discovery and excited capture led to
a general exodus from church.

Seven species of largely terrestrial feeding habits, which utilized both
secondary and primary forest and had broad altitudinal distributions, were,
like the bandicoots discussed here, regularly trapped. They contributed
nearly 19 percent to the annual tally and comprised a larger and a smaller
marsupial carnivore, *Dasyurus albopunctatus* and *Myoictos melas,* respectively; a wallaby, *Dorcopsulus macleayi;* and five medium-sized rodents,
*Anisomys imitator, Macruromys major, Uromys caudimaculatus, Uromys
anak,* and *Parahydromys asper.* From 77 to 100 percent of the captures of
each of these species was by trapping, nearly always in deadfalls, although
a few *U. caudimaculatus* were caught in tree traps. The two marsupial carni-
vores yielded 29 captures, many of which were obtained because the animals
had visited lines of deadfalls to feed on carcasses of other game. The wallaby, with 143 captures, was commonly taken in unbaited deadfalls and, 21
times, by theft from dogs. There were another 11 records where wallaby
skulls were delivered to me with the information that the dog concerned had
greedily eaten everything but the head. Although these latter records are
excluded from the annual tally, they pose a puzzle. Only nine wallabies were
obtained on hunts. For unknown reasons dogs could capture wallabies more
easily when they hunted alone than when they hunted with a person. The
practice of fitting a bell to hunting dogs was not frequent enough to account
for the observations. Among the rodents, *Macruromys major* was taken least
often; it yielded only eight captures, presumably because it was uncommon.
For the two species of *Uromys,* captures obtained by methods other than
trapping differed in that most *U. caudimaculatus* were as casual encounters
and most *U. anak* were from hunting excursions. This difference arose be-

cause the former species was more abundant below 1,200 meters and the latter more abundant above this altitude. Figure 12 shows the temporal distribution of captures for the wallaby *D. macleayi* and the rodent *U. caudimaculatus;* in both cases captures were concentrated in the cloud season.

Animals caught in traps were taken at night while they were active. Those caught during hunts were taken during daylight hours when they were at rest. Species of game mammal that usually fed arboreally were not often exposed to deadfall traps but, if they occurred in primary forest at higher altitudes and occupied dens that dogs or people could locate, were likely to be obtained on hunts. There were five species in this category. Each weighed more than one kilogram, and together they contributed 31.7 percent to the annual catch. About 90 percent of the captures were obtained during hunts. Two of the species were ring-tailed possums, *Pseudocheirops corinnae* and *Pseudocheirops cupreus*. These animals rested in the hollow bases of trees, among root tangles and in hollow logs where dogs could locate them but seldom dislodge them. Many were taken when people hunted with a dog. Another two species, *Phalanger carmelitae* and *Phalanger sericeus,** were chocolate brown cuscuses that occupied dens high in trees—in hollows or beneath epiphyte tangles. They were obtained when hunters spotted likely den sites. *P. corinnae* and *P. carmelitae* were much less common than their respective congener and, thus, yielded far fewer captures. Occasional individuals of each of the four species were from tree traps people had built in primary forest, but because most animals were taken during hunts, captures were concentrated in the pandanus season; figure 12 shows records for the ring-tailed possum *P. cupreus* and the cuscus *P. sericeus*. The fifth species of game mammal that fell in this category was the tree kangaroo *Dendrolagus dorianus*. With some individuals weighing more than 10 kilograms, it was the largest game mammal available to Etolo. Only seventeen were taken in the year, and although all derived from hunts, the captures were spread through the year rather than being clustered in the pandanus season. This was because one man contributed to the capture of many of the animals, and unlike those of most other hunters, his hunting trips were fairly regularly spaced.

The largest rodents found at Haliago were two black and long-furred

---

Phalanger sericeus is currently the accepted name of a common, higher altitude, silky cuscus that has been long known in the literature as *Phalanger vestitus*. Recent taxonomic revision of the Papua New Guinean cuscuses restricts the name *vestitus* to a much less common, middle-altitude species from far western Papua New Guinea. In this book I follow Menzies and Pernetta (1986) in naming the similar middle-altitude form from Mt. Haliago as *Phalanger permixtio*. In much recent literature both these forms have been usually identified as *Phalanger interpositus*; see App. 2 for further details.

species, *Hyomys goliath* and *Mallomys aroaensis*. The former exceeded 1 kilogram, and the latter sometimes attained 2 kilograms. Both were present at higher altitudes, usually in primary forest, and combined terrestrial and arboreal feeding habits. They were seldom taken in casual circumstances but were almost equally vulnerable to trapping and hunting. They yielded 122 captures—nearly 7 percent of the annual tally. The temporal distribution of captures for *M. aroaensis* is shown on figure 12; the distribution is bimodal with peaks corresponding to major periods of trapping and hunting, respectively.

A few species of game mammal were present within the zone where trapping was frequent but were immune to deadfalls because they were strictly arboreal. They comprised a cuscus, *Phalanger permixtio;* a spectacularly striped possum, *Dactylopsila trivirgata;* and a rather small, orange-faced ring-tailed possum, *Pseudocheirus forbesi*. The cuscus yielded 123 of the 190 captures of these species. All three species were commonly captured when people felled trees to make gardens. Most striped possums were obtained in this way, but many of the cuscus and ring-tailed possum were from tree traps. Indeed, the abundance of the cuscus within secondary forest and its relatively large size (2 kilograms) made it the focus of this sort of trapping. Because it did not occur above perhaps 1,300 meters, it was not often taken on hunts. The ring-tailed possum, *P. forbesi,* was also uncommon in the hunter's bag but not because it was absent within the zone of hunting. This species built spherical nests within tangles of epiphytes or beneath pandan fronds. Presumably the nests were inconspicuous to hunters or were not worth the search when larger game were in the offing. Because both garden preparation and tree trapping occurred in the latter half of the cloud season, the captures of these three species peaked at this time. Records for the cuscus *P. permixtio* are shown on figure 12.

There were six species of game mammal whose captures did not clearly fit any of the patterns described thus far. A small marsupial carnivore, *Murexia longicaudata,* yielded seventeen captures, most in casual circumstances when people cleared garden areas or processed sago near the village and five from lines of deadfalls. A species of striped possum, *Dactylopsila palpator,* rested by day in hollow logs and fed by night on insect larvae that it extracted from rotting logs. It occurred in primary forest and advanced secondary forest at altitudes above 1,000 meters. Most of the twenty-three captures were from deadfall traps or obtained when people, usually accompanied by a dog, flushed animals from resting places as they walked through forest to check their traps. The large long-nosed echidna *Zaglossus bruijni* yielded only six captures in the year. It was present at higher altitudes, was highly prized for its meat, and when captured, its spines were kept as probes and its skulls as mementos. It was probably not common. This species fed on earthworms that it dug from the ground, but though these habits implied it may have been vulnerable to deadfalls, only one capture was from a trap. The bulk of the animals may have either prevented them entering deadfalls or saved them even though they triggered the trap. Four animals were located by dogs during extended hunting trips high on Haliago and were dug from their hiding places by men or youths.

Two species of medium-sized rat, *Hydromys chrysogaster* and *Crossomys moncktoni,* were associated with the numerous streams and torrents on Haliago. They fed on animals that they captured in the water. Nearly all of the twenty captures were obtained when people were otherwise engaged collecting frogs, searching for fish, or swimming. Both species sometimes foraged during daylight, particularly in the hours after dawn. They were very agile and capable of bursts of speed; presumably many that were seen escaped capture, and the modest catch does not reflect abundance.

The final species to be mentioned is the terrestrial cuscus *Strigocuscus gymnotis.* It yielded 134 captures that were more regularly distributed across time and among techniques than the captures of any other species of game mammal (see fig. 12). Eleven percent were from tree traps, 24 percent from deadfalls, 40 percent from specified hunts, and 14 percent as either casual encounters or from brief hunts. Some of the captures in deadfalls were from special traps built above dens. Another four percent of captures were stolen from dogs, and the fresh carcass of one youngster, already thoroughly chewed, was collected from the lair of the marsupial carnivore *Dasyurus albopunctatus* together with the live occupant of that lair. *S. gymnotis* grew to 3 or more kilograms, was abundant, was distributed across the available altitudinal range, and was present in all types of forest. It rested in terrestrial dens and fed both terrestrially and arboreally. It was a generalist, and its human predators responded accordingly. The relationship between this species and the hunters of Haliago epitomized their response to all game. The people were opportunistic hunters.

The widely differing habits and habitats of game mammals available at Haliago required of the people that they adopt an array of tactics in the pursuit of animal protein. That they accomplished this was demonstrated by the magnitude of the annual catch and the variety of species it included. The seven species that contributed most were obtained by diverse techniques. The ring-tailed possum *Pseudocheirops cupreus* and the cuscus *Phalanger sericeus* were hunted. A second cuscus, *Phalanger permixtio,* yielded to both tree traps and to casual collection during periods of garden preparation. The wallaby *Dorcopsulus macleayi* and the bandicoots *Peroryctes raffrayanus* and *Microperoryctes longicauda* were most often taken in deadfall traps though the last named frequently granted a meal when gardens were being cleared. And the terrestrial cuscus, though seen most often in the hunter's

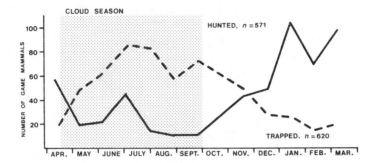

Fig. 13. Seasonal changes in species of captured game mammals. The figure shows pooled four-week tallies of five species that were most commonly obtained by hunting (i.e., *Phalanger sericeus*, *Phalanger carmelitae*, *Pseudocheirops cupreus*, *Pseudocheirops corinnae*, and *Dendrolagus dorianus*) and of eight species that were most commonly obtained by trapping (i.e., *Dasyurus albopunctatus*, *Microperoryctes longicauda*, *Peroryctes raffrayanus*, *Dorcopsulus macleayi*, *Anisomys imitator*, *Uromys caudimaculatus*, *Uromys anak*, and *Parahydromys asper*).

bag, shared its favors among all techniques. Alert eyes and quick hands produced the small, ring-tailed possum *Pseudocheirus forbesi* from concealed nests, striped possums *Dactylopsila trivirgata* from tree hollows, and the water rat *Crossomys moncktoni* from streams. The air of casualness about many captures was deceptive because, in fact, people were ever watchful for a likely catch and seldom left a possible resting place unexamined.

Two sets of circumstances patterned the annual catch. The first concerned altitudinal effects upon the distribution of species and the fact that people trapped or hunted within certain zones. Some species of game mammal were missing or poorly represented in the annual tally because they occurred at low altitudes and were seldom encountered. Species that were abundant in the middle altitude range, from 900 to 1,200 meters, were vulnerable to being trapped, and those restricted to higher altitudes were most likely to be captured during hunts. But it was the change from trapping to hunting, corresponding in part to the shift from cloud season to pandanus season, that gave most pattern to the catch by imposing a quantitative switch in the species taken through time. This pattern is summarized in figure 13.[5] Species that were trapped, the bandicoots and the wallaby, were major sources of animal protein through the cloud season and into the early pandanus season. Thereafter, these species gave way to an abundance of hunted game, particularly the ring-tailed possum *P. cupreus* and the cuscus *P. sericeus*. The terrestrial cuscus and the two largest species of rodent made their contribution throughout the year because they fell victim to both traps and hunters, but three other species, *Phalanger permixtio, Dactylopsila trivir-gata,* and *Pseudocheirus forbesi,* reinforced the seasonal theme because many were captured when gardens were prepared in the cloud season.

CHAPTER 7

By Whose Hand?

The pursuit of animals was influenced by their availability and the capacities of people. Chapter 6 showed how people had accommodated different techniques of capture to the variety of game mammals. They behaved as opportunistic predators sampling the fauna extensively and matching modes of pursuit to constraints of animal distribution and abundance. The end result was a large catch. Through much of the chapter the particular species of mammal or, to turn a cliche, their adaptations to their ways of death were central to the discussion. Here I turn to the people themselves. The emphasis is now with who trapped or hunted. Differences between sex and age classes of people, and among longhouse communities, are examined in terms of both performance and time committed to the chase. Most of the information concerns game mammals; trapping, hunting, and casual encounters are treated separately. The pursuit of other animals is considered at the close of the chapter.[1]

Trapping

Within nine weeks of arriving at Bobole I had received skulls of more than 100 game mammals. Twenty-two species were represented, but the ring-tailed possum *Pseudocheirus forbesi* was not one of them. I had expected this species to be present at Haliago, even moderately abundant. Early in the tenth week the first specimen appeared. The animal had been captured at night when it was feeding in a tree near a longhouse. In the same week 4 more were received in as many days. With them came a trickle of skulls from cuscuses and another species of ring-tailed possum. Some were delivered by boys, others by men. They were not returns from a hunting expedition because on those occasions a small, or large, flood of skulls came on the one day. In the following weeks the same people produced carcasses and skulls of bandicoots and wallabies; more of these species than they had previously delivered. They said the animals had been trapped. Through the next two months the same sequence of events was repeated several times. Some men

85

and youths would leave Bobole and, a few days later, return with skulls of half-a-dozen ring-tailed possums and cuscuses. The next week they and female kin would bring bandicoots, wallabies, and giant rats that had been trapped. This was the start of the trapping season.

Between mid-April and mid-July fifteen lines of deadfall traps were repaired. These had been out of action for about six months. Each line was owned by one or two families who were always members of the same long-house community.[2] Most were repaired within four or five consecutive days by small parties of men and youths who camped in the forest. A father and his sons, or several brothers, worked together. Coresidents, who were not blood relations, or male kin who were not coresidents, helped each other. While they worked, they disturbed and caught some mammals that were near the trapline. A few men interrupted the work to go hunting. The skulls of ring-tailed possums and cuscuses I received were a bonus; a side effect of repairing the lines of traps. At some lines the work was spread over several weeks, and at a few a man without sons old enough to help worked with his wife or a young daughter. The last line to be repaired was owned by an elderly woman. Her son was not interested in trapping. He married in May, and his wife provided the stimulus and much of the work that brought the traps to operating condition.

Once a line of traps was operating, it had to be checked and maintained. This work was shared widely. It required that someone visited the traps once or twice a week, collected the catch, reset the traps that had been sprung, and repaired damage to traps or fence line. Men and women and children older than about nine years contributed to these tasks. The journey to and from the traps took two or three hours. It could be accommodated within a relatively busy period of gardening. For more distant traplines a man usually retrieved the catch. He might combine his walk with a brief hunt but, more often, the trip was hurried because he would want to return to fencing or felling a new garden site. Some men routinely timed trap checks for Sunday since on this day no one was supposed to work and they did not regard a walk through the forest as work. When traps were closer to the village, women, youths, and children often collected the catch. Small groups of boys treated the task as an enjoyable adventure. If a family had left the village for another purpose, perhaps to process sago, someone was appointed to check their traps and receive any animals that resulted.

Early in the period of trapping people visited their traps every four or five days. Some made two trips a week; a few made one only. Commitments to gardening, the distance to the traps, and preferences for the quality of meat influenced these decisions. Regular visits guaranteed reasonably fresh meat. They also decreased the risk of scavenging by carnivorous marsupials. The number of animals trapped declined with time, and the frequency of visits decreased accordingly. Figure 14 depicts the effort in hours devoted to these large-scale trapping ventures. One-quarter of the annual total of around nineteen hundred hours was for initial repair of the traplines. After July effort decreased, and by January the trapping program was effectively over. The figure provides a second measure of effort. For each four-week period this tallies the number of weeks during which each of the traplines was operating. It makes no allowance for the initial phase of repairing traps. It is really a measure of the trapping pressure exerted upon populations of the animals being trapped. Trapping pressure increased to August and then declined. The values shown after December are not reliable. In the new year a few people visited their traplines if they were in the vicinity for some other purpose. But by this time few of the traps were functional and, after January, only three animals were trapped.

The number of captures in each four-week period increased rapidly to about 90 by June and July and then fell until January (fig. 14). Between 501 and 573 mammals were obtained from the fifteen lines. This is 1 mammal for each three or four hours of effort. The minimum count is of all mammals that were specified as taken in traps of this sort. The maximum includes bandicoots, the terrestrial cuscus *Strigocuscus gymnotis,* wallabies, and large rodents that were probably trapped but for which I failed to obtain clear details of capture technique. In addition to game mammals the traplines yielded some jungle fowl and small rats. I do not have details of these. The number of small rats was probably low because the traps were set so that animals of this size would be unlikely to dislodge the trigger.

The functional life of traplines varied from fourteen to about thirty-nine weeks. At one trapline there were occasional visits up to forty-five weeks. Most families ceased trapping in response to a fall in the rate of capture. It was the decrease in the number of captures each week that discouraged them (fig. 15). Changes in the number of captures per hour of effort were less important because people adjusted the frequency of visits to the size of the catch. Toward the close of the trapping period captured animals were often rather smelly but, unless decomposition was well advanced, they were still judged suitable for eating. If several smelly or inedible carcasses were obtained together or on successive visits, then for a few weeks people checked their traplines more regularly.

Through the first twenty weeks of trapping the rate of capture per hour of effort and per week decreased. This was largely because fewer bandicoots were trapped; indeed the spiny-furred *Echymipera kalubu* was never trapped after twenty weeks. People who persisted with their traps beyond about twenty-four weeks were rewarded with an upsurge in yield; this was due to an increase in the rate of capture of four species of giant rat. The wallaby *Dorcopsulus macleayi* gave a relatively stable yield for forty weeks.

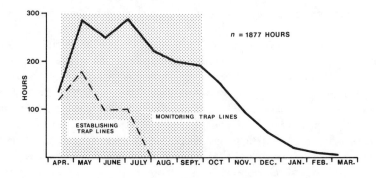

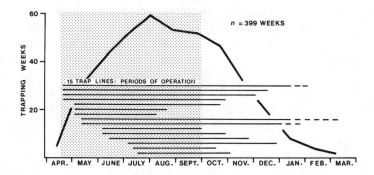

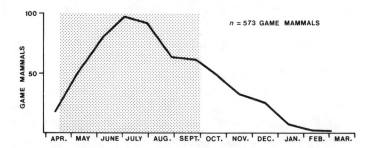

Fig. 14. Trapping with lines of deadfalls: effort and returns. Effort is recorded as person-hours and as trapping weeks; one line of deadfall traps that was operated during four consecutive weeks contributes four trapping weeks to the tally. In the central panel of the figure dashed lines indicate intermittent use of lines of deadfalls. Data points on figures 14, 16, 18, and 19 are from thirteen four-week periods, commencing on March 25, 1979, distributed across twelve months.

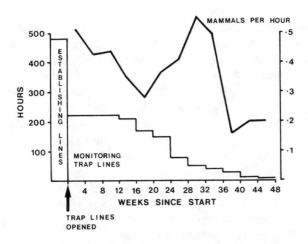

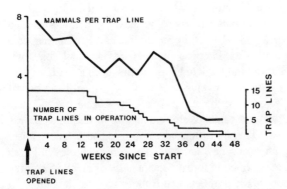

Fig. 15. Trapping with lines of deadfalls: success rates. On this figure records from traplines are standardized by taking the time when each line was opened as time zero.

Four traplines were closed after only fourteen or sixteen weeks although three of them had maintained a relatively high rate of capture. Those of Muga and Watabu were the last to be opened in 1979, and the latter had produced few captures. The lines of Gamia and Sagobea were inconveniently placed; they were high on the mountain, distant from Bobole, and in directions opposite to those where the families concerned were working new gardens. For all other families traplines were closed when the rate of capture, averaged over twelve weeks, fell below one animal each week. Some people deliberately sprang all drop logs on a final visit. Others simply ceased repairing broken traps while continuing to check any that remained functional.

Trapping with isolated deadfalls or with short series of traps complemented the large-scale ventures already described. It did so in terms of the
people who trapped and the times when they trapped. Thus, the families of
Fuago and Gawani did some trapping of this sort before they established their
traplines, and Sagobea, with his sons, built a line of five traps after they
closed their larger system. Gafaiya and Fuma, with their wives, and an older
bachelor, Silima, did not operate traplines, but all of them captured some
game mammals from single traps or short lines. The returns of all these
people together with four from women, four from youths, four from young
children, and one from an elderly man accounted for forty-seven of the
fifty-two reported captures. The distribution of captures through time
reflected a concentration of effort from September to November, when the
yield from traplines was falling (fig. 16), and the distribution among longhouses revealed that people from House IV, who had committed the least
effort to traplines, obtained more than half the tally.

Tree traps were made by men and older youths and were checked by
men, women, and youths. Children contributed little; they could have retrieved captured animals but would not have been able to set the traps. Most
tree traps were placed so they could be checked in the course of other
activities. Many were in regrowth near gardens and some were placed in
forest where a walking track led to a trapline or to a snare set for cassowaries.
Ninety-five captures of twelve species were said to have been taken in tree
traps. Forty-three were the cuscus *Phalanger permixtio*. Captures were concentrated in the latter half of the cloud season and into the early pandanus
season (fig. 16). This was after most traplines had been established and when
people were preparing new gardens. The three captures in February and one
in March were obtained in forest when a party of men had contracted for three
weeks to improve the trail between Bobole and the highlands.

I have no direct knowledge of the effort devoted to tree trapping. Some
people who made traps failed to obtain animals. If success was a measure of
effort, then people varied in their enthusiasm. Two of the four adult men
who did not operate traplines obtained twenty-two of the animals; Gafaiya
trapped thirteen over twenty weeks, and Silima obtained nine *Phalanger
permixtio* in a three-week burst of trapping. The tallies for Houses I to IV
were thirty-two, thirty, nine, and twenty-four, respectively. Within House I
the families of Ilabu, Ololo, and Gago made all the captures; they had
operated traplines. Ololo and Gago, who combined in their trapping ventures, captured the three *Dendrolagus goodfellowi* that I saw during my stay.
Ololo was elderly. He was reputed for his ability to obtain this species. He
was less popular for deciding to eat one of the animals. It stank! It was a
slimy, tree kangaroo soup even before it was cooked. I had refused to weigh

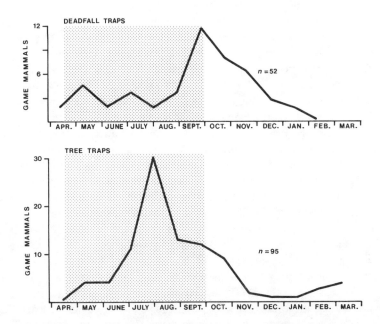

Fig. 16. Returns of game mammals from isolated deadfalls and tree traps

it. Ololo's coresidents went into hiding until the meal was over. They did not want to offend by declining their share.

Table 4 brings together the tallies from each sort of trapping. For each longhouse it provides estimates of the effort devoted to trapping with lines of deadfalls and of the success of these ventures. People from House IV spread their effort widely among available techniques but ended up with the lowest per-person tally of game mammals. People from House III concentrated their effort on traplines and achieved the highest per-person tally. Although the same species of mammals were available to everyone, it is clear that people did not utilize the fauna in the same way. But trapping was only one way of getting meat. The picture changes when we discover who hunted.

Hunting

Ololo's reputation as a trapper of tree kangaroos was a little gratuitous. The species he obtained was uncommon and distributed patchily at lower altitudes. Ololo alone held rights to trap and hunt within the area of its occurrence. He had relinquished some of those rights to Gago. But there was a second species of tree kangaroo at Haliago. *Dendrolagus dorianus* lived at higher altitudes, where it was hunted and had to be dispatched by hand. When cornered, this large tree kangaroo became enraged; it was all teeth and claws. It was safer if two people combined their efforts, and a brave dog was helpful. Two hunters working together gave another advantage. The animals were often in pairs or small groups, and two people could sometimes make more than one capture. Maga deserved his reputation as a hunter of this species. He contributed to the capture of eleven of the seventeen that were obtained during the year. He captured a female with a large youngster while hunting alone. No one else duplicated that feat. Two were captured when he hunted with another man, and seven when he was with his wife, Nowalia—the reputation was not his only.

Nowalia and Maga were the most enthusiastic hunters at Bobole. Maga was in his early to mid-forties; Nowalia in her early to mid-thirties. He was a tall man, lean, and handsomely bearded, a deacon of the church. Her smile was sudden and generous. Every four or five weeks they left the village at dawn, climbed the ridge toward the highlands, and turned east into the watershed of Woromo, where Maga had been granted hunting rights. He was of the Waisado people and a decade or so earlier had not owned land near Bobole. During these trips they left their four children in the care of other adults. Their dog named Dog (Uguno) was always with them, and they both carried axes, Nowalia's usually half-hidden in her string bag. On nine one-day hunts, two hunts of two days, and one hunt of four days, they captured

TABLE 4.   Returns of Trapped Mammals to Longhouses

	Longhouse			
	I	II	III	IV
Total catch	155	237	189	139
Percentage of catch from				
Lines of deadfalls	78.1	83.1	88.3	63.3
Single deadfalls	1.3	4.2	6.9	19.4
Tree traps	20.6	12.7	4.8	17.3
Mammals per person (52 weeks)	5.4	8.2	9.4	4.5
Effort and success with lines of deadfalls				
Number of operating lines	5	3	5	2
Effort in hours	568	465	585	259
Effort in weeks	116	107	117	59
Total catch	121	197	167	88
Number per hour	0.2	0.4	0.3	0.3
Number per week	1.0	1.8	1.4	1.5

eighty-one game mammals. Maga added forty-two to the tally in the course of seven other hunting trips that Nowalia did not join. And when Maga left the village on church business, Nowalia captured five more in one busy day. It would have been six, she said, but she had fallen on rocks while chasing a cuscus. Nowalia was then three months' pregnant; she stopped hunting at about six months. The game mammals Nowalia and Maga obtained on these occasions were 17 percent of all that were successfully hunted in the year. Only one other person came near to half their combined tally.

Gamia was a loner; a stocky, muscular man in his mid-thirties. He was one of the few Etolo men who had worked in the lowlands and one of very few who maintained the custom of wearing cane hoops around waist and calves. He smoked. He never wore European clothing, attended church, or helped with the pastor's garden. He was always one of the first to contribute to village tasks provided they were secular. With his wife and children Gamia lived one ridge to the west of Bobole. He built there in 1977 after a storm had destroyed part of the longhouse where he had lived. His large and comfortable family house, in a huge garden, looked down upon the full extent of Bobole. And he looked forward to the call for labor that would come from a pending mining venture in the Western Province. He had plans to open Bobole's first trade store. Gamia was more attuned than most to the ways of the Western world, and though he might let that world serve him, he would not be subordinated to it. He was a capable hunter. Maga had gone on nineteen hunting trips; fifteen were one-day hunts and only four were by himself. Two of his longer hunts were associated with church functions. Gamia's seven hunting trips lasted between two and four days. Only once was he not on his own. He camped in the forest with his dog, Bark, and during about twenty days captured fifty-four game mammals. On one of his trips he repaired his trapline; on another he closed it down. One four-day trip removed him from Bobole through the hectic rush of Christmas services. Once, with his brother-in-law, Ilabu, he contributed game mammals for a feast of welcome to a Christian outreach group. He abandoned the village for the duration of their visit.

At Bobole the attitude to trapping was matter-of-fact. Everyone did it or could do it. Yamini's line of traps had produced thirty-seven animals. When Yamini retrieved the catch, which was often, he crawled through the forest on wrists and knees. He had been afflicted by leprosy and had lost all fingers, most of his palms, and all but the heels of his feet. Neither Yamini nor anyone else thought much about it. In the cloud season people trapped; it was one of life's routines. Hunting was never routine. There was passion and delight here, not merely in the pleasure of the feast. Hunting was an individual act, a moment of privacy in a crowded social world. Yet by hunting, people could and did fulfill social obligations. When a person went hunting, most others knew it. The imminent return of a party of hunters created a mood of unspoken excitement.

Many factors motivated people to go hunting. For Maga and Nowalia, and for Gamia, hunting was fairly regular. For most other people it was intermittent. A few hunts were to relieve tension, some to resolve awkward social situations, and many early in the pandanus season because the pressure of gardening had eased. At the start of the cloud season hunting was often associated with repair to traplines, and some hunting was because men I employed to carry equipment into the forest chose to camp and hunt until their services were needed for the return trip to the village. In July some men and youths hunted to provide animals at a farewell feast to Pastor Damule and his family, and in March, 1980, more than half the hunting effort was for game to present to a visiting Christian group. Gift giving was the overt motivation for seven hunting trips between January and March, 1980, and, in late January and early February, there was a spate of hunting when men repaired the track to the highlands.

The combinations of people who hunted together were varied. A common theme was for males who were brothers, who called each other "brother," or were related as "uncle-nephew" to hunt together. Even where hunting parties were moderately large, kinship ties dominated their composition. The exceptions were usually strongly motivated. The hunting parties that sought game for church functions were of diverse composition, and men from Houses II, III, and IV hunted together soon after a difficult compensation case had caused tension between two of those households. On another occasion six youths from three longhouses went hunting for three days. Hunting trips that occurred after December were likely to include more people and last longer than trips before that month. Of twenty-six trips after December, seventeen lasted more than one day, and sixteen included more than one person. Before December only fourteen of thirty-six trips had lasted more than a day, and only nineteen had included more than one person. Nearly half the hunting trips that occurred in one year were undertaken by a woman, man, or youth on her or his own. Gamia from House I; Hamaga, Ega, Gafaiya, and Maga from House II; and Fuma and Sailo from House IV obtained half of all the mammals captured during specified hunts. Very often it was their own company they kept.

Although women shared in trapping ventures and captured game mammals in the course of gardening and other activities, they did not often join specific hunting ventures. Apart from Nowalia the only other woman who hunted was Esopa. She did so for three days with her husband, Siagoba. Their catch was twenty, three tree kangaroos included. No one said that women should not hunt. It was their own decision. Any inhibitions were probably developed early because hunting was not appropriate for young unmarried women. This was because it was considered improper that they go alone to the forest. It was after marriage that women were free to hunt; their husband's encouragement could be a turning point. Nor did anyone say that men should hunt, though, in fifty-two weeks, there were only three males older than fifteen years who never did—Yamini, who couldn't, and Ololo and Saliya, who were the oldest people at Bobole.

Boys were introduced to hunting early. Before they were ten, they camped in the forest with their fathers or older brothers. They built deadfall traps, practiced with axes, and received some formal instruction. They might accompany older people for a few hours but were not successful hunters and probably interfered with the success of others. Most of their time was spent in the vicinity of the forest camp. As boys aged, they experimented on their own, combining trips to check traps with hopeful hunting or spending a morning or afternoon in a lighthearted search for game. When they did make a catch, it was often fortuitous. Only twice was I confident animals were taken when boys were intent on hunting. Halia, about twelve years old, captured a wallaby, and Taiaro, on the brink of fifteen years, obtained a striped possum from a hollow log. Hunting was a more serious pursuit for youths of fifteen to twenty years. This was the age when they began to garden on their own. They were diffident as to their purpose and easily discouraged. They were conscious that much was expected of them but usually lacked the endurance to perform well. Five youths in this age class notched at least 350 hours of hunting among them and were rewarded with only twenty-six animals. Gundu obtained half the catch in a quarter of the hours.

Some men seldom hunted, a few because they were physically handicapped and others through lack of interest. Gago was one of the latter; he hunted only when camped in the forest for other reasons. But for people who did hunt, the effort devoted to hunting increased with age up to about the mid-forties, decreased slightly for those between mid-forty and mid-fifty and dropped abruptly among the elderly (fig. 17). For example, Sabaiya was the youngest of five men who were older than their mid-fifties. He hunted more often than the others but seldom did so for a full day or joined longer hunting excursions. He would occasionally hunt for a few hours after a morning spent gardening.

Hunting success increased sharply with age (fig. 17). Hunters who were younger than twenty years obtained, on average, one game mammal for every 13.5 hours they hunted. Hunters whose ages were between about mid-forty and mid-fifty were most successful; they captured one game mammal for every 3.5 hours hunting. Although twenty-seven different species of game mammal were taken by hunters, the increased success rate of older hunters was evidenced in the return rates of two species only. These were the ring-tailed possum *Pseudocheirops cupreus* and the cuscus *Phalanger seri-*

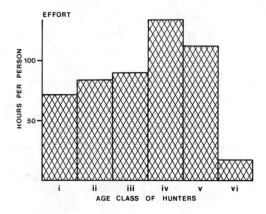

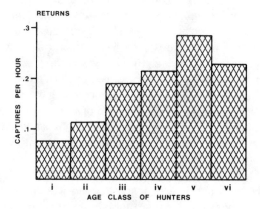

Fig. 17. Hunting effort and returns according to age class. Age classes are as follows: (i) approximately 15–19 years, (ii) approximately 20–25 years, (iii) approximately 26 years to early 30s, (iv) early or mid-30s to early 40s, (v) early or mid-40s to mid-50s and (vi) older than mid-50s.

ceus. The former were taken from terrestrial dens after dogs had located them and the latter from tree hollows. At Haliago the essentials of successful hunting were skill at spotting likely dens, skill with an ax, a capable dog, and the endurance to work with it. All these, including ownership of a dog, were enhanced by age. Older men who were capable hunters were less inclined to hunt if they did not own a dog, and the most successful of youthful hunters were those who could borrow a dog.

The temporal distribution of effort devoted to hunting complemented that spent on trapping. The latter activity was most intense through the cloud season, as the former was through the pandanus season. Figure 18 shows the

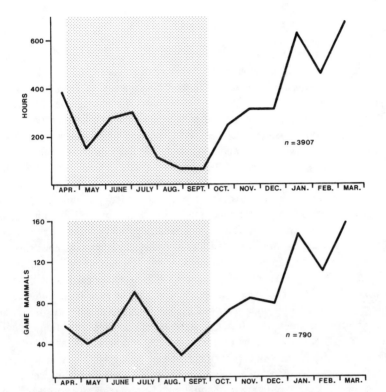

Fig. 18. Hunting effort and returns: the annual pattern

spread of hunting effort through the year; nearly half the aggregate of 3,900 hours was in the first twelve weeks of 1980.[3] Between late July and early October few people hunted; they were busy with gardens and processing sago. This pattern was common to all four longhouse communities, though the aggregate effort and the success differed among longhouses (table 5). Only 11 percent of hunting effort was by people from House III. They obtained 10 percent of the catch of about 790 animals. People from House II were most successful; they obtained 39 percent of the catch in 30 percent of the hours. For House I, the equivalent values were 22 percent of the catch in 27 percent of the hours; and, for House IV, 29 percent of the catch in 32 percent of the hours. People from House III, who had fared best in terms of trapped game, each received an average of only 3.8 game mammals from hunting during a fifty-two-week period. People from House II, whose share of trapped animals was generous, each received almost three times as many animals from hunting as did the residents of House III.

Casual Encounters

When people were repairing traplines or had contracted for road work, they sometimes hunted. This gave relief from routine tasks and increased the pleasure of evening meals. Some of the animals captured at these times were obtained fortuitously. A bandicoot may have built a nest near the abandoned trapline, or a striped possum may have been sleeping in a log that had to be moved. It was not possible for me always to be sure which animals had been hunted and which were lucky finds. When people hunted for just a few hours or found game as they checked their traps, I had the same difficulty. The previous account positioned many of these ambiguous captures within the hunted tally. In particular, two species of ring-tailed possum and two of cuscus were unlikely to be captured unless people had hunting in mind. This was because these species were usually found in primary forest above 1,200 meters. I assigned captures of these four species, plus those of other species taken with them, to hunters. This procedure left 260 captures of game mammals in the category of casual encounters. Their temporal distribution is shown on figure 19. They were captured when people were processing sago, felling trees, or pulling undergrowth for new gardens. Some were found as people walked between longhouses at night, others on frog-collecting expeditions, and a few when groups of youths were swimming. Males older than fifteen years produced 78 percent of them, and young boys obtained 4 percent. Females older than fifteen years obtained the remaining 18 percent.

Women were more likely to encounter and capture certain species. They collected eight of the sixteen water rats; boys and youths obtained another five. These animals were often captured when people were searching for frogs. Women also obtained a relatively large share of terrestrial species that occurred in regrowth; for example, one-third of casually obtained bandicoots were taken by women. But there were two categories of mammals that women seldom encountered, terrestrial species that were largely confined to

TABLE 5. Returns of Hunted Mammals to Longhouses

	Longhouse			
	I	II	III	IV
Total catch[a]	175	306	76	222
Total hours spent hunting	1,050	1,148	426	1,230
Success as mammals per hour	0.17	0.27	0.18	0.18
Mammals per person (52 weeks)	6.1	10.6	3.8	7.1

[a]Eleven unattributed mammals are excluded.

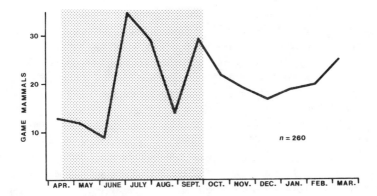

Fig. 19. Returns of game mammals from casual encounters

primary forest and all arboreal species. Women obtained only 7 percent of the casual takes of these game animals; more than fifty *Phalanger permixtio* were included in the tally, but only two were taken by women. The reason was that women seldom climbed trees. Nor were they often equipped with axes. Their success with bandicoots from regrowth was because they cleared much of the undergrowth from the new garden plots.

Differences in the tallies of longhouse communities were pronounced. People from Houses I and III obtained 14 percent and 11 percent, respectively, of the casually encountered mammals. Those from Houses II and IV fared better with 34 percent and 41 percent, respectively. People who were enthusiastic hunters were more attuned to stray captures and routinely checked places where mammals might rest. Another influence was the places where people made gardens. Residents of House IV had a clear advantage in that most of their gardens were at higher altitudes near undisturbed forest. The cloud season peak of casually encountered game mammals reflected increased gardening activity at this time.

Other Animals

While game mammals were the predominant sort of wildlife taken, the people did capture and eat many other animals. These ranged in size from cassowaries to tiny frogs and in appearance from birds' eggs to parasitic worms. Some were taken rarely and others at particular times of the year. For some I obtained reliable information and for others had to infer their importance.

After wild pigs, cassowaries were the largest animals in the forests of Haliago. The birds were more common than pigs and present at higher altitudes. Their flat, seed-filled droppings were often seen, and sometimes an individual cassowary would crash explosively through the undergrowth, panicked by the approach of a person. Men told stories of futile chases, of vigorously flung axes, and of the broken handles that resulted. The tales caused much merriment, but no one really expected to take an adult cassowary in this way. They were too dangerous; their feet were lethal weapons. One, a half-kilogram youngster, was caught by a dog during a hunt. The other eight cassowaries I knew of were from snares that men had made. They were caught through the latter half of the cloud season and into the early pandanus season when several species of wild pandans dropped fruit to the ground. The count of eight will understate the annual catch. Suguia, who contributed one bird to the tally I recorded, said his total catch had been four, though one had rotted in the snare. He was proud of his effort because he had been setting snares for some years and had never before caught a bird. Persistence and acquired skills were important to success. Suguia was certainly persistent, leaving the village for several days at a time to camp alone while tending to his snares.

With the exception of cassowaries, a few jungle fowl taken in deadfalls, and the eggs of these species, birds contributed little to diet. No concerted effort was directed at the many species available. Children and youths flung stones at stray birds but usually shrugged off a faulty trajectory. The half-dozen or so captures I saw were fledglings that had been stolen from nests. Eggs were eaten more regularly. I saw two large cassowary eggs that a man found in the forest, and I was often offered eggs of jungle fowl to purchase. The latter weighed up to 200 grams; they were available through most of the year from large mounds of leaf litter that the birds had scraped together. People who found an active mound claimed it until it ceased to yield.

Large hauls of the fruit bat *Dobsonia moluccensis* were obtained on two occasions. The animals were roosting in a cave in the rock wall of a mountain torrent. Sixty-six were captured in January and February by men who were hunting. People described other caves where fruit bats might be found but, despite stated intentions, did not visit these. Access to the caves was hazardous and often required a risky swim. Six additional fruit bats were captured during the year, two at night when they were feeding in shrubs and the others by day when they roosted in foliage. They were dislodged by stones and sturdy sticks.

Species of small mammals, mostly different varieties of rat, were available throughout the year. One species of rat was taken from its nests in grass, another when people visited pandanus orchards, and six terrestrial species, abundant in forest or gardens, by using lightweight deadfall traps. Tree hollows yielded some small bats, pigmy possums (*Distoechurus pennatus*), and groups of five or six pixie-eared tree mice (*Chiruromys vates*). The tree mouse was taken most often when people lived at their temporary sago camps; it gave relief from the monotony of a sago diet. Other bats were found beneath the fronds of banana trees and, when youths were exploring streams, under overhanging rocks. Three colonial species of soft-furred rat (*Pogonomys*) were dug from burrows, one by men who were hunting in the forest, the other two from regrowth when it was being cleared for new gardens. Captures of a second species of pygmy possum (*Cercartetus caudatus*) were also associated with garden clearance because the animals commonly spent the day in hollows of old tree fern trunks. The animals from regrowth dominated the catch of small mammals with the result that more small mammals were eaten at the time gardens were prepared; many were obtained by women because they cleared much of the undergrowth from garden sites.

Larger skinks were chased when they seemed accessible, and many were probably eaten. Some lizard eggs were dug up, and people wandering near streams were always watchful for water dragons that grew to 80 or 90 centimeters. Frogs and fish were taken regularly, the former as casual captures or on nocturnal expeditions and the latter by either stoning or poisoning in special dams. Expeditions to capture frogs were more common in the cloud season, and fish were eaten more often at the time when the yield from mammal traps was falling. Most hauls of fish were small, but on a few occasions groups of people visited swampy streams many hours' walk from Bobole and obtained as much as 20 kilograms of fish.

Finally, many invertebrate animals, especially insect larvae, were eaten. These included crayfish, land crabs, orb-web spiders, and roundworms and tapeworms from the bodies of marsupials, grasshoppers, mantids, and stick insects.[4] The crayfish were not available near Bobole, but, although small, they were regarded as tasty, and older men, women, and youths sometimes made special trips to collect them. Grasshoppers were usually eaten by children and they provided excellent tuition in the arts of stalking. Indeed, I was often distracted from the full force of a church service by the sight of several children, led by a very determined Matali, creeping stealthily around bushes experimenting with their own skills.

Insect larvae were the main source of invertebrate food. Several species—most were beetles—were used, and a clue to their importance was the rich nomenclature that referred to them. There were names for different kinds and for larvae, pupae, and adults, as well as names for look-alike grubs that people did not eat. The grubs of paper wasps were a delicacy, though hazardous to collect, while a reckless boast found me raiding a hive of European bees to steal grubs, which were eaten with pleasure, and honey that was found to be distastefully and disgracefully sweet. It did not again feature on the menu. The larvae of longhorn beetles were collected from rotting logs or deliberately felled trees and hauls of these were sometimes substantial. Moth larvae (Saturniidae) were collected for both food and the strongly woven cases that enclosed them; these were available only at altitudes below Bobole and during the early months of the year. It was the larvae of thickset rhinoceros beetles that contributed most. They were incubated in specially felled fish-tail palms and sago palms and, with elegant simplicity, were named *nudigi,* "food exists." Incubation time at Bobole was three months but at lower altitudes was shorter by as much as a month. Many were collected two to three months after people had processed sago. They were usually eaten with sago, and their strong, lingering, rather rancid smell was clear evidence of the meal. Olfactory clues told that moderately large collections were made through the middle months of the pandanus season.

The diversity of animal foods used by Etolo people was impressive. Yet what was striking for many items other than game mammals was the air of casualness surrounding their capture. Cassowaries were snared. The egg-producing mounds of jungle fowl were so conspicuous they invited plunder. Frog-collecting forays were moderately organized and a lot of fun as well. Fish were poisoned in temporary dams, and beetle larvae were carefully husbanded. But small mammals had almost to invite capture before they were taken; small birds were all but ignored; lizards were worth a brief dash or a quick lunge but might otherwise go unhindered while invertebrates, other than beetle larvae, were often waved aside. Many of these animals, together with casually taken frogs and a few fish that were stoned, provided small amounts of protein, especially to children, on an almost daily basis. They were always available, and people knew where and how to obtain them. Yet it seemed little deliberate planning went into their capture. It was rather that the daily round almost routinely placed people where they might add some animal snack to their meal or to that of a child. The walk to a garden would flush a lizard or reveal a bird's nest or a new spider's web. The path would cross a stream tempting a few minutes' pause to watch for frogs or to throw stones and concuss several fish. Clearing the undergrowth for a new round of planting exposed burrows of rats while a glance into the trunk of a tree fern before it was tossed on the rubbish heap might yield a pygmy possum. There was an inevitability about the capture of at least some items, and for many this is apparent in the link between the pattern of capture and the activity phase of the people. Some were associated with phases of the gardening cycle, others with work in pandanus orchards or with the processing of sago and so forth. These species contributed a small but regular quantity of dietary protein, and for many of them the relevant search image was effectively built into the daily routine of the people.

CHAPTER 8

Gela Pusa Hawio: *A Note on Techniques*

Every fourth week we suffered what we called "mad Friday." On the preceding Monday we would have gone to a forest camp at Magidobo, 350 meters higher than Bobole. Magidobo was one of the places where I studied the ecology of small rats. At first light each morning there were traps to be cleared, and in the late afternoon, usually in the rain, the traps had to be rebaited. Between these tasks we explored the steep forested ridges of Haliago, sat in flimsy hides watching Queen Parotia birds of paradise display on their arenas, or followed parties of legionary ants carrying red and black millipedes to their nests. The days at Magidobo always seemed a peaceful respite from the bustle of the village.

On the Friday we returned to Bobole, arriving late in the morning as everyone assembled for church and for us. From bushes, tangles of grass, and ever-present string bags there emerged offers of unlimited food. Mounds of sweet potato, huge bundles of watercress, beans we could never resist, chokos, and pumpkins were laid out inside our house as an instant market. Gago might be tying a bunch of bananas to the rafters. Someone would be negotiating in a whisper concerning our supply of sago, and Fuago, his son Biabe perched on his shoulders, would be leading shy, little Gisemae with a pawpaw that had been guarded for a week from the depredations of fruit bats. All we wanted and needed was one of our acrobatically modest, fully-dressed-while-changing-clothes washes in the invigorating stream below the village. But business had to be concluded first, and this was twofold.

Our larder had to be replenished and the purchases dispersed fairly among the too numerous sellers. At the same time I had to buy skulls of all game mammals that had been captured and eaten during our absence. On some Fridays there might be more than thirty but on one day only seventeen were delivered in the hour. They had to be labeled, the details of their identity and capture had to be recorded, then they had to be paid for and only later cleaned, dried, measured, and stored in plastic bags to grow fungus and be

103

cleaned again and again. Old, tall, lean Sagobea carried six skulls, more than he had ever brought, and for each of them I asked my ritual questions. *Go ei etolo*? as he presented each skull, "What is its name?" He named one as *fagena*, two as *hatagaui*, and three as *gedigi*. But two of his *gedigi* were not cuscuses as he asserted; they were skulls of ring-tailed possums. *Nufili*? I asked, "Were they captured by hand?" No, they were all trapped. *Noi ei sane*, "Whose traps?" I asked. They were all from Sagobea's traps, the giant rat *fagena* from a deadfall and the others from tree traps.

I singled out the ring-tailed possum skulls and showed them to Sagobea. *Gedigi pusa made*, "These are not cuscus skulls," I informed him. I was approaching the limit of my knowledge of the Etolo language but had embarked upon the slippery part of our conversation. My agreement was to purchase all skulls that originated from the people of Bobole. Skulls from other places were not acceptable, and now perhaps I was being put to the test. Monetary considerations aside, the skulls were quite valueless unless I was confident of information supplied with them. Our small house was overflowing with people who would delight in the interchange but would aid neither Sagobea nor myself.

Marshaling my fragmentary Etolo, sprinkling it liberally with pidgin that Sagobea did not understand, and, I suspect, tossing in some English as a personal comforter, I retraced the details Sagobea had given. He confirmed them and remained adamant that the ring-tailed possum skulls belonged to cuscuses. He had caught them himself. I disagreed, asserting that had he caught them, then he would not have misidentified them. Possums and cuscuses were distinct; their fur was quite different; and, I suggested, he was far too experienced to make an error of this kind. The words were probably incomprehensible but perhaps the mood was grasped. Or my irritation: I was weary, and I wanted to wash.

We circled around the problem. The key was the identity of those skulls, and in this area I now had to demonstrate my experience and expertise. I argued that I had lived at Bobole for many months and had seen more skulls than anyone else. I reminded Sagobea that I purchased skulls from everyone whereas each person saw only his or her own. Sweeping a hand across 100 or so skulls drying near the fire, I demonstrated the truth of my words. Where skulls were concerned, it was I, or so I asserted, who had the *dau digiti*, "the knowledge," and these wretched skulls belonged to ring-tailed possums. They could not be from cuscuses that Sagobea had trapped. Where had he obtained them, I demanded?

My argument or insistence won the day—or the fact that Etolo people were very disinclined to lie. The ring-tailed possum skulls had come from Gela, an Etolo community four or five hours' walk to the southwest. They had been given to Sagobea to sell to me, and he could hardly refuse the request. He had not been told their identity and had guessed. But, he insisted, only the ring-tailed possum skulls were at fault; the others were his own. I made a fine speech, hurled the guilty skulls into the fire with a dramatic *Gela pusa made,* "I will not buy skulls from Gela," and told whoever listened that if this happened again, I would not buy skulls from anyone. Then I paid Sagobea for his legitimate skulls, and we all subsided into a quieter mood as the vegetable pile grew, and more skulls appeared from their cockroach-filled leaf packages.

A group of youths sitting around the fire giggled and whispered of my (comic) forcefulness and Sagobea's shame and told late arrivers of the exciting moment. On the sidelines Sagobea mumbled about justice, the fact that he had caught four mammals and that only two skulls had come from Gela. They had been given to him, and he had been obliged to try and sell them. After half an hour he left. *Gela pusa hawio,* "goodbye Gela skull," one of the youths called cruelly, renaming him as he left the house, and then, when he was out of hearing, the youths collapsed in mirth telling and retelling each other the tale.

Sagobea came back the next day to sell us food. The disagreement was over, and we were friends. I was glad his new name did not stick.

Fortunately, there were few incidents of this kind. The technique I had adopted to study hunting and trapping was vulnerable to abuse. It could easily have collapsed. Within a few weeks of arriving at Bobole I established a market in skulls. I spread the word that skulls of all newly caught game mammals were now worth money. Payment would vary with the condition of the material received. If I was able to weigh the specimen intact, record biological information from it, and later obtain its skull in good condition, then I would pay fifty toea. For intact skulls from specimens I had not seen, the payment was thirty toea. Damaged skulls or a missing lower jaw meant forfeiture of ten toea on either count. But isolated lower jaws would not be bought since it was likely, and this proved correct, that some of these might be stored in the roofs or walls of houses as mementos to hunts and feasts that had been enjoyed in the past.

My concern was to obtain skulls from freshly captured animals so the information given with them would be current and reliable. I had no inclination toward accumulating a vast collection of skulls and acquiring curatorial skills. In reality, the market was in information, and the skulls were mere epiphenomena. This intrigued some people. The notion that the greater part of this hard-won, ever-growing collection would be abandoned to the Papua New Guinea National Museum was indicative of mild, if harmless, insanity.

The graded series of payments was designed to counter traditional eating practices. The brains of game mammals were a delicacy and were obtained most readily by breaking open the back of the skull. But this damage would disallow certain measurements needed to estimate the weight of animals from their skull lengths. The monetary incentive had the desired effect, and the people quickly became adept at cleaning the interior of crania without inflicting injury to the skulls. The smallest children learned to tease out the brains with the end of a slender stick. Only the dogs were offended.

Three problems were associated with this financially based technique. First, there were reservations and constraints operating within Etolo culture regarding the proper way to behave with captured game mammals. My research wants were an intrusion upon propriety, and together we had to resolve this dilemma. Second, it was essential that the information received was reliable and that purchased skulls did indeed derive from Bobole. I had initiated a highly localized cash economy in mammal skulls and was surely tempting anyone with entrepreneurial talents to look beyond Bobole for a source of skulls. Third, and thoroughly conducive to sleepless nights, were possible consequences for the pattern of hunting and trapping. I wished to record what the people did in a normal year and had just rendered the year far from normal. My own attachment to wildlife was such that I had no desire to increase unduly hunting pressure upon animal populations. In addition, the study would be futile if the information gathered were an artifact of the technique used. These problems and their resolution form the topic of this chapter.

In a small and crowded community there can be little privacy that is not sanctioned. Most adults and many children are intensely aware of the activities of other people They are also very interested in those activities. Family quarrels, irritating or sick children, disputes that arise when pigs damage gardens, personal grievances, visitors bearing gifts for relatives, and a person absent on a trading mission and expected to return shortly having made unknown purchases at a distant trade store are all highly visible and enormously interesting. Gossip is a commonplace, probably a necessity because the unceasing daily interactions between people require that each can position others within a mosaic of shifting moods and relationships. As well the bearer of gossip acquires that transient prestige that flows from being the center of attention. But gossiping, like all forms of human behavior, has its rules and conventions. Etolo gossip was shrouded with reserve. You could share information you had gained—that was your prerogative—but you could not ask, at least not directly. For example, late one evening, as we prepared dinner, Hesi was loudly and publicly berating his relatives. The entire village listened, and I asked a youth, who was leaning from our door to catch every nuance, what the quarrel was about. *Dau mati,* "I don't know," Yola replied, with the implication he had no idea a quarrel was in the air. My approach had been wrong. I had demonstrated ignorance, and the ignorant do not deserve enlightenment. Or worse, I had offended against conventions of privacy. The appropriate strategy was to participate by seeming to initiate gossip. To glean fragments of information and boldly state one's guess: "Hesi's foster daughter is leaving to live with his sister." (This was not entirely correct; Hesi was excitable.) Both participants to the exchange now appear to be on equal footing, they can trade information and may be obliged to. In the process they can cross-check, confirm, or elaborate their own knowledge.

At Bobole the obtaining and eating of meat were conspicuous affairs. Feasts that featured pigs or game mammals and markets at which cooked portions of pig were sold were public. Nestling birds, small lizards, and spiders intended for children were never concealed. On still evenings, as mist settled on the village, the smell of singeing fur could waft to every hearth. Nostrils would quiver and glances be exchanged, and someone might whisper her guess at the identity of the animal other people planned to eat. An hour after dawn Esopa and Siagoba might leave for their garden, Esopa with a small pig in her string bag and Siagoba carrying their son, Wanjebi. On mornings when they were accompanied by other children, then the message was clear. The children's parents, Nowalia and Maga, must have gone hunting, and since their catch was unlikely to be small, it could pay to be available in the evening. Telltale tufts of fur caught in heaped firewood where someone had sat or the acrid, lingering smell of a terrestrial cuscus told of meals that might not have been shared.

While everyone knew what was happening or was likely to happen, there were rules that guaranteed privacy. The first was that you should not ask. The second was that you should not see into another person's string bag. Fur might be bulging through the mesh from a pile of unwrapped game; plaited entrails might have slipped from an abdominal cavity to dangle free; and the smell might be mouth watering. You could talk of the gardens or of the trading party that passed through the village or would rest overnight, but you had to be oblivious to the contents of the string bag. To peer into it, to mention what you had not been shown, would be grotesque. It would be to request a share of the catch, the entirety if there was only one item, and that request could hardly be refused. To express interest was equivalent to asking, and to ask and not receive would shame the other party. For, clearly, success on the hunt or good luck at the traps meant a hunter or trapper and his or her family did not go short of meat, while your interest was tantamount to an expression of hunger. A successful hunter would be callous indeed if he or she failed to forgo this one meal. In shame the hunter would release it.

I entered this milieu with an interest in every game mammal that was captured but with no desire personally to eat the year's take. Ray Kelly had warned me of complications attached to even dispassionate expressions of interest; a decade earlier he had lived with Etolo people to the southwest of Bobole. It was advisable to proceed gradually. The introduction of a system of payments would ensure at least some skulls were obtained. It had the added advantage for research, though not for the development of personal relationships, that my requirements could be rationalized as having no connection with Etolo norms. My monetary arrangements placed me outside their system of obligations and responsibilities. A trickle of skulls commenced, and late one evening as people settled into a night's rest, a man came surreptitiously to our house, produced a live cuscus, and gave it to me to weigh. He spread the word that fifty toea could be obtained for a skull without risk that the animal attached to it would be lost as well. More people took the same risk or, to avoid the possibility of an unwanted encounter in our ever-crowded house, called me to their houses.

We made some mistakes. An enthusiastic remark from one of us that a cuscus, delivered for weighing, had an exceptionally fine coat . . . and it was ours to eat. An intended joke to a man with a bandicoot that he was certainly eating well tonight for had not we all just returned from the pig feast . . . and it was we who would eat well. Refusing an offer was difficult. It could be construed as insult and, in any event, was a pointless gesture. A person whose offer had been declined was already irretrievably committed; he or she would have to off-load the given animal in some other quarter. I developed a businesslike manner. I took the carcass and weighed it, commenced my routine questions as I measured and recorded other details and, only with the animal securely back in the string bag, digressed in search of further information—when had the hunt commenced and where had it occurred, who else had gone, what happened to the suckling youngster I was sure must have been present, and so forth? With nervous door-watching clients I remained ready to return the carcass if an unwanted visitor was seen approaching.

The people developed their own strategies. Some attempted to come privately. On weekdays the call to an evening church service often signaled Nowalia's appearance at our house, giggling as she disengaged endless carcasses from her string bag. Once, in the descending gloom, the whimpers we thought were her youngest child emerged as a struggling, firmly bound tree kangaroo. Some people, if the house was occupied, attempted to sit out other visitors in a room that reeked of fresh game; some of those visitors had the patience of Job! Others arrived on the pretext of selling vegetables, a large pumpkin or a pile of sweet potato concealing their real intentions. Many sent the children. Wagibe, Dugume, Sagolia, Buliba, and Mane trekked in and out of the house. The smaller the children—what loads they sometimes carried—the less vulnerable they were to the dictates of sharing. A few men preferred never to appear in person and burdened their wives with the task. Aro and Yabage, who regularly hunted together, often delivered for each other; if it was not their game they carried, then they could not relinquish it. Some sent messengers for me, particularly if there was a large haul that would be eaten within the confines of a single longhouse or if a highly prized animal, an echidna or a tree kangaroo, had been taken. Indeed, the money I had offered was not enough to warrant showing these prestigious animals before they were eaten and for them I eventually doubled the prices. Literacy (but not spelling) gave special advantages to one person. This signed note was delivered one afternoon: *Pida mi lak tok save long yu kam kuk haliap long haus bilong mi. Yu kalim sgel bilong gabuli. Mi igat wanpela Samting. Em tasol.* Carrying my scaling (*sgel*) equipment, I hurried (*haliap*), as instructed, to the cook house (*kuk haus*), where the game mammals (*kapuls* with an Etolo 'g') were waiting to be recorded for posterity!

There were a very few people who rode with careless ease through it all; they delivered their catch unabashed by the presence of others and carried it off openly for family consumption. Sometimes they offered to sell the entire evening meal, but here we had our own rule. We bought no game mammals. To have done so would have positioned us beyond the network of giving and receiving meat. When we were given game, we accepted with pleasure, reciprocated on a later occasion, and still paid for the skull. The skull was business; it was outside the terms of reference of the gift; though when Siagoba gave, to us or to others, he gave both meat and skull. Only rarely had skulls from gifts we received suffered rough treatment and, officially though too late, a reduction in value because the unfortunate animal had been too forcefully dispatched.

These individual strategies continued throughout our stay. Yet what really happened was that our house gradually became a sanctuary where conventional norms no longer applied. Our house was neutral ground; it held different rules. It was very rare that anyone forfeited part of a catch because it had been delivered for weighing. A few children sometimes pulled cultural strings, and one small, fiendishly delightful girl successfully wheedled an undeserved meal on more than one occasion. Her greatest feat—she was born an entrepreneur—was to accept my gift of two small rats, animals that I had trapped, and return the following morning without the knowledge of her parents and with two superbly prepared skulls and a demand for payment.

The first four weeks at Bobole produced ten skulls. Most were from a four-day trip into the forest where the small hunting party that remained with us, uncertain I imagine whether we could manage alone, was released from the crowded constraints of village life. Their catch was immediately visible, and I wielded my balances with impunity. That trip convinced many people that payment was possible. And the time to establish traplines was approaching. In the second four weeks, commencing March 25, I received ninety-nine skulls—the research program was underway and so was the endless cleaning. With the data floodgates opened, my next task was to be assured the information was reliable and fraudulent skulls were absent.

Early on, a few skulls did arrive from outside Bobole. There was no ambiguity; they were stated to be what they were. They were tests of the geographic sweep of my generosity, in one case brought by the visitor himself and, in the second case, delivered experimentally by Bobole children. I declined to purchase and did not return the skulls. It would be too easy for them to reappear later with a genuine batch. When carcasses had been weighed, there was no doubt as to recency of capture or the identity of skulls expected the next day. Transfers of ownership were complicating, but the necessity to ratify the higher value of skulls for animals that had been weighed resolved this. In fact, many adults who sent children with carcasses came themselves with the skulls, providing the opportunity to confirm or clarify information that was apt to be less than perfect. Very small children were willing informants but poor taxonomists. They would answer my questions with seriousness but often with no knowledge of the details of capture or of what they were carrying. On different occasions Gisemae carried bandicoots, ring-tailed possums, cuscuses, wallabies, and giant rats. With the convincing authority of her four years of age she named them all *awini*— predatory marsupial cats! With small children I could be confident only that the owner of the animal was correctly named; its identity and manner of capture were often in doubt. Within a day or two I would try to obtain further details from the primary source. There were as well several grizzly clues that told how a creature had died. A flattened appearance hinted at a deadfall trap; dirt adhering to the fur of the belly or caught between claws and in the mouth confirmed it. Bulging eyes or a narrow constriction along the torso showed that the noose of a tree trap had held fast.

Most care had to be taken with skulls from animals that I had not weighed. The majority were relatively fresh, with adhering tissue or morsels of brain that had escaped the delicate feeding procedure newly introduced to Bobole. These could safely be assumed to be recent and, hence, local in origin. Some skulls had been dried for a night or more, tied in a leaf package, and hidden in the roof, to be invaded by battalions of cockroaches but remain secure from malingering dogs. When at times the latter intention failed, the cringing culprit suffered fifty toeas' worth of punishment.

The procedure for checking reliability of information was based on one assumption—that people knew what they had caught or what they had eaten but were less likely to be able to identify skulls. A few were good at this but most had never been interested. With some practice I became accomplished at on-the-spot identification of skulls as scientific species of mammals. With rather more effort I learned the basic set of names Etolo people applied to these species. There were numerous nomenclatural intricacies to be acquired later. My early tool kit was the short list, the names in regular use. Armed with this list, I was able to check the identity of the skull against the name given with it. No match, no money would be a harsh parody of the technique. Not everyone in a community is equally attentive to matters of nomenclature, and there were, of course, many legitimate forms of error. Some of the large rats had distinctive skulls but were superficially alike in external form; they were candidates for justifiable misidentification. A person delivering three skulls might employ the correct set of names but attach each of them to the wrong specimen. This was acceptable. And poor Sagobea, on another occasion, brought the skull of a giant rat declaring it to be from a cuscus I had weighed the previous evening. Nothing could dissuade him, and I paid up guessing at the truth. Later that day his cuscus skull arrived and was named as the giant rat that also had been seen the evening before. The meal had been shared and the skulls inadvertently swapped in the gloomy interior of the longhouse.

In fact, I really need not have worried. Cross-checking was useful in confirming information and in expanding that information. Only twice that I know of were false skulls delivered: the two from Sagobea, in the incident described earlier in which he had been positioned by obligation to pursue an awkward, probably unwanted, scene; and on a second occasion when a Bobole lad carried several skulls from the neighboring Huli, where he had been visiting, and foolishly attributed them to his father, who had been elsewhere processing sago. In the latter instance all elicited identifications were correct, but my knowledge of everyone's whereabouts solved the problem. Only for one skull in a collection of more than two thousand was I in doubt about its origin and the accompanying story.

The information I received was usually correct. The reason was beautifully simple; the Etolo were exceptionally honest. Frequently they withheld information that they did not wish to share or that they considered none of my business, but they were extraordinarily disinclined to lie. Two hours' walk from Bobole was Namosado. People traveled between these villages every week. Yet at Namosado everyone stored his or her mammal skulls month after month because I had said that eventually I would come and buy them. They did not attempt to feed them into the Bobole collection and guarantee an income as it came to hand; a different composition of species would have informed me had they done so. The Etolo were simply a pleasure to do business with.

A digression is needed, an embarrassing footnote to the technique described above. The technique required sufficient knowledge of the names Etolo people attached to animals and of errors they might make in using those names, that—to put it bluntly—I could beat them at their own game should the occasion arise. As it happened this proved unnecessary; the game was not on. But, although I applied the technique modestly, feeling my way into it, there was a smell of arrogance about it. I had arrived entirely ignorant of

Etolo nomenclatural procedures. I was equipped with a set of scientific names and could fit these to the species that appeared. A list of Etolo names was accumulated quickly, but at the outset this was vacuous because only my hosts could teach me how to connect the two sets of names. I was in their hands. And, of course, an early aim was to penetrate and understand Etolo classificatory practices. To do this successfully, one needed an attitude of ignorance: to remain the pupil, slow to master the art, to ask and ask again and, only at the end, cautiously combine all identifications given to numerous examples of a single scientific species, preferably obtained in a variety of contexts, and deduce how the people dealt with that species. This need contrasts starkly with the procedures outlined above. The technical dictates of buying skulls and of discovering names were in conflict. No sooner did a skull form itself into a question mark than I found myself trying to instruct my teachers! Elsewhere, though not in this book, I shall discuss Etolo classification and will have to consider this problem to the satisfaction of critical readers. Here, I offer two brief defenses: first, for the majority of game mammals, Etolo nomenclature was simple and unambiguous; and, second, I always gave first say to the person carrying the carcass. Well, not quite always! Nowalia and Yabage, in particular, enjoyed delicious and instructive name games with me, teasing my grasp of Etolo nomenclature with a host of seldom used synonyms.[1]

The third problem I encountered concerns possible impacts upon the frequency and pattern of trapping and hunting. This emerged as a potential difficulty from the moment skulls were rewarded with money. It was exacerbated by comparison of information I obtained with that of Ray Kelly. From May, 1968, to July, 1969, Kelly lived with Etolo people at Gabulusado, 11 kilometers southwest of Bobole and 325 meters lower in altitude. He studied the social structure of the people and provided valuable information about their ecology. On two counts his observations concerning game mammals differed from mine. First, the number of game mammals eaten at Gabulusado was, per person, very much less than at Bobole. Second, at the former community most game mammals were obtained during the cloud season while at the latter community captures were distributed across all months. There was an implication in Kelly's report that the animals may have been less available or less easily procured outside the cloud season. These discrepancies need careful attention. They could imply that introduction of a cash economy based on skulls led to changes in the seasons when animals were sought and to a greatly inflated tally. If these implications were true, my report of events at Bobole would be seriously in doubt.[2]

At both Gabulusado and Bobole two-thirds or more of animal protein came from nondomesticated species. Game mammals were the most important source of wild animal foods at Bobole but, at Gabulusado, the contributions from jungle fowl eggs, wild pigs, and cassowaries all exceeded that from game mammals, and the contribution from fish was two-thirds that from the mammals. Several of these differences in the composition of the hauls of animals are directly attributable to altitude. Wild pigs, cassowaries, and fish were more abundant at the lower altitude while game mammals were both more abundant and more varied in kinds at the higher altitude. Differences in the relative importance of eggs from jungle fowl are less readily explained though I suspect the larger size and greater permanence of the Bobole community may have led to local reduction in populations of the birds through the past decade.

Altitudinal effects upon availability of potential animal foods jeopardize comparison of tallies between Gabulusado and Bobole. A better basis for comparison might be between Gabulusado and the small community at Namosado. The latter was at roughly the same altitude as Gabulusado and in 1979–80 also showed less emphasis upon game mammals and more use of diverse faunal types. During forty-seven weeks 65 game mammals were eaten at Gabulusado while, at Namosado, I recorded 223 game mammals during a forty-five-week period; the former community averaged 25.5 residents; the latter included 33 residents.

At Gabulusado Kelly recorded game that was brought to the longhouse and remarked that additional animals were presumably eaten at distant garden houses. Others may have been eaten in the forest where they were captured. Records from Namosado suggest that a rather high proportion of animals may never have reached the longhouse. Stored collections of skulls were obtained from this community in September, 1979, and March, 1980. Several people produced more than one parcel of skulls: a set that had been stored in the communal longhouse and others from garden houses. Minimum tallies of 46 in 102 skulls in September and 32 in 94 skulls in March came from garden houses. One man, who maintained two garden houses over this period, delivered 30 skulls from garden houses and only 16 from the longhouse. These few data suggest that as much as 40 percent of game mammals may not have reached the longhouse and reduce apparent per-person differences between Gabulusado and Namosado. Indeed, if we assumed that males older than fifteen years captured all the mammals, the annual capture rates per male would be 13.3 at Gabulusado and 17.2 at Namosado. (To derive these estimates I boosted the Gabulusado count from 65 to 108 to allow for animals eaten away from the longhouse. The discrepancy between the two values would nearly vanish if flying foxes were included in the estimates; many were captured at Gabulusado and none at Namosado). There is little cause to think that the Namosado tally was inflated by skulls acquired from outside the community. My visits to Namosado were announced well in advance and did not coincide with influxes of visitors who anticipated possible payments and, further, people at Namosado competently named the skulls that they offered for sale.

The second difference between Gabulusado and Bobole relates to the seasons during which game mammals were captured and eaten. At Gabulusado most were taken in the cloud season while at Bobole they were taken year-round. At the latter community most cloud season captures came from traps, and most pandanus season captures came from planned hunting excursions to higher altitude primary forest. Comparable hunting excursions did not occur at Gabulusado in 1968–69. Indeed, most of the 65 animals eaten at Gabulusado longhouse were taken in isolated deadfall traps scattered through secondary forest and from terrestrial and arboreal dens that were spotted during the course of other activities. These latter captures would, for the most part, fall into the category that I chose to call casual encounters; their association with cloud season matches the situation at Bobole. Traplines located to the north of Gabulusado and hunts that took place in association with their use contributed few animals to the tally recorded by Kelly. Indeed, only one of these lines of traps was operated by Gabulusado residents; the others were associated with people at Turusato. In 1979–80 traplines were not used at Namosado, and during the period I purchased skulls, hunting did not take place at higher altitudes of Haliago; here more game mammals were taken in the cloud season than in the pandanus season. (One man from Namosado hunted with men from Bobole during April, 1980, to obtain animals for our farewell.)

One final consideration concerns the implication in Kelly's text that availability of game mammals was reduced in the pandanus season. Etolo conceptions are relevant here. At Bobole, people articulated the separation between their two named seasons as a difference in available foods: "in the cloud season we eat game mammals, in the pandanus season we eat *marita* pandanus." The connection between cloud season and game mammals was, additionally, specifically linked to the trapping program. Further, people said often that game mammals disappeared in the pandanus season, but they did not behave as though they believed this general statement and their catch belied their words. The statement can refer only to trapping and to the fact that sustained use of a line of traps resulted in a local and short-term reduction in the abundance of game. It was this effect that provided the stimulus to close a trapline after some months of operation. Trapping and hunting differed for Etolo in that the first was a routine activity and the second a passionate activity. Trapping was highly visible and communal, and the effort was synchronized across households and was sustained. In consequence trapping was thought of in calendric terms. For example, Efala's text at the head of this book opened by positioning trapping within a cycle of food-producing activities. That text made no mention of hunting that in contrast to trapping was relatively private, invisible by convention, and intermittent. At no time did anyone suggest that hunting was tied to a particular season. When Kelly lived at Gabulusado, most game mammals were taken in the cloud season, but any implication that they were unavailable in the pandanus season was, I suggest, influenced by Etolo conceptions rather than biological facts.

These remarks go a long way toward removing apparent disparities between observations from Gabulusado and Bobole. The fact that the catch of game mammals per person at Bobole was far in excess of that at Gabulusado was, primarily, a function of the variety of animal foods available at different altitudes. The concentration of captures in the cloud season at Gabulusado may have arisen because people seldom hunted within high-altitude primary forest; it did not arise because the animals were unavailable in the pandanus season. The distance from Gabulusado to the forest and the distribution of lineage territories may have reduced opportunities to hunt in the very places where mammals were most abundant. Both these explanations are reinforced by similarities between Namosado and Gabulusado despite the fact that skulls were exchanged for money at the former community.

Not all cause for concern is removed by the foregoing. It remains possible that by purchasing skulls I promoted additional effort. It is possible also that hunting at Bobole in 1979–80 was released in some way from former constraints without accompanying change in conventional forms of discussing the activity. Two sorts of information are useful here. First, a comment on the motivations underlying particular hunts and, second, the response that followed the fateful day when I ceased buying skulls. The day itself deserves a word.

The people of Bobole behaved as though trapped mammals were not suitable for inclusion in important prestations. Trapped animals often changed hands; but when they did so, the mood was rather casual. All large-scale, or even moderately large-scale, prestations within Bobole or from people in Bobole to those at other communities comprised game that had been hunted. Most of these prestations took place in the pandanus season. A feast in July, 1979, to farewell Damule, the Huli pastor, included game mammals. In the four weeks preceding and including this feast 102 animals were trapped. None appeared at the feast. Instead six men and youths undertook a specific hunt that produced 27 animals. It seems unlikely that my interests dictated the timing or the frequency of hunts that were motivated by gift giving. Other major hunts, organized along house lines, occurred early in the pandanus season as responses to a relaxation of gardening and sago-processing pressures. Finally, 32 animals resulted from three weeks in

January and February, 1980, when a party of ten men was commissioned to upgrade the walking track from Bobole to the border with Huli. Again, I was hardly responsible.

On March 23, 1980, I announced that the era of buying skulls was over. Bedlam erupted briefly on what would otherwise have been a quiet Sunday. The announcement had been awaited with growing anxiety. For several weeks people had tried, without success, to cajole the deadline from me, appealing at times to my better nature and sense of fair play. A sadness of expectation both for our impending departure and for the loss of income had fallen upon Bobole. Nowalia, the huntress, had cried *Ne muni,* "my money!" to express her dual grief. The second service for the morning was over, and people had gathered outside church to talk or groom each other's hair or fill water bottles at the tank before drifting quietly away. My declaration fractured the relaxed mood. After today skulls were not for sale. It was over. There were, I knew, some outstanding skulls from twenty-three animals weighed the day before. The word swept through the community, and people vanished. Within half an hour there was pandemonium. Our house was crammed as skulls and money changed hands in unending transactions. Nowalia and Maga, with their four children, were clustered on the floor eating flesh from half a dozen detached heads. Hamaga appeared toting four animals to weigh plus three skulls that were already picked clean. An hour produced forty fresh skulls that were not accounted for in weighings from the previous day and a contract on ten others that were already simmering in an earth oven. This had never happened before. Sunday was for rest and for worshipping Jesus. People might check their traps or visit and maintain pandan orchards, but gardening and hunting did not occur. Even Saturday's tally of animals had been unusually high. I needed to invoke psychic powers to comprehend this final avalanche of skulls. How else had people known that today the shop would close?

It was in a sense God's gift to Bobole. We had fallen behind with the gossip. On Monday two pigs were killed, and the afternoon feast of pork and fifty headless game mammals, two tree kangaroos in pride of place, was a splendid welcome to Bobole's three visitors. They were Huli people, a Christian Endeavour Group, who had arrived to promote a week of sport and religious instruction before traveling on to the next large community. We hung the skulls over the fire, abandoning them to five days of physical and spiritual enrichment, and fled to the comparative peace of Namosado. The touring Christians ate well that week for on that Thursday Hamaga provided fourteen more animals; I did not see their skulls, nor did I want to.

Six weeks remained before we would leave Bobole. This was a critical time during which I needed to discover if hunting would abruptly cease once the flow of money dried up. In the first two weeks I was tested with four skulls but remained resolute. A year's exposure to the style of Etolo gossip was the prerequisite to gleaning the required information. A face missing for one day, and I would be recklessly asserting to a likely source that "so and so has gone hunting, what will he (she) catch?" There were many stone walls, but I drew some blood. And there was some assistance. Gafaiya came a few times, always alone, and with an embarrassed laugh would give me an immaculate skull. He alone had decided they had value beyond money. Several youths gathered at our doorway to gnaw symbolically the rear ends from two skulls and relish sucking brains in the traditional manner. Amid much merriment they answered my joking questions.

For some hunts I was told the size of the catch, for others only who went and for how long. It was necessary to estimate the count on the basis of past performance; to convert my knowledge of hunting into a predictive science. The opportunity to try my hand at this arose in the form of an unexpected compliment in the fifth week. From Monday to Friday twenty men and youths dispersed as half a dozen hunting parties into the forest above Bobole. Their purpose was to accumulate sufficient game mammals to mark our imminent departure with a feast. While they hunted, I burrowed through notebooks to predict their catches. And upon their return, some after 4 days out and others after 4.5 days, I spied when I could and asked questions when it did not seem too rude. The results from these efforts are summarized in Table 6, which shows predicted and recorded catches for six individuals and for a group of eight who camped together.[3] The values agree fairly well. Sailo's performance was below expectation; he was working against an extraordinary statistic. And Suguia did remarkably well, though he, I discovered, had the assistance of a dog whereas usually he hunted alone. For the remaining six hunters, those of whom I learned no details, past performance gave a conservative figure of 40 animals. For our farewell 150 game mammals must have been captured. There was not one hint for money; instead there were numerous offers of skulls.

The six weeks in which I spied, gossiped, and predicted people's hunting tallies accounted for 209 game mammals, 2 fruit bats, and a four-meter-long python. Much of this total was from one week. There was nothing unusual about this; weekly tallies through the pandanus season were consistently erratic. Casual takes, usually of bandicoots, obtained in the course of a day's activity would barely intrude into this total because these items were typically eaten soon after capture, perhaps at a garden site and away from the obligation to share widely. They might add another 5 animals each week. Even without these, the average count for the last six weeks at Bobole was 34.8 game mammals per week; for the preceding fifty-two weeks the average was 34.7 animals. When the flow of money stopped, hunting remained a passionate interest.

The Pigs That Ate the Garden

TABLE 6. Predicted and Observed Catch of Game Mammals by Six Individual Hunters and a Group of Eight Hunters

Hunter	Average Success (Hours/Mammal)	Predicted Catch (4 to 4.5 Days)	Actual Catch[a]
Wahene	5.17	7.0–7.8	≥6[b]
Suguia	6.42	5.6–6.3	10
Efala	7.54	4.8–5.4	8
Fuago	7.00	5.7–6.3	≥4[b]
Maga	2.46	16.2–18.3	15
Ilabu	3.50	11.4–12.6	10
Wosia	17.64	2.0–2.3	
Sianda	10.30	3.5–3.9	
Haboyado	22.57	1.6–1.8	
Aro Yabage	6.03	6.3–7.1	
Silima	2.95	13.6–15.3	
Sailo	2.40	16.7–18.6	14
Fuma	4.49	8.9–10.0	12
Group total		52.6–59.0	56
Grand total		103.3–115.7	>109

[a]The size of the actual catch is known for two men in the group of eight.
[b]Additional animals may have been eaten in the forest.

It would be foolish to argue that I had no effect. Retrospectively, there seems no good reason for viewing the seasonal switch from trapping to hunting as an artifact. Some people added a few extra deadfalls to their lines of traps, but repair and replacement were presumably annual events. One short trapline, built by two youthful hunters only a few years earlier, lay idle for half the season until another man and his wife, commencing a garden nearby, operated it for a few months. Three other men, one in his thirties, two in their early forties, were not tempted to reopen traplines they had used in past years. I doubt there was any significant increase in the frequency of trapping; the effect was of a different sort and was not particularly productive. Several families seemed loath to close their lines of traps. For them the trapping season may have been a little longer than was usual though the yield was probably not much greater. Some people may have hunted more than they usually did. I cannot quantify this though the information here does not suggest a major effect. My opinion is that the people of Bobole may have routinely hunted more often than did Etolo who lived at lower altitudes. Hamaga, at least, assured me this was so and spontaneously gave, as reason, the ready access to forests where the ring-tailed possum *Pseudocheirops cupreus* and the cuscus *Phalanger sericeus* lived. He had named the two animals that dominated the hunted tally.

There remains one final consideration. It is possible, I think likely, that hunting within higher-altitude forest in 1979–80 was a more frequent activity than it had been ten years earlier. In the decade of the 1960s hunting was, of necessity, sanctioned by the forest spirits, the *segesado*. They communicated their advice through men who, in trance, acted as mediums. The abode of the *segesado* was the forest that clothed the upper slopes of Haliago. Thunder in the mountains signaled their activity and, because they could take offense, the forest held an element of danger. It might have been wise or at least comforting to hunt with a companion and take few risks with the weather. It was through the pandanus season that sudden, violent storms were most common.

In the decade of the 1970s the role of the forest spirits as guardians of game mammals had been usurped—more than usurped, it had evaporated. The metaphorical language traditionally spoken in the high forests, spoken in obeisance to the *segesado,* was now forgone. The ritual offering of sweet potato as exchange for the right to take game no longer occurred. The *segesado* had dissolved to be replaced by God, and His concern was with the souls of people, not with hunting propriety. Religious change will penetrate deep into a people's existence. At Bobole the frequency of hunting, by men on their own and through the season of storms, may have increased as the *segesado* faded from the forests.

CHAPTER 9

Hu Hedabi: Animals Are Good to Eat

Etolo did not eat ants, but they named them. Their lexicon of animal names was large. It included labels for species that they used and for many others that they seemed to ignore. The names for cicadas, crickets, frogs, and birds often mimicked the sounds made by these animals. A catbird was named *awa;* its call was a drawn-out, nasal *a-wa, a-wa.* A frog was named *ego* after its call. Other names were descriptive of a prominent feature or of the habits of the animal: one cuscus was named "red nose," and another was "rock dwelling." Fireflies were "stars," and earwigs were "it forks." The ecology and behavior of the animals were important in the nomenclatural practices of Etolo. The name of a bird might recall its song: the song might prompt the name. The labels might be literal or figurative; they might depict features or colors or be statements about the likely location of the species concerned. But there was also a host of names whose etymology was either obscure or lost in language change. These names were no different from the others. Names facilitate communication. They connote associations between people and wildlife. They serve as a grid or map that both guides and constrains people in their responses to nature.

The ways in which people classify wildlife say something of how they order their relations with nature. In Western societies most people can label categories of broad scope—butterfly, ant, fish, lizard, bird, and so forth. They are less concerned with, or knowledgeable of, detail within these categories. It is not part of their everyday experience. There are specialists, of course, to whom, for reasons of economics or curiosity, it is important to know breeds of sheep or of dogs or the intricacies of spider nomenclature. To people who use wild animals as food, as decoration or in magic, who regard them as spirits or find in them metaphors for their own lives, the themes of classification will be different. To them the particular will be more important, the general less relevant. The classificatory system they use need not be monolithic. There may be several systems that intersect: different

121

frames of reference for different contexts—dietary, ritualistic, and so on. Etolo classification gave emphasis to particular kinds of animals as species or as clusters of species. It was not concerned to gather those kinds under an umbrella of a few inclusive labels. The skill of Etolo was in identifying the world about them and, through this process, recognizing familiar relations with it. For those who did not know the proper distinctions the world was inaccessible.

The flesh of vertebrate animals was named *hu*. It was considered vastly superior to the flesh of invertebrate animals. Among the latter, crayfish were specially favored, and their flesh was *dunamini*, but there was no term for the flesh of other invertebrates even though many were eaten.

Not all vertebrate animals were eaten. Some frogs and snakes were strictly avoided, and people behaved cautiously with other kinds that, though they were classed as edible, might be confused with the inedible species. Among frogs this resulted in avoidance of many small species and, with snakes, it meant that few species other than pythons were ever eaten. All fish, lizards, and birds and all mammals, except dogs, were edible. The prohibition on dogs was reinforced by the belief that if people killed a wild dog its kin would, in turn, steal a child.

At Bobole few birds were eaten despite the declared edibility of all. Several factors probably contributed to this. First, because larger mammals were readily available, small birds, though abundant, may have seemed less worthy of pursuit. Second, people said that a shotgun was useful in obtaining birds and through my stay the only shotgun belonging to the village had been confiscated by government officers. Third, people asserted that they obeyed government injunctions concerning the hunting of birds of paradise. Fourth and perhaps most important, I think people were somewhat ambivalent regarding birds. These animals had been strongly linked with the world of spirits and of ceremonial events; the plumage of some species had been incorporated in elaborate costumes, and the songs people sang had often featured birds. By 1979 there were no traditional ceremonies and no songs in the old style; the world of spirits—and by association of birds—was officially out of bounds.[1]

People varied in their preferences for the flesh of different vertebrates. Pig and cassowary ranked very high while catfish and game mammals were always acclaimed. The eggs of birds and the flesh of smaller mammals were not described as exceptionally tasty, but the care taken in preparation and the evident pleasure while eating left no doubt as to their high standing. It was game mammals, however, that brought out the gourmet in Etolo. Preparation was elaborate. The stomach and intestines were stripped of their contents and the intestines then neatly woven in a series of running loops. Internal parasites from some species were wrapped in leaf packages for later cooking. Fur was singed from the carcasses; limbs were disarticulated but left attached; and paws were discarded. After cooking, the animals were carved to a set pattern. The merits of different species, or of particular individuals, were discussed with enthusiasm, and different people held different opinions. The flesh of the giant rat *Mallomys aroaensis* and the terrestrial cuscus *Strigocuscus gymnotis* was considered excellent; in both cases glandular secretions gave a strong flavor. Immature cuscuses were popular though some people complained that the flesh was too soft. The distinctive, rather dry flesh of echidnas was a particular treat to some people but was disparaged by others. All agreed that tree kangaroo was fine meat. There were people who considered fatty animals to be best, and others who preferred the lean. Arboreal herbivores or animals captured in the cloud season were most likely to be fatty; terrestrial animals or ones caught in the pandanus season were more often lean.

Making the proper distinctions was important for naming animals and knowing their qualities as food. It was also important at a deeper level because food and eating food raised moral issues and matters of etiquette. Etolo people used many animals as food and, traditionally, there had been many restrictions upon what could be eaten and in what circumstances. Some animals had been taboo to everyone, others to certain lineage groups, and yet others during different phases of each person's life. Most of these practices had been abandoned by 1979, and I did not learn details. People asserted that the old ways had been unfair to women, though this opinion probably did little justice to the complex suite of beliefs and prohibitions. It remained important, however, to make the proper distinctions that underlay the sharing and giving of meat or the presentation and distribution of meat and other foods when feasts were held. The remainder of this chapter discusses these matters.[2]

Sharing and giving are very different acts. When we camped in the forest with people who hunted, we always received a portion of the catch. It might be a cut of cooked carcass or an entire animal to singe and cook at our pleasure. We were with the hunters and could not be excluded from the meal. When we were at Bobole, the mood was different. The game mammals or portions of pig we received were gifts. They were delivered to us. We had not situated ourselves at the dinner table, and thus there was no obligation to share.

Sharing meat with those who were present was obligatory for those who had the meat. It was an unavoidable social act. At a forest camp an unsuccessful hunter would exclaim *nesigei*, "thank you," as his successful companion dropped a bulging string bag to the ground. There was no ambiguity. Everyone would eat well. As likely as not it was the unsuccessful hunter who immediately prepared firewood and set to stripping entrails and singeing fur from carcasses. No one hesitated to pluck roundworms from body cavities and eat them at once. The successful hunter rested content, perhaps instructing his companions regarding animals to be saved for later eating or for carrying to the village. In this setting, sharing created a mood of pleasurable companionship.

There were other occasions when sharing was burdened with awkward restraint. A stray bandicoot taken in a garden would not go far at the longhouse, and many such captures were eaten at the garden or in the comparative privacy of a family house within the village. If they were not seen, there was no obligation to share. A persistent house guest, even from within the village, would never be denied food, but if he failed to reciprocate, then for some days little food and no luxuries would arrive at the longhouse. The residents would send their unwanted guest to dietary Coventry and in this way encourage him to move on. No words would be spoken, but the mood would be clear. Sharing was obligatory; it could be avoided only by avoiding people with whom you did not wish to share. And this was accomplished by either eating elsewhere or declaring the catch to be smaller than it was and channeling the concealed animals to other quarters.

Sharing was normal practice for hunting companions and for co-residents. It was easiest to avoid when game had been taken by casual encounter. It was impossible to avoid when game had been stolen from bitches returning to feed pups at a longhouse and was difficult to avoid with game that had been trapped. Within each longhouse people were thoroughly aware of each other's trapping efforts, and, indeed, it was often children who collected the catch. Only a small proportion of trapped animals was not included in the communal evening meals. There were two major exceptions to this. When people lived for extended periods at garden houses, they kept most of the catch to themselves. And, when male members of a family were absent from the village, the women who collected the catch often took the opportunity to share with sisters or other female kin who were not co-residents. There were few other occasions, except when game was taken casually, when women who did not hunt could control the distribution of game mammals. Sharing of trapped mammals with people who were not coresidents could be achieved by either surreptitious eating or invitation to the evening meal. Unmarried males were the major beneficiaries of these practices, which served to establish bonds of friendship between the primary parties to the meal. Indeed, when visitors from Namosado arrived at Bobole, males would sometimes address each other by the name of a mammal that they had once eaten together.

With game obtained by hunting, the extent of sharing varied. People who hunted on one day regularly shared their catch with coresidents. They might invite others to join the evening meal or make gifts to particular individuals within or outside their own longhouse. On longer hunting excursions some, or even all, of the haul was eaten at the forest camp. The amount depended upon the size of the catch and the motivation underlying the hunt. Male-only hunting parties, prompted by my rat-trapping activities or by the demands of upgrading walking tracks, sometimes ate the entire haul at the forest camp. So, too, did nuclear or extended family groups when they camped in the forest. If a hunter camped alone or a group caught many animals, then proportionately more would be brought to the village. A lone hunter might eat entrails only, and small groups might eat one carcass each night together with several sets of entrails. The remainder of the carcasses, singed and seeping grease, would hang on a rack near the hunting shelter.[3] These were times when the hunters, not necessarily in words but implicitly by their absence, had declared themselves obliged to others. They had, it appeared, temporarily relinquished gardening or other responsibilities of village life but would reciprocate with meat. They were not bonded to other people in the same way if it seemed they were employed by government or by me. When hunting was motivated specifically by gift giving or communal feasting, then the amount eaten at the forest camp was usually small.

The preceding comments highlight times when people may have failed to share widely. In fact these formed a minority of occasions. Most game was distributed among many people. During weeks that I was resident at the village, 1,219 game mammals were eaten. At least 65 percent of these had arrived at the village as either intact carcasses obtained that day or singed carcasses obtained in the preceding few days. Virtually all these animals would have been shared among residents of a single longhouse. Some were shared more widely. The value of 65 percent is based upon carcasses for which I am reasonably confident of their fate. It will understate the true value. Broadly based sharing of 75 percent of the catch may be a more realistic guess.

Giving meat differed from sharing. It was a means both of fulfilling and establishing obligations. A person might give meat to someone who had assisted with a garden or in building a family house. The gift of a game mammal might restore equilibrium to a tense relationship, enhance the bond between in-laws, express sympathy to someone who was ill, and so forth. Giving meat to the pastor and his family or to the Europeans served two purposes. The act generously acknowledged our lack of access to game as it manipulated us, the beneficiaries, for spiritual favors on the one hand or material favors on the other. On most occasions gifts of game were from one person to another. The relationship negotiated by the gift was between individuals. But the overt transaction was not always the intended meaning. A gift to a child might be a message to a parent or a gift between women might contain a message between men. The privacy of these acts and the lack of public ostentation made understanding difficult. It was seldom possible to separate acts of giving from those of sharing for persons who resided together. It was easier to be sure with some exchanges between residents of different longhouses. And it was easiest to know what had happened when we, the pastor's family, or people living beyond Bobole were the recipients of a gift.

Game mammals were shared in appropriate circumstances irrespective of the technique by which they were obtained. This was not the case with game mammals used as gifts. Trapped animals were less likely to be used as gifts than hunted animals (table 7). All game mammals known to have left Bobole as gifts had been obtained by hunting. They included four species; nineteen ring-tailed possums (*Pseudocheirops cupreus*), eleven cuscuses (*Phalanger sericeus* and *P. carmelitae*), and one giant rat (*Mallomys aroaensis*). Trapped animals may have been less suitable as gifts because they were often partially decomposed. But it is more likely that hunted game was chosen for important prestations because there was no ambiguity concerning the effort made by the donor. This is reflected in a difference between the origin of game mammals given to kin and that of game mammals given to nonkin who were not coresidents of the donor. Eight of eighteen known gifts to kin had been obtained by trapping; only five of thirty-five known gifts to nonkin had been obtained in this way. Similarly, the relatively high proportion of casually encountered game included in gifts made to us reflects the spontaneous generosity of particular individuals. When people obtained game in this way, they were less likely to feel committed to others in the manner of disposal. Nearly all gifts of game mammals made within Bobole were of a single animal only. There was one notable exception to this. When Sio miscarried, her brother and sister-in-law, Siagoba and Esopa, went hunting. Three of the animals they captured were presented to Sio and her hus-

TABLE 7.   Gifts of Game Mammals

	Sample Size	Number of Species	Technique of Capture		
			Casual	Trapped	Hunted
Total catch[a]	1,843	35	14.5%	39.0%	46.5%
Gifts to:					
outside Bobole	31	4	0	0	100
other Bobole longhouses	53	20	13	23	64
pastors' families	24	11	17	29	54
Europeans	39	16	38	18	44

[a]Catch includes 72 fruit bats; 13 of these are included in the tally of gifts.

band. The remainder were eaten within the longhouse of the hunters, though some were gifts to residents of that house.

Six hunting trips were to obtain game for prestations outside Bobole. All were in the pandanus season. Hamaga and Siagoba captured animals to present to their married sisters. Ilabu gave to his wife's kin and, another time, to Saiopa of Namosado who cared for some of Ilabu's pigs. In November Aro's nephew, Nabu, lived at Bobole for four weeks. Nabu was about sixteen years old, an age where he might show interest in hunting. Aro twice arranged for him to join hunting parties on Haliago. Nabu himself was not successful but did not go empty-handed to his parents. Aro and Yabage sent four mammals with him. Two months later they carried ten animals to Gemisado for Yabage's kin. This was the largest of the gifts sent beyond Bobole. The others were of four or five ring-tailed possums and cuscuses. They were gifts from one person to another.

Animal foods other than game mammals and pigs were often shared. They were seldom used as gifts except for small items that were specially saved for children. Beetle larvae that had been incubated in palms may have been another exception, though no instance came to my attention. In any case, at Bobole, people complained that their incubation efforts gave low or miserable returns. Most cassowaries were shared among coresidents, and a few were distributed or sold to everyone. At least one was eaten by a group of families and invited youths who were not all kin and were affiliated with three longhouses. It is probable that people who snared cassowaries and shared with coresidents gave portions of cooked meat to kin who lived at other houses. This was normal practice when small domestic pigs were eaten. Large hauls of fish were also shared with coresidents. Most other items of animal food were small—a few jungle fowl eggs, some small rats, a fledgling bird, a lizard, two or three frogs, and so forth. They were seldom brought to the longhouse unless it was intended to give them to a child. Most were cooked and eaten as daytime snacks and shared with the few people present at the time. Almost certainly children received a disproportionate share of these items because either a parent (usually their mother) gave most to them, they received the entire item as a gift, or they demanded the item (often from their father) and threw a tantrum if they did not receive it immediately.

Customary practices concerning the sharing and giving of animal foods were undergoing revision during the period I lived at Bobole. I often detected elements of tension, ambiguity, and even mild deceit connected with these exchanges. Selling pork was new, and selling cassowary, which was done by one Bobole man, appeared extraordinary given that these animals, more than any other, had recently been the embodiment of forest spirits. With small pigs or cassowaries and with game mammals people sometimes avoided sharing with coresidents but chose instead to invite others to impromptu feasts away from the village. Gifts were often directed to either persons who were nonkin or those whose kinship connections were remote. There were, as well, new categories of indebtedness. When Esopa and Siagoba (House III) took care of the children of Nowalia and Maga (House II) while the latter hunted, they routinely received a share of the catch. As child minders they *knew* of the hunt and, in this sense, were ex officio coresidents who shared by entitlement. In truth, of course, they were neither coresidents nor kin to the hunters and thus were beholden to them. Siagoba and Esopa sometimes reciprocated the gifts they had received. Because four longhouse communities now lived in proximity and perhaps because people strove toward a Christian brotherhood (Siagoba and Maga were both deacons of the church), it was necessary that new forms of sharing and giving emerged. The latitude to explore new forms may have been granted by reduced fears that improper behavior and witchcraft were connected. Thus, Ray Kelly reported that failure to share pork from domestic pigs would anger the forest spirits who would then withdraw protection from attack by witches. In 1979–80 not everyone was either certain about or comfortable with the changing expectations and obligations.[4]

The preceding account of Etolo practices concerning sharing and giving meat is too meager by far. It does justice to neither the intricate web of exchange relationships that bound people nor the warmth that sharing and giving generated. My purpose has been to recreate a little of the complex pathways meat followed as it traveled from those who obtained it to those who ate it. This was as a prelude to commenting on the contribution meat made to diet. I have estimated that the average yield from game mammals (including fruit bats) amounted to six grams of protein per person per day. Domestic pigs contributed, on average, another three grams of protein per person per day, and all other sources of animal protein—cassowary, eggs of jungle fowl, fish, and so on—may have added another two or three grams to each person's daily intake. Meat foods therefore made a useful contribution to the diet, though the availability of protein from different sources was not uniform across the year. Figure 20 shows variation in the availability of protein from game mammals and domestic pigs. Four-week averages in protein yields from game mammals were remarkably consistent while those from pigs varied a great deal. In combination pigs and game mammals contributed less protein to diet from September to December than at other times; through these months of scarcity cassowary and fish were eaten more often.[5]

From a nutritional perspective it is important that protein foods are eaten regularly; the human body cannot store protein for times of shortage. On this count the supply of game mammals to people at Bobole takes on particular significance. Despite the seasonal switch from trapping animals to hunting

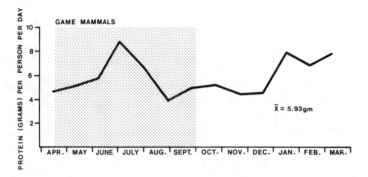

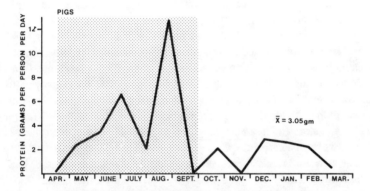

Fig. 20. Yield of protein per day from game mammals and pigs. On this figure the trace based on game mammals includes protein derived from fruit bats. In the four-week period commencing December 30, 1979, fruit bats contributed 4.7 percent of the total and in the four-week period commencing January 27, 1980, they contributed 16 percent of the total. Data points are from thirteen four-week periods, commencing on March 25, 1979, distributed across twelve months.

them and the associated switch in species eaten, game mammals provided a reliable and regular input of protein. Many of the smallest animal foods (insects, frogs, lizards, and small mammals) also would have contributed protein on a regular basis. By contrast the irregular availability of pork means that this source of protein was less important nutritionally. Indeed, most of the pigs eaten at Bobole were consumed at a few feasts. The feasts celebrated different events, and the foods displayed and eaten, together with the form or theater—for that is what it was—of the feasts, altered accordingly.

The Pigs That Ate the Garden

July 13–14, 1979

The mist was slow to disperse on Friday 13. It hung low over the village chilling the air. It was the sort of morning when people normally would gossip at their fires, warming themselves with excuses before leaving for gardens. This day they were committed. At first light men from Houses I and IV went to a garden where pigs had foraged for the previous two weeks. They worked swiftly, killing five pigs with blows to the head. Then, with the pigs bleeding and kicking, the men bound them to poles and carried them to the cleared area in front of House I.

This was the day when people from Bobole and Namosado would gather to mark the departure of Damule, his wife, Ligae, and their daughter, Ali. "We shall kill and eat pigs," I was told. "We shall think of Damule and be sad that he is leaving." Damule had been pastor at Bobole for nearly four years. The mission wanted to transfer him to a western Etolo community, but Damule was fearful of lower altitudes, anxious that he himself and his family would suffer recurring attacks of malaria. After previous trips to the west, he often had been ill and so he resisted the transfer. The mission decided he had faltered in his commitment; it decided he could no longer work as a pastor; and he chose to return to his own people, who were Huli, and seek work as a carpenter.

Through the week there had been desultory preparations. Men and youths from House I cut grass and weeds in front of the house, and they heaped logs of wood in readiness. Careful attention was given to the site of an earth oven. An area 3.5 by 1.75 meters was dug to a depth of nearly 20 centimeters. This shallow pit was leveled; a narrow drain was dug from one corner; and stones were piled nearby. Different individuals contributed to this work when they had time to spare; there was no coordinated effort.

On Friday the mood changed. As the dead pigs were dumped in front of the longhouse, men arrived through the mist carrying huge logs. Women went to gardens and nearby areas of regrowth to collect vegetables and fern fronds. Piles of leaves cut from banana plants appeared as if from nowhere while men and youths split the long logs that would be burned to heat stones. The pigs were laid out on leaves. They were gutted and then singed by men, and the entrails, carried by women and by old Ololo, were flushed out in the torrent Bobolegi. Other women began to arrive laden with greens, pumpkins, chokos, and packages of sago while the men, using steel and bamboo knives, butchered the pigs. Each pig was treated in the same way. The sternum was separated with heart and lungs attached. The head and backbone were removed as a single piece and long fillets carefully cut from the vertebrae. Ribs, in sets of twos and threes, were sliced from overlying flesh, and for this task the bamboo knives came into their own. Favored cuts of fat were placed separately. Livers, kidneys, and portions of gut disappeared into string bags and bamboo containers and vanished from the main arena of activity. With them went the sternal portions, the heads, and the backbones. Urinary bladders and gallbladders were emptied, blown up, tied off, and used as balls by small children. The five pigs were reduced to ten sides of pork, each comprising a foreleg and a hindleg held together by a boneless flap of skin, fat, and meat. Onto each of these Gago placed fillets, sets of ribs, and cuts of mesentery with intestine attached. He counted the portions out, swapping short sticks from a bundle in one hand to his other hand as an aid to memory. Ilabu assisted him, and others prepared the oven. Long slabs of wood were placed across the fire pit. Stones were spread across these, more firewood at right angles to the first layer, and more stones liberally heaped on top. The fire was lit. Smoke billowed across the ridge enveloping people who laughed and chattered as they moved busily between tasks. Children watched from the sidelines; youths sat holding babies; and dogs yelped from the blows they received for approaching too closely to the meat.

When the sun came overhead, it was time for the first distribution. Moving gradually along the line of sides of pork Gago would select two portions from the meat piled on top. He held these aloft, one in each hand, and loudly called the names of two males. Married men and youths older than about sixteen years were named in this distribution of raw meat. All residents of Bobole and visitors from Namosado were included. Either the person named or a proxy came forward to receive the share, and within moments the recipients had delivered most of the meat to women, usually their wives or mothers. A few small portions were retained by the males, draped on sticks, cooked at the edge of the fire, and eaten at once. Some men toasted and ate lumps of sago. Women and one older man from Namosado prepared family dishes. They took previously prepared banana leaves, folded at the midrib and often warmed on the oven, and used these to wrap a mix of greens, meat and fat of pig, and crumbled sago. Watercress, hibiscus, acanth spinach, or pumpkin tips were chosen by different women as their preferred green.

As women completed their packages of food, the men and youths turned to the fire. The wood had burned away, and the stones were hot. Some had exploded, but none had hurtled dangerously from the fire. Using long poles and giant wooden tongs the men rearranged the stones, working rapidly to retain the heat; and when the stones were ready—or even sooner—they were covered with the packages that women had prepared. These were buried beneath fern fronds; and the ten sides of pork, interspersed with pumpkins, chokos, and a dozen or more game mammals, were laid on top and smothered under more fern. No tubers were included. Stones from the edge of the oven were repositioned among the slabs of pork. People called to others who they thought were being slow, jostled through the crowd to the oven, or shouted angrily that someone else had taken the very place they had chosen for a package of food. The heap grew. Water was poured over it; and as steam billowed up, everyone, shouting, laughing, and calling for others to help, threw huge leaves over the food. The steam was contained and the heap buried beneath dirt. It was done. The excitement dissipated, and for two hours the food cooked.

It was midafternoon when the oven was opened. People reached through the steam to the food while dogs slunk at their feet. Fern fronds, now soaked in grease, were sucked and eaten at once, and pumpkins and chokos were quickly distributed. Men leaned across the oven to lift out the sides of pork and laid these on leaves where, earlier, the pigs had been displayed and butchered. They carved the pork into large slabs of skin and fat and smaller portions of meat and placed the pieces into piles, counting them out, debating details of the distribution, checking, and rearranging. Some of the heaps included a few game mammals. Women removed their sago packages from the oven, opened them at once, and either cut or ripped off small portions of vegetables that were now jellied in sago. People who were not working feasted on the fern that had lain beneath the pigs; these fronds were rich in grease.

Gago initiated a second distribution of meat. Moving once more along the line of cooked and carved portions, he called the names of all married men. Some took their share and departed. Those who remained either relinquished their portion to women who wrapped it in leaves and hid it away or, in a few cases, commenced cutting part of what they had received into mouthful-sized pieces. There was an awkward lull when no one was eating, when it seemed they were undecided whether to stay or depart. Some sat down as family groups or according to residence affiliation. Grace was said, and people began to eat modestly from their own sago packages, or they huddled over this food, dividing it up, and carried offerings to other families. Gago moved through the crowd with a bowl heaped with cubes of fat. He gave one piece to each person and, unless someone resisted, placed the morsel directly into each one's mouth. Then he carried the bowl from group to group until it was overflowing with small pieces of meat. He shared these among everyone present, saying *hu hedabi*, "meat good," to each person as he or she received a portion.

Then it was finished for that day. There had been no speeches. Damule's presence had been barely acknowledged, though Ligae was burdened with gifts of food. A great deal of food had been cooked, but very little had been eaten. People wandered singly or in small groups toward their own longhouses. There were a few handshakes and calls of farewell. But the feast was not over; the next day everyone was to gather again.

Saturday began at a leisurely pace. People ate a hearty breakfast of sweet potato, bananas, and sugarcane. Some men helped repair the roof of Gamia's garden house while others split firewood. The women were busiest, collecting vegetables for the afternoon meal. By midday a new oven, 1.5 meters in diameter, had been made and the stones heated in readiness. Gago, from House I, and Yabage, from House IV, had prepared uncooked pork left over from the previous day. They carved meat from the heads, reducing the latter to gaunt skulls. Sago packages were again made by the women. Some of these were placed as a ring at the outer rim of the small oven. Pumpkins, choko, and pork were placed inside with the pig's skulls positioned carefully in the center of the heap. A few yams were included, and the completed mound, buried beneath leaves and mud, was almost 1 meter high. The larger oven, used the day before, was piled with sago packages and a layer of vegetables to a depth of 30 centimeters. This day there were no guests from Namosado, and the men and youths of Bobole played football while the food cooked. The mood was relaxed.

Late in the afternoon, everyone was called and the ovens were opened. The cover of leaves was turned back on the ground and the food heaped on top. People reached for items they had placed inside or held food aloft and called for a claimant. Gago and Yabage shared the meat with everyone. They did so without ceremony, and people settled down to eat at once. The hesitance and ambivalence of the previous day were missing. People sat in family groups, often as nuclear families; they were animated, endlessly passing gifts of food back and forth to other groups; and they ate remarkably little. Gago and Fuago moved from group to group giving morsels of meat and fat to each person and accepting reciprocal donations into the bowls they carried. Twice they distributed pork to the crowd. It was nearly dark; and people commenced to disperse, calling their goodnights, laughing with each other, and chatting. They returned to their own longhouses, and the night was quiet. Occasionally someone strummed a guitar. Several youths wandered through the settling mist singing of contentment: *walio hamade, walio hamade,* "now sufficient, now sufficient."

On Monday Damule and his family left Bobole. A dozen people assisted with their pigs, other belongings, and recent gifts. The day before, Damule had killed and cooked a large captive cassowary. He took the meat with him to sell to Huli because he needed to raise money to support his family through the months before new gardens yielded. Efala and his wife, Daieme, went with the group. Efala was to become pastor and, with Daieme, was about to undertake two weeks' training in medical care. For days after the departure people moped at Damule's house or sat disconsolately in his cook house raking through the hearth. This was not unusual. All departures from Bobole induced similar behavior. When trading parties or other groups stayed a night or two at the guest house, it was the same. A moody group picked at the debris left behind, marking the absence, acknowledging the loss.

August 13–14, 1979

It was said that pigs had ruined a garden and might damage others. They were to be killed, though no one mentioned they had been placed in the garden. The venue for the feast was House IV, and since some people from this longhouse had a flare for show, preparations began early. Large heaps of firewood were made ready, and an elaborate pen was built to hold the pigs on their last night. Twenty Huli from the northeast and fifteen people from Onabasulu and Etolo communities to the southwest arrived up to four days before the feast, the latter carrying heavy loads of sago, the former with one rifle and three dogs. The Huli came both as guests and to supervise the killing and distribution of three of their own pigs that, till now, had been fostered with Gawani of House IV.

The appearance and form of this feast were like those of the last. It spanned two days, with guests from outside Bobole absenting themselves for the second day. Parcels of sago, pork, and vegetables, together with fern fronds, pumpkins, and chokos, were prepared and cooked; and once again, there were no tubers in the large oven. Eleven pigs and one piglet were killed; an earlier plan to shoot them was abandoned after unsatisfactory results with the first two victims. The remainder were clubbed to death. Raw meat was distributed to youths and older males irrespective of marital status, cooked meat and fat to married men, and cooked skin and fat to unmarried men and youths. Some pork was sold at a tense market, and the Huli visitors or their dogs were frequently abused in the Etolo language as incompetent or a nuisance. Morsels of fat and of meat were distributed to everyone. On the first day of the feast most people moved off early to eat in private; on the second day the Huli departed early carrying much of their own pork; it rained, and the afternoon meal was underdone; people complained loudly or looked disgusted, but they stayed at the longhouse and ate together till well after dark.

April 12–13, 1980

This feast was impromptu. On April 11 a huge renegade boar was located by dogs that belonged to some visiting Huli men. The dogs put the animal to flight, and about twenty men and youths ran it down, killed it, and carried it triumphantly to the village. It had once been Ilabu's pig and was dumped outside House I in front of an excited crowd. Nothing else happened that day, but early the following morning one of Gago's pigs entered a garden, was declared a renegade, and was killed with arrows. Gago bowed to pressure from the Huli and allowed this animal to be gutted and singed at the garden; the visitors wanted to eat liver and lungs, and since their dogs had found Ilabu's pig, they were not prepared to wait longer.

A large oven in front of House I was used to cook Ilabu's pig and part of Gago's smaller one. Fern fronds were included, but there were no other vegetables. When the meat was cooked, Ilabu distributed large quantities to people from each longhouse other than House I. With the exception of half a dozen youths and unmarried men, these people departed as soon as they received meat. Visitors from Namosado were given a share, and the head of the boar in its entirety was carried through the corridor of the longhouse by Fuma, who presented it with measured courtesy to the Huli visitors. Their protestations were for form's sake as they accepted the magnanimous gift.

A second, smaller oven was made beneath the overhanging verandah of House I. This contained a large part of Gago's pig, together with "sago specials," greens, bundles of highland pitpit, many sweet potatoes, and red pandanus. The oven was opened after the main distribution of meat and when most people had dispersed. Some residents of House I gave vegetables to their guests; others prepared three bowls of sauce from pandanus; and Ilabu and Gago carved and distributed portions to each family. The Huli ate pandanus from one bowl outside the men's entrance to the longhouse; women ate their sauce under the verandah, saving some that they squeezed onto sweet potato for the next morning; and Etolo men ate the third bowl outside and at a discreet distance from the women. With the sauce finished, people gathered in family groups under the verandah where they ate and shared with each other, sitting so close that gifts could be passed among families without the need to stand. Food was carried to the visitors, who ate alone within the longhouse. Gago collected portions of meat and fat from each family and distributed these to everyone. The next evening people from House I feasted again with their Namosado guests; the Huli and their dogs had departed in the early morning.

April 26, 1980

This feast of game mammals marked our imminent departure. In the four days preceding the feast, twenty men and youths had hunted, and in the early afternoon of the 26th, at least 100 singed carcasses lay amid a splendid array of vegetables in a newly prepared oven. Taro, sweet potato, pumpkin, and choko were interspersed with corn cobs, tied bundles of greens, fern fronds, and red pandanus. There was no sago. The colors, arrangement, and quantity drew appreciative comments from everyone, and then it was all covered and allowed to steam for 2.5 hours while a threatening storm blew away. People

gossiped, joked at the thought of so many mammal skulls that were no longer
worth money, and waited for the food.

When the oven was opened, people retrieved what they had placed
inside. Everyone shared and ate vegetables at once. Some prepared bowls
of pandanus sauce. Successful hunters claimed carcasses of the animals they
had captured and commenced to arrange these, entire or in portions, on six
growing piles of food or to make special gifts to us. Two tree kangaroos and
one echidna were carved and distributed in the same way. Each of the heaps
included tubers, pumpkin, choko, and corn contributed by different households, and when completed, Fuago called the distribution. He named a senior
resident from Namosado and from each of Bobole's four longhouses; the
sixth heap was for Efala in his capacity as pastor. Efala's share and that for
Namosado were distributed further by the formal calling of names, young
men in the first case and family groups in the second. The piles of food
intended for longhouses at Bobole were carried away to be eaten later; and
as all this food was dispersed, people ate pandanus sauce, most men eating
from one bowl, some boys and elderly men sharing with the women from
another bowl. At no time on this day did people segregate as either family
or household groups; they intermingled and, as always, ate modest quantities
in public.

At all these feasts there was a further set of distinctions that concerned who,
from within Bobole, should or should not attend or who absented themselves
because they judged this as appropriate. Gamia, for example, was not a
churchgoing man and did not attend Damule's farewell feast, although he
gathered firewood and, on the first morning, with his wife, Emele, assisted
in a variety of tasks. The families of three men were missing from our
farewell feast, though, in one case, they contributed vegetables and assisted
in preparing food. The men concerned were skilled hunters who had not
contributed game mammals, and at least two had different commitments for
the period before the feast. It seemed that in failing to contribute meat, they
were required by courtesy to stay away because neither before nor after the
occasion were our relations with them strained. Men who rarely or never
hunted and who had not hunted for this feast were present at our farewell.

When pork was eaten, old traditions and ancient animosities came near
the surface. Waisado men from House II did not attend the early phases of
the first day of Damule's farewell feast, but, as the oven was opened, all but
two of them drifted inconspicuously into the crowd. On the second day these
men came earlier. The two nonattenders of the day before made a late
appearance limping slowly, side by side, toward the feast; each man had a
bandage of leaves, moss and cloth. The injury each had apparently sustained
was at the same height on the same leg! At least one of the injuries was a

fiction. Waisado men were again missing from the feast of early April, 1980, that was also hosted by House I, and in turn some Gaibi families from this longhouse did not join the feast at House IV. The difficulties existed between senior males from Houses I and II but were expressed only in the presence of pork; these men ate together without hesitation when the menu was game mammals. A young man said, "It is a hard custom; people should put it aside." He did not elaborate, but a connection with past accusations of witchcraft seems likely.[6] Those who did not attend feasts were included in formal distributions and were additionally compensated by gifts; they ate as well as or better than everyone else.

Finally, some ambivalence at the presence of Huli was often evident. In part this may have related to an Etolo perception that the eating behavior of these visitors was characterized by greed. At feasts where Etolo seemed to eat so little food despite the bountiful supply, their visitors appeared immodest of appetite, eating what they received at once in front of everyone and carrying little or none away. The ambivalence surfaced again at our farewell feast when a few Huli arrived in the afternoon. They were election-eering, were allowed to speak, but were not invited to join the feast. Instead a substantial gift of food, including much red pandanus, was carried to them at the guest house. In one month's time the candidate they were sponsoring would not be receiving votes from Bobole. One person expressed the mood of all the plateau peoples: "As children we supported the Huli; now we should support ourselves."

CHAPTER 10

The Shape of Things

The food-producing practices of people who lived at Bobole were diverse. In earlier chapters different practices—gardening, orcharding, hunting, and so forth—were treated more or less separately. Each made different sorts of demands upon the people and was accomplished by assigning the tasks to groups of particular size or to people who assumed particular roles. The manipulative input varied from almost nil with some collecting activities to extreme as with gardening where fences were built, trees felled, soil prepared, plant cuttings carried from old to new sites, weeding done, and, only months after the project was initiated, crops harvested and transported to the household where they were cooked and finally consumed. When the manipulative input was greatest, then returns were more likely to be delayed. Some activities occurred at higher altitudes, others at lower altitudes; some took place near the village, and others, such as processing sago, required a temporary shift to shelters built elsewhere. The periodicity of the practices also varied with major trapping ventures and hunting excursions concentrated in cloud and pandanus seasons, respectively, but with gardening work spread, though unevenly, through the year. Again, different practices called for different combinations of workers. Processing sago was nearly always a family affair, but hunting was often solitary. Felling trees was perceived as a task properly for older youths and men whereas retrieving game from deadfall traps could be done by quite young children.

When considered apart, each food-getting practice imposed different requirements upon people in terms of necessary manipulative input, geographic location, timing, the number of participants, and the roles assumed by people of different sex or marital or age status. Yet it was the articulation of this diverse set of practices that comprised the Etolo system of subsistence and provided people directly with adequate and ongoing energy and nutritional returns and, indirectly, with the capacity to fulfill lives rich in social needs and wants. This chapter shows how the food-getting practices were connected as a viable, unitary system and how different family groups achieved essentially the same ends by somewhat different means. It describes the shape of Etolo subsistence.

Information about food-getting practices varied in quality. For example, there are no quantitative data about labor inputs and food returns from harvesting eggs of jungle fowl, collecting frogs, poisoning fish, incubating beetle larvae, or gathering fern fronds. With these practices and some others, I could observe any associated technology and perhaps detect gross seasonal trends. The sorts of practices where data are few are those where either the combined effort of people or the manipulative input was relatively slight. Yet these practices should not be regarded as inconsequential merely because they did not occupy many hours in a day or yield much of the quantity of food eaten by people; they may have contributed much to the variety and nutritional quality of diet.

High visibility and ease of measurement influenced my decisions to record detailed information about some activities. These were fencing new garden plots, felling trees in the plots, processing sago, trapping with lines of deadfalls, and hunting game mammals. Collectively they were components of procurement systems that contributed most quantity, energy, and animal protein to diet. The sort of data recorded differed for each practice. With trapping and hunting I estimated the hours committed to each; gardening effort was measured as meters of fence built and hectares of forest felled; and time spent processing sago was indexed as the number of days people were absent from the village for this purpose. Values for gardening and processing sago could not be translated into hours of work, but this was not of great concern. I did not seek to specify the actual effort or returns associated with particular tasks. Instead, I wanted to know what the activity in question looked like—its shape in time—to enable comparison of the temporal dynamics of different activities. The graphs and plots appearing in earlier chapters should be regarded as traces, etched out as the people interacted with the environment. Like the slime trails of snails or the vapor trails of jet airplanes, those traces of themselves cannot reveal truths about the relationships that produced them. Rather, as with any other texts, understanding depends upon the way in which they are read.

It is convenient to describe themes of Etolo subsistence by commencing in mid-April when, in 1979, some families repaired lines of deadfalls and the period of trapping game mammals was under way. This time coincided with changes in weather marking the onset of the cloud season and a rapid decline in availability of fruit pandanus. But the choice of mid-April is not influenced by these coincidences. Nor is it influenced by Etolo perceptions, since I know of none that might suggest opening the discussion at one time rather than another. The reason is artifactual. I arrived at Bobole in late February, 1979, and the commencement of trapping was the earliest I was aware of seasonal patterning in any type of food-getting activity. The patterns that I subsequently detected are displayed on figure 21.

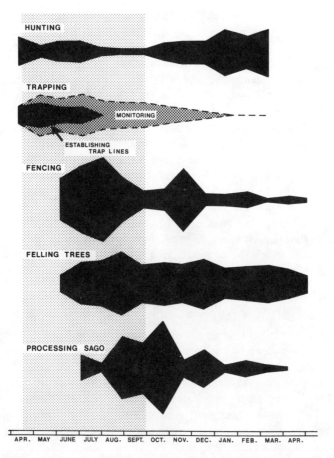

Fig. 21. Scheduling of major tasks: the village pattern. The kites shown on this figure are based on data from figures 5, 11, 14, and 18. They depict the temporal flow and sequence of different activities but are not standardized with respect to effort. Data points on figures 21, 22, and 23 are from consecutive four-week periods.

Two features of the figure are important. The first is that peak periods of effort for the activities were separated in time. The separation was of a quantitative, not a qualitative, sort such that as one activity declined in emphasis another came to dominate the work schedule. The period during which lines of traps were repaired gave way to a time when many new garden plots were made. At these plots the peak period of building fences was followed closely by felling trees within the enclosed areas. By September effort committed to these gardening tasks—particularly to building fences—

was greatly reduced, and more family groups spent more time at lower altitudes, where they processed sago. After October emphasis shifted to a second round of gardening, and, finally, this work declined, and much more time was allocated to hunting game mammals.

The second important feature of figure 21 is a corollary of the first. At Bobole the 109 residents lived as twenty family groups—some with affiliates who were not blood kin—in four longhouse communities. Peak periods of effort committed to establishing lines of traps, preparing new garden sites, processing sago, and hunting were much the same for all family groups. Within moderately broad limits the food-getting schedules of the people were synchronized. Factors that may have necessitated or motivated this synchrony and produced the sequence of traces shown on figure 21 are discussed in the next chapter. There are, however, some preliminary matters to consider. These are (a) possible biases caused because I emphasized work done by males, (b) some implications of scheduling arrangements for diet, (c) differences between longhouse communities within Bobole, and (d) comparative data from two other Etolo communities where the patterns were different.

Complementary Roles

Most work entailed in repairing lines of traps, building fences, felling trees, and hunting was done by men and youths. In a few cases a married couple or father and daughter repaired traps, and with most families everyone older than nine or ten years visited traps to retrieve animals. Women and children rarely helped build fences or fell trees, and there were only two women who hunted. By contrast, processing sago was a family affair with men and women contributing in different ways and with children older than about ten years assisting where they were able.

The activities I recorded in detail occupied the greater part of time male members of the community allocated to subsistence. Yet, except with hunting, tasks performed by males called for complementary work from females, work that coincided with, or followed closely upon, the work of men. Once lines of traps had been established, their owners, male and female, old and young, had to allocate several hours each week to checking and maintenance. As men and youths built fences and felled trees, so women were committed to clearing undergrowth at the new garden plots, gathering cuttings from older sites, and planting and weeding. All these tasks had to be coordinated. Planting could precede or follow the felling of trees by about one month; weeding was essential within two to three months of planting; and if men embarked on sago work, the preferred distribution of tasks meant that women should be present to beat and wash the pith that men had chopped from the palm. With some tasks there was a fair degree of latitude as to when they could be performed. When new garden plots had been enclosed, trees were felled only as areas were wanted for planting, and people could alternate periods of planting and weeding with a week spent at a sago camp. With other tasks there was less latitude. Fencing was done rapidly because, until completed, it was risky to plant crops.

In general, the sorts of work done by women meant that, relative to men, effort they allocated to different activities was less sharply separated in time. The data I collected were prejudiced toward males, yet the traces recorded on figure 21 index part of a complementarity between the sexes that was essential to the unified food-producing system. There was no overt quantitative difference in the ultimate contributions of the sexes. The scheduling of tasks by men or, more accurately, of tasks depicted on the figure specified the temporal dynamics of many complementary tasks performed, for the greater part, by women. In a sense, therefore, the figure presents a caricature of the scheduling arrangements at Bobole, but that caricature represents an underlying dynamic of those arrangements.

Diet

The traces on figure 21 record effort allocated to processing sago, to hunting, to some gardening tasks, and to some forms of trapping. They do not depict yield profiles of either carbohydrate foods or animal protein. This is because, relative to periods of intense work, yields were often delayed and more spread across time. Relevant data are summarized on figure 22. The profile for sweet potato, based on the area of garden producing during thirteen four-week periods, shows that availability of this food was reduced from late September to early or mid-January. Sago starch was the primary carbohydrate substitute through the months of shortfall. The period of maximum effort allocated to processing palms was timed so that fresh and stored starch would be on hand as the abundance of sweet potato waned. The figure includes yield profiles of protein from game mammals and domestic pigs. The former contributed at least half the animal protein eaten at Bobole, and despite the seasonal switch from trapping to hunting the animals, the yield was very uniform across time. The supply of protein from domestic pigs was irregular, and the nutritional importance of these animals must have been less than that of game mammals. It is of note, however, that from September to December when game mammals and domestic pigs contributed least to diet, people snared cassowaries and spent more time catching fish. These data about yield are few but show that both carbohydrate staples and animal protein were available to the people on a regular basis. The separation of different tasks through time did not result in pronounced fluctuations of major dietary components.

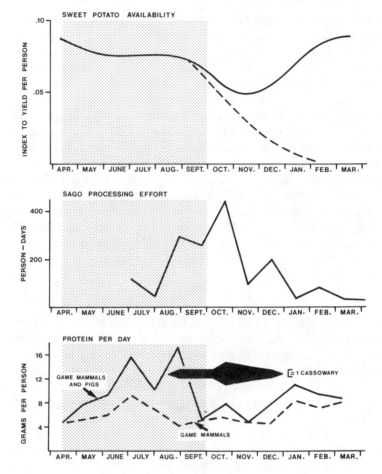

Fig. 22. Availability of sweet potato, sago starch, and animal protein. The traces shown on this figure repeat information from figures 7, 11, and 20. The kite in the bottom panel of the figure records periods when cassowaries were captured.

This brief analysis does not assert that the overall quality of diet was particularly high. It ignores many plant and animal foods that were eaten either regularly or on a seasonal basis. The single intention of the analysis is to show that key food-producing activities that were characterized by very irregular inputs of labor resulted in yields of carbohydrate and protein that were well spread across time.

Choice and Constraint

Because the variety of food-producing activities was great, people at Bobole had the option to obtain most of their carbohydrate or animal protein by concentrating effort, for example, on gardening rather than on processing sago or on trapping rather than on hunting game mammals. But in these matters the choices people made were not entirely free. Lineage affiliation and the recent history of the lineage constrained choice of sweet potato or sago starch as the primary carbohydrate food, and, in turn, the places where and the times at which people gardened and processed palms constrained choice of trapping or hunting as the means of getting game mammals.[1]

Some families obtained most of their carbohydrate-derived calories from sweet potato. These families usually relied on trapping game mammals more than on hunting them. With other families, dependence upon sweet potato was far less, and as much as half of their carbohydrate-derived calories were from sago starch. The latter families tended to hunt game mammals more than they trapped them. Most families from Houses I and III concentrated on gardening and trapping, and most from Houses II and IV concentrated on processing sago and hunting. The data on figure 21 averaged out these differences between family groups. On figure 23 the same data are re-sorted according to the two combinations of longhouses mentioned. This arrangement does not disrupt primary themes inferred from the earlier figure. Major subsistence tasks remain separated in time; the sequence of tasks is the same; and different family groups are still seen to have been doing similar tasks at similar times. Indeed, the synchrony between family groups is sharpened on the new figure. Differences between the two sets of longhouses, those who favored sweet potato and trapping and those who favored processing sago and hunting, are quantitative. Relative to people from House II and House IV, those from Houses I and III each committed twice the effort to repairing lines of traps, 1.75 times the effort to maintaining the traps, 1.25 times the effort to building garden fences, and 1.30 times the effort to felling trees at gardens. By contrast, people from Houses II and IV each exceeded the effort of people from Houses I and III by 1.46 times with sago work and 1.33 times with hunting. (These values are based on eligible workers only.)

The option to use sweet potato as the primary carbohydrate food was, in the first instance, a consequence of history. The people and families who had been first to live at Bobole or whose recent ancestors had lived in the area had customary rights to land near the village. People and families who had arrived more recently, through the late 1950s and the following decade, had fewer rights; their access to gardening land was dependent upon the generosity of customary owners or acquiring rights through arranging suitable marriages. The Gaibi families at Houses I and III had historical priority

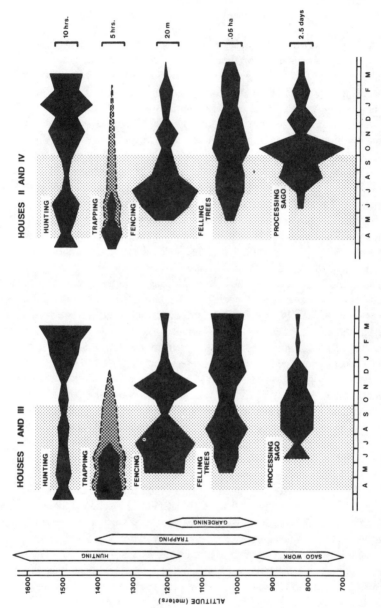

Fig. 23. Scheduling of major tasks: Houses I and III compared with Houses II and IV. The figure shows altitude zones within which different activities took place. Effort is standardized (as hours, meters, hectares, or days) according to the number of participants in each activity; the scales to the right of the figure index effort per participant.

over all the families within the lineage of Waisado and the subdivision of Gaibi that was named Habalo. These latter families lived at Houses II and IV, and their rights to land near the village were more tenuous. Because they had come relatively recently from lower altitudes, their ownership of sago palms was reasonably secure—sufficient, in fact, that some Waisado families had been able to exchange palms for rights to hunting areas on Haliago.

Families who placed higher reliance upon sweet potato were committed to a sequence of tasks—fencing, tree felling, planting, weeding, and harvesting—that needed sustained effort during many months of the year. They worked frequently within the altitude range 900 to 1,200 meters, and their opportunities to hunt at higher altitudes for three or four consecutive days were limited accordingly. On the other hand, the altitudinal zone within which gardens were made was the same as, or contiguous with, the zone where trapping took place. Once a line of traps was operating, it was easy for one member of a gardening family to spend a few hours each week checking and maintaining the traps. The connection between higher reliance on sweet potato and trapping mammals was conditioned by the proximity of locations where these activities took place and constraints on available time imposed by gardening tasks.

Families who placed less reliance upon sweet potato and hence more on sago starch encountered different constraints. As with gardening, the altitudinal zone where sago work was done precluded simultaneous hunting. But work with sago differed from gardening in one important respect: the former could be accomplished within a short period during which much starch was prepared and stored for subsequent use. This meant that families who relied on sago had more blocks of time available within which they could hunt. Families who processed many palms were away from the village often and so had less opportunity to maintain and regularly to check a line of traps. Higher reliance on sago starch and on hunting game mammals was, thus, connected because each required intermittent runs of consecutive days to facilitate the work best. With sago a run of five or more days was prescribed by the nature of the tasks; with hunting a run of three or four days was preferred but not prescribed. The key difference between the two subsistence emphases at Bobole lay in the contrast between sustained and intermittent effort, but in part this contrast was a construct of the people themselves; it was because they chose to organize the tasks in these different ways.

The broad constraints I have described were not absolute. They were influenced by the size and composition of family groups, by opportunities to adopt other food-getting activities, and by altering conventional procedures. Thus far, comment about trapping has concerned the use of lines of deadfalls. Three families with relatively high dependence on sago did not operate lines of traps but used baited deadfalls and tree traps more often than other families did. These techniques yielded some game mammals through the cloud season but did not entail sustained commitment to building and maintaining the facilities. The three families were relatively small—married couples with up to four children. When they left the village to process sago, it was usual that all members of the family went and remained away for the duration of the venture. Because at Bobole an ethos of economic independence was strongly developed, there was little opportunity for small families who were reliant on sago to operate lines of traps. Had they done so, captured animals would have rotted during periods when they were away. Larger families, whose membership was older or whose affiliates included older bachelors (not necessarily sons), did not always go to sago camps in their entirety or, if they did so, some individuals were likely to travel between the camp and the village. With these families it was easy to organize someone to check traps near Bobole while others processed sago elsewhere. Opportunities to trap game mammals were thus enhanced among sago-reliant families whose teenage and adult membership was moderately large. In one case the same outcome was achieved by two smaller families, one Gaibi and one Waisado, whose children were young but who combined in a large-scale trapping venture. By avoiding overlap in the times they went to process sago, there was always an adult at the village to tend the traps.

Namosado and Gabulusado

Although the people who lived at Bobole shared the same environment and had access to the same technology, there was much variation in the ways they patterned subsistence. Historical circumstance, scheduling demands, and family demography influenced the options open to them. The magnitude of differences between families in the ways they satisfied needs was sometimes large. Given the options available and the differences existing between household groups, community-wide synchrony seems unlikely. Yet there was synchrony. It is useful to ask whether concordance of action existed at other Etolo communities and, if it did, whether the timing of tasks was the same.

Thirty-three people lived at Namosado, five kilometers south of Bobole, at an altitude of 800 meters. I visited the community several times through 1979 and early 1980 and obtained some information about food-producing behavior. Nearly all subsistence activity took place between altitudes of 700 and 900 meters. Here lowland pitpit, taro, fruit pandanus, bananas, and sago palms were more prolific and more important food plants than at higher altitudes. Lowland pitpit and pandanus were available earlier in the pandanus season, and the individual inflorescences and fruit were larger, at Namosado, than at Bobole. At the lower altitude taro and bananas contributed more to

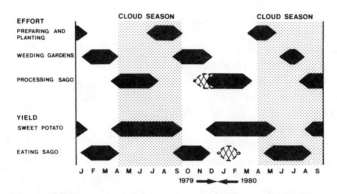

Fig. 24. Gardens and sago palms at Namosado: effort and consumption. The cross-hatched portions indicate additional periods of processing and eating sago that were related to the program of building.

diet, and the proximity of sago palms to the longhouse permitted people often to prepare the starch without moving to a temporary residence.[2]

The increased role of the listed plants in the diet of Namosado people was matched by less attention to sweet potato. The planting regime at sweet potato gardens was not as seen at Bobole. New gardens were initiated at intervals of eight to nine months (fig. 24) with the result that sweet potato was plentiful for five or six consecutive months and scarce or absent during the following two or three months. Although the gardens were not measured, the area under sweet potato was less per person than at Bobole, about one-half to two-thirds of the average value at the higher altitude. At Namosado most effort allocated to processing sago was at times when sweet potato gardens were yielding profusely. Stores of sago flour were readied about five months before periods of greatest demand. The reasons they scheduled tasks in these ways related, in part, to the peculiar demography of the community.

Seven of the thirty-three people who lived at Namosado were bachelor males, older than their late teens, who did not have living close kin. Two of them acted as foster fathers to orphaned boys, and there were two other bachelors whose only resident relative was either a young unmarried, or an elderly widowed, sister. These males were awkwardly placed in terms of fulfilling subsistence needs yet would be expected to be economically independent. Thus, many males had to do work that might otherwise have been the province of women. Having contributed to all phases of garden preparation and planting, they later had to weed. When weeding, they could not commit blocks of time to processing sago, and, of course, the periods when weeding was necessary were dictated by the times of planting. To spread effort they processed palms in the interval between weeding one set of gardens and preparing for the next. Bachelors, it seemed, favored tasks associated with processing sago over those associated with gardens. At Bobole older bachelors were more likely to receive help from women with sago work than with gardening tasks. If this were true at Namosado, then the work load of bachelors would have been reduced by an emphasis upon sago.

Work at gardens and at sago palms left few blocks of time when men from Namosado were free to establish lines of traps or hunt at higher altitudes, and these practices did not occur. Instead, most people operated baited deadfalls and unbaited tree traps that were scattered singly in forest, near either the longhouse or garden houses. They tended traps close to the place where they spent the night; the yield, and presumably the effort, was greater through the cloud season than through the pandanus season. Insect larvae, fish, frogs, lizards (including moderately large varanids), birds, and birds' eggs contributed more animal protein to diet at Namosado than at Bobole. Catfish weighing up to 1 kilogram and large eggs of jungle fowl were important and available during many months. All these animals could be obtained without the commitment of much time, and their capture easily was accommodated within the scheduling regimes I have described.

At Bobole scheduling of work at gardens and sago palms conformed to an annual cycle; at Namosado the cycle had a periodicity of about eight months. But at the latter community, as at Bobole, the schedules of everyone in the community were more or less synchronous. This was so even though family groups were not limited by labor in the way bachelors were. Other factors, however, may have affected subsistence patterns at Namosado. Through much of 1979 and early 1980 the community as a whole and some families acting separately engaged in an extensive program of construction. The major project was a new longhouse and several associated buildings. This was planned by May, 1979, and in July a wedge-shaped block of land was secured from pigs by digging a deep ditch, 150 meters long, between two streams. A comfortable guest house, large enough for twenty visitors, and a pit lavatory were built on this land by September. Work was then diverted to felling a huge tree, cutting and trimming a massive log from the trunk, hauling the log several hundred meters through the forest, and positioning it as a bridge across a narrow gorge of the torrent Sioa. The new longhouse was built in January and February, 1980, and in the same months two family houses were completed; a new church with attached dispensary was started; and adjoining ground was leveled as a sports field. In March the trail leading to and from Namosado was upgraded. Within twelve months Namosado changed from a small, cozy retreat tucked to one side of a major walking trail into a fresh and flourishing hamlet astride the trail. It was not important that many people planned to live at garden dwellings away from the main settlement. The new arrangements were to satisfy government officials who had, in the 1979 census, complained that existing buildings were squalid and the footbridge across Sioa was hazardous. The officials demanded new accommodation for everyone by the time of the next census. The people were more than obliging; they had not liked the hint that they should relocate and join larger Etolo communities.

People from Bobole offered much assistance to those who lived at Namosado. They helped dig the ditch, shared building the longhouse, and during November and December some participated in sago-processing ventures. In these months many bundles of sago fronds were readied to be used as thatch. Because much sago starch was prepared before construction of the longhouse commenced, there was always a supply of food for resident and visiting workers. And, of course, the months of building were when fruit pandanus was abundant. Thus, scheduling arrangements at Namosado may have been influenced by the continuing program of construction; the organization of gardening and sago tasks may have been planned to provide sufficient uninterrupted time for building and a surfeit of food for those who did the work.[3]

During sixteen months in 1968 and 1969 Ray Kelly lived at Gabulusado, a western Etolo longhouse community 10 kilometers west of Namosado at an altitude of 775 meters. The community included up to thirty-five residents. The general themes of subsistence described by Kelly were like those I observed at different communities ten years later.[4] But there were differences in particulars and, sometimes, differences of interpretation. As at Namosado, plant foods that grew better at lower altitudes were of greater dietary importance at Gabulusado than at Bobole, and sago flour contributed more calories to diet than did sweet potato. Effort allocated to major tasks was very variable between months indicating, once again, synchrony among family groups though, from Kelly's data, this was less pronounced than I observed at Bobole. The actual scheduling of tasks at Gabulusado was unlike patterns at either Namosado or Bobole. At the former community most sweet potato was planted in October when large, communal gardens were made; these amounted to 78 percent of all the plantings in a twelve-month period. There were minor peaks of planting in February and June when some families made small gardens.[5] (At Bobole, only 7 percent of planting was in October and, at Namosado, no sweet potato was planted in this month.) The planting regime at Gabulusado gave a high yield of tubers from February to June, a reduced yield in the following months, and a period of scarcity in December and January. While some sago palms were processed each month, the peaks of effort in November and December and from June through August meant that quantities of starch were available when the yield from sweet potato fell. Again, these periods did not match the times when people at Bobole or Namosado allocated most effort to processing sago palms.

The variety of animal foods eaten at Gabulusado was more like that at Namosado than at Bobole. So, too, was the bias that wild foods were most often eaten in the cloud season. These differences between Gabulusado and Bobole related to the difference of altitude that separated the communities and the influence this had upon availability of species. At both the lower-altitude communities most game mammals that were eaten were captured in scattered traps or when they were located in the course of other activities. At Bobole, by contrast, the vast majority of game mammals were taken from lines of deadfall traps or when people hunted at higher altitudes of Haliago. Large-scale fish-poisoning expeditions in which rivers were dammed by groups of people working together occurred at Gabulusado, as did nocturnal hunting of flying foxes (*Pteropus*) at second-growth trees that bore fruit in May and June. Altitude precluded use of these strategies at Bobole. At Namosado, in 1979–80, larger catfish were captured from rivers by line fishing and not by poisoning, and the flying foxes failed to migrate from lower altitudes. Finally, Kelly reported that most domestic pigs were killed in the pandanus season during the months when relatively few wild animals were eaten. On this count, too, the pattern seen at Gabulusado differed from that at Bobole ten years later.

As at Bobole and Namosado key components of subsistence at Gabulusado were temporally separated. This was true of gardening work, processing of sago, the pursuit of wild animals, and the killing of domestic pigs. Different families often did similar work at similar times. There remain, however, important matters of interpretation in which Kelly's account does not coincide with mine. These relate to connections he described between processing of sago and the gardening cycle and to the possibility that patterns at Gabulusado were, ultimately, constrained by environment.

At Gabulusado sago was processed more often during months when the yield from sweet potato gardens was low. Often, in fact, the sago work was done when large gardens were being made. It was useful that planted sago palms matured at the same time as, and in the neighborhood of, areas of secondary forest that were ready to be felled as gardens. This lent a spatial and temporal dynamic to these major endeavors. If palms were planted at the time a garden was established, the palms themselves and the fallowed land were both ready to use in approximately two decades. That is, the maturation time of the palms regulated the length of fallow periods. Thus, Kelly reported the people as saying that "at about the time of his marriage, a man will return to the garden land and sago stands utilized by his father when he was born".[6] Kelly thought this connection was beneficial in two ways. First, it allowed an effective allocation of labor in that, through the morning, men might fell a palm or fragment pith while women cleared undergrowth from the nearby garden site and, through the afternoon, women would beat and wash pith to extract starch while men fenced the garden or felled trees within it. Second, the arrangement satisfied needs of defense in ensuring that armed men were always on hand if women and children were threatened.

Kelly considered that both gardening and sago processing could be undertaken at any time. The temporal patterns of effort allocated to the tasks were not imposed by environmental circumstance. By contrast, he thought that many species of wild foods, both plant and animal, were available only or were procured most easily in the cloud season. Seasonal factors, therefore, directly influenced access to certain wild foods—the eggs of jungle fowl, game mammals, flying foxes, and wood grubs. By limiting gardening effort through the cloud season, people made time available to capture desired animal foods. The result was that gardening itself and, thence, processing of sago emerged as seasonal activities. Kelly wrote: "Thus the seasonality of hunting, trapping, and collecting imparts a seasonal patterning to all subsistence activity, influencing the timing of garden starts and consequently the scheduling of sago working".[7]

Neither before nor after contact could people from Bobole often process sago near the site of a new garden. This was because groves of sago and gardens were usually at different altitudes. Even near Bobole where palms were not plentiful, they were seldom close to current gardens, and none that was felled and processed was near a garden. Indeed, most palms that were close to the village were located as a single patch in a swamp that never could have been used to grow sweet potato. They had been planted through a period of many years and were not of uniform size. This difference between Gabulusado and Bobole was a consequence of altitude and not of history. Before contact people who lived at Bobole must have satisfied defense needs in ways other than Kelly described. Indeed, the relative isolation of Bobole from other communities meant that the location of itself gave security. Some people told of precautions they had taken when working sago at lower altitudes. It had been advisable to choose times when the moon was full, to work as large parties, and to have men standing guard. They related cautionary tales in which men or entire families had been ambushed and eaten while engaged in the work. Kelly's description of events at Gabulusado showed one way in which defense needs and effective use of labor could have been met, but that option had never been available to people who lived at higher altitudes, where the palms did not grow well. A spatial connection between processing sago and gardening was not seen at Namosado though, of course, in 1979–80, there was no need for defense. Further, although three longhouses had been occupied by this community during the previous six or seven years (including the house built in 1980), the sites of these were close together, and a sustained period of gardening in the one area may have disrupted former connections between preferred garden locations and mature sago palms. Even at Gabulusado, however, the ideal expressed by the people themselves that after one generation they would return to particular gardening lands and sago stands must sometimes have been difficult to put into practice. Accusations of witchcraft would have often resulted in long-term changes of residence, and the ideal ignores the fact that married couples might garden and process sago on the woman's land.

My account of the wild foods eaten at Bobole does not reveal the cloud season bias that Kelly detected at Gabulusado. This was primarily because game mammals dominated the catch at the higher altitude and many were captured in both seasons. But additionally, at Bobole, cassowaries, fish, and sago grubs were all eaten more often in the pandanus season, and the eggs of jungle fowl were collected in both seasons.[8] Cloud season captures of some smaller items such as burrowing rats and many bandicoots and cuscuses were associated with gardening work, but it was the work that gave the opportunities to capture the animals; it was not availability of the animals that guided times when people made gardens. Thus, at Bobole seasonal patterns of availability of animal foods did not govern work regimes either at gardens or when processing sago. The same, I think, may be said of the lower-altitude communities: most wild animal foods were available throughout the year, but people chose to concentrate effort in the cloud season. At Gabulusado, of course, this choice would have then influenced scheduling options in other spheres. Further details concerning seasonality and analyses of possible environmental constraints appear in the next chapter.

The subsistence patterns exhibited by longhouse communities at Bobole, Namosado, and Gabulusado were variants within a common theme. Some primary differences between the communities may be readily explained in terms of altitude: these relate, first, to the relative emphases upon sago or sweet potato as the primary source of carbohydrate; second, to the importance of crops such as taro and bananas; and third, to the sorts of animal species available near at hand. On all these counts Bobole stood apart from Gabulusado and Namosado; at the higher altitude sweet potato took precedence over sago starch; taro and bananas were minor crops; and game mammals were available in large numbers from primary forest. Again, at each community the schedules adhered to by different families tended to coincide; subsistence action was often communal, though this, it seemed, might be motivated in different ways—by, for example, considerations of defense at Gabulusado and, in the absence of this need, of demography at Namosado. What, though, of the ten years that separated the reports of subsistence at Bobole and Namosado from that at Gabulusado? An important source of potential change arose because communities no longer shifted location every three to four years and, in consequence, were obliged to alter the spatial connections that had once existed between longhouses and the sites where gardens were made and sago was processed. At Bobole and Namosado these places were more dispersed than had been the case at Gabulusado ten years earlier; the effect was greatest at Bobole where more than 100 people lived together. Lesser effects arose from access to a wider array of crops and from opportunities to experiment with alternative gardening techniques, though by 1979 these impacts remained minor at Bobole.

The effects of change had intruded more into people's social lives than they had upon basic themes of subsistence. By 1979 there was almost no use of purchased foods—canned fish, rice, etc.—at Bobole, and there was no dependence upon them. The use of hooks and lines to obtain catfish was new. The cessation of raiding and cannibalism may have enlarged scheduling options and minimally reduced variety in diet, and there were two reasons why the frequency of hunting may have altered. First, constraints upon hunting frequency that had been governed by forest spirits were relaxed. Second, before 1968, the initiation of youths entailed long seclusion at hunting lodges within the forest, and because this custom had ceased, one motive to hunt—the assertion of manliness—may have declined.[9] Ecological differences between Gabulusado and Bobole had little to do with effects of contact. In the main, they reflected effects of altitude and the varied options open to people. Without knowledge of the differences, it would be less easy to interpret patterns at either place. My review of Ray Kelly's account finds no quarrel with the details. A few interpretations were, I think, overgeneralized, but this hazard is universal.

CHAPTER 11

Timing, Sequence, and Synchrony

In November, when the march flies came, people remembered that soon there would be much fruit pandanus. The winds blew from the northeast, and on gusty days people said it would not be long before they ate lowland pitpit. Those days recalled my childhood, and I made a kite. It was of simple design with a light bamboo cross as the frame, a plastic sail, and a long string tail with pieces of paper tied at intervals. None of the pieces of paper was colored.

My recollections had been faulty. In weather seemingly perfect for the job, the kite refused to fly. At best, by running across the sports field I could make it rise 5 or even 6 meters before it stalled and fell headlong to the ground. It never once paid the courtesy of an aerobatic roll or an elegant, if downward, swoop. It merely plunged. I do not know whether the fault was with the materials chosen or the way they were connected. Was it the cross-piece of the lack of color on the tail? The design itself may not have suited the idiosyncrasies of those gusts, coming sometimes from one side, some-times from the other, of the ridge where we all lived. I had got it wrong and never understood why. One day I shall try again. In this chapter many kites of very different construction are flown. Their robustness will vary; some may never get off the ground; and others may flutter briefly and then fall. They are about Etolo subsistence and environment, about human choice and the causes of patterns depicted in the previous chapter.

At Bobole, Namosado, and Gabulusado scheduling arrangements were different. In particular, major periods when sago was processed and gardens prepared did not coincide across the three communities. But at each commu-nity key subsistence tasks were organized such that people did similar things at similar times. This was true of the relatively isolated longhouse communi-ties at Gabulusado and Namosado and of the amalgam of four longhouse communities at Bobole. The question arises: why were food-getting activities synchronized among different families within a single community? Was there

157

no choice in the matter? Did the observed patterns emerge as necessary responses to the environments within which people acted? Was the scheduling of one crucial food-getting activity dictated by environmental circumstance and the scheduling of others contingent upon this constraint? Or were the patterns relatively free from environmental necessity and, rather, motivated from within the communities themselves? These questions have three components: they are about factors that regulated the timing, sequence, and synchrony of food-getting activities within a community. With focus upon patterns at Bobole, I first consider possible environmental causes of the times when people hunted, trapped, gardened, and processed sago. Then I turn to the themes of sequence and synchrony.

Timing of hunting and trapping could be influenced by seasonal factors intrinsic to the animals or others connected with people. In the first category behavioral traits of the animals might make them easier to capture at certain times of the year or, because they migrated, inaccessible at other times. Breeding regimes might produce seasonal changes in abundance or restrict production of vulnerable youngsters to particular months. And, if people pursued animals to obtain fat as well as protein, seasonal shifts in body fat content of different species could alter their attractiveness as prey. In the second category the effectiveness of techniques used by people could alter in response to the weather. None of these potential factors appears to have been causally tied to the timing of hunting or of trapping with lines of deadfalls at Bobole.

There is no information about the biology of game mammals to suggest any were more vulnerable during particular months. All species were available in all months, and for those where data are sufficient, breeding and hence recruitment of young animals continued through the year. People who hunt or trap often seek game at likely feeding locations or even at specific food plants. When flowers or fruit are used as food by the animals, then seasonality among the plants may shape hunting and trapping strategies. This did not occur at Haliago. Game mammals obtained by hunting were usually located at their daytime resting places, and when deadfalls were used, the traps were not placed near known food plants. Indeed, Etolo knowledge of, or declared interest in, the feeding habits of game mammals was less detailed or precise than that of other Papua New Guineans who live in regions where abundance and variety of the animals were less than at Haliago.

I lack explicit information about the body fat content of game mammals. Etolo perceptions were that this was higher among arboreal than terrestrial species and, within species, higher in the cloud season than in the pandanus season. Given that most game taken in the cloud season was terrestrial and most taken in the pandanus season was arboreal, the shift from trapping to hunting might have sustained a yield of animals with intermediate levels of fat. At this juncture no good case may be made for or against the idea that changes in the body fat of game mammals influenced people's behavior. I return to this problem later.

Most hunting at Bobole was done in the pandanus season, from December to March, when clear days were followed by late afternoon or evening storms. These conditions may have enhanced the comfort of hunters but did not enhance success; on average, hunts during the cloud season yielded one game mammal in 5.3 hours ($n = 124$ game mammals), and hunts during the pandanus season yielded one game mammal in 5.0 hours ($n = 470$ game mammals). People may have preferred to hunt on days when the likelihood of rain was low, but even if true, this is hardly a compelling constraint on the scheduling of hunting.

Possible influences of weather conditions on the success of trapping are hard to untangle. Trapping with deadfalls got under way early in the cloud season, and some families continued to trap well into the pandanus season. The yield was high at first and progressively declined, but this was almost certainly because local abundance of animals was reduced as more were captured. Three additional observations hint that trapping could have been effective at any time of the year. First, my own extensive trapping activities were sustained through twelve months, and though techniques used and species obtained differed from those of the people at Bobole, there were no overt changes in rate of capture through time.[1] Second, at Namosado, at least some people trapped game mammals through the year—admittedly, they used baited deadfalls and not lines of unbaited traps. Third, if effective trapping with lines of deadfalls was environmentally constrained, it might have been expected that synchrony among families would have been tighter than observed; in fact, the interval during which fifteen lines of deadfalls were brought into operation spanned thirteen weeks, and the last of these lines was commenced only two weeks before the first was closed down.

Scheduling options related to trapping were apparently flexible, but some comparative information raises other problems. The pioneer anthropologist F. E. Williams visited Lake Kutubu, 60 kilometers east of the Great Papuan Plateau at an altitude of 800 meters, in 1939–40. His report included some tantalizing remarks about trapping that were based on what the people said.[2] They thought of the cloud season as a time when game mammals were abundant—the animals had come down in the clouds—and available to be trapped with deadfalls. The people of the Lake Kutubu area are named Foi, and Jimmy Weiner, who lived among eastern Foi speakers in 1979–81 and on later occasions, provided further details of their subsistence and its seasonal themes.[3] There was a customary association between trapping and hunting of game mammals and periods of higher rainfall. The connection was mediated in part by the availability of certain ripe fruit that were eaten by the animals. The Foi said that game mammals and cassowaries "descend from their houses in the sky when the cloud cover forms during the rainy season," and Weiner added that it may have been "fruitless to go hunting during the time of the year when (the animals) have returned to the sky." But seasonality of the kind depicted by Weiner need not be inevitable. He noted that such rhythms may be "intelligible in terms of the social and moral oscillations of a particular society" and, very tellingly, reported that "young unmarried men today often abandon their responsibilities in the village to go on hunting trips at any time of the year." They would not have done this if no animals were available to be captured: "it is the manner in which the Foi themselves interpret the variation in seasonal rhythms that is important."

Another anthropologist, Robin Hide, with John Pernetta and Tara Senabe, studied hunting and trapping by Yuro people at Mt. Karimui, Simbu Province, through 1981 and 1982.[4] The people used deadfall traps to obtain large numbers of the bandicoot *Echymipera kalubu*. Between March and October they set the traps in secondary forest at altitudes between 1,100 and 1,400 meters. The traps were baited with either insect larvae or ripe banana and placed near fruiting ginger plants or wild figs. Animals seeking food at the plants were lured into the traps by the alternative baits. Major periods of trapping overlapped broadly at Mt. Haliago, Mt. Karimui, and Lake Kutubu. This implies an underlying, presumably environmental rationale. But the techniques used by Yuro and Etolo were very different. The former sited baited traps at specific locations and caught large numbers of a single species while the latter obtained many different species by using unbaited deadfalls that were positioned without reference to likely feeding locations of animals. Yuro people seem to have taken advantage of seasonal foraging behavior of one species but, perhaps, could have placed traps as effectively at different food plants at different times. On this count, differences between the two groups of people suggest that similarities in the times when trapping was likely to be done were no more than coincidence. The comparative data, however, return me to the problem of the fat content of game animals.

Some ecologists assert that animals, including people, feed in ways that ultimately maximize their fitness—that is, the number of offspring that survive and reproduce. The food-getting decisions of the animals may be the best compromise possible—the optimal solution—within a given environment. In environments where access to one nutrient was problematic, food-getting patterns might be organized around obtaining this nutrient. The diet of inland Papua New Guineans is typically low in fats and oils. If access to these nutrients was both crucial to well-being and problematic, then recorded patterns of capturing game might be explicable. Fruit pandanus is an extraordinarily rich source of oils within the middle altitudinal range of Papua New Guinea. The trees are grown at small or large orchards, and with increasing altitude, the size and abundance of fruit decreases, and there are fewer months when the food is regularly available. Of the localities mentioned, it was at Gabulusado and Lake Kutubu that fruit pandanus was probably most prolific, and at Bobole that it was least prolific. In parallel, the pursuit of game mammals (and, perhaps, all wild animals) altered from extreme concentration in cloud season months to a pattern of year-round captures. At Mt. Karimui, which was ecologically—though not altitudinally—intermediate between Gabulusado and Bobole, much less emphasis was directed toward the capture of mammals during months that fruit pandanus was most abundant. The same association was detected at Lake Kutubu. These observations allow the thought that pursuit of wild game was influenced strongly by a need or desire for fats and oils. The hypothesis contained in the thought may be worth exploring. This cannot be done here. In relation to patterns at Bobole, an implied hypothesis is that fat from wild animals was of nutritional importance in all months. That hypothesis says nothing about how the animals should be captured and, hence, does not specify times when people should trap rather than hunt.

Seasonality among major plant foods could be influenced, as with animals, by changing patterns of growth and maturation or of the effectiveness of management techniques. With both sweet potato and sago starch these factors did not constrain scheduling options. Some sweet potato was planted, and some palms were processed in almost all months. At gardens people often altered the sequence of felling trees and planting sweet potato runners to adjust success of the runners to seasonal weather patterns. But the variability in planting times at Bobole and the different periods of peak planting at Namosado and Gabulusado indicate that sweet potato could have been planted at any time. Similarly, while individual sago palms had to be processed before they flowered, this did not confine the possibility of making starch to a specific period. There is one proviso here. When sago is processed, it is important that the pith neither dry out nor become saturated. The risk was greater that one or the other of these might happen in the pandanus season when daytime temperatures and the chance of midafternoon downpours were relatively high. In each case the risk could be offset by either pouring more water onto the pith or building roofs over the felled palms and troughs. These solutions increased work loads but were not prohibitive; at Namosado and Gabulusado much sago starch was made in the pandanus season months of November and December.[5] Thus, the regimes of processing sago and preparing sweet potato gardens at Bobole were not directly motivated through either environment or limitations of techniques. This opinion was shared by Kelly and the people. With rather less confidence the same conclusion applies to many other garden foods; taro, acanth spinach, aibika, beans, highland pitpit, sugarcane, cucumber, corn, and bananas. The availability of many of them altered through the year, but this was a response to planting times and little influenced by seasonal effects of weather on growth.

The preceding discussion has not revealed substantive constraints on scheduling options concerning several major food-getting activities. But I must be careful here. I have asked whether the recorded work regimes connected with particular facets of some procurement systems could have been other than they were. The answer is yes; trapping with lines of deadfalls, hunting, growing sweet potato, and processing sago could have been done, without penalty, at other times of the year. Work regimes, however, need not coincide with times when the foods produced by the work are eaten. Sago flour can be stored; building a line of traps can produce game several months after the event, and so forth. Constraints can arise in regard to periods of consumption, and these, in turn, may exert control over scheduling arrangements. At Bobole some food-getting practices that did not need a great input of work produced foods at particular times of the year. The practices concern both animal and plant foods; their possible connections with overall scheduling patterns need comment.

The cuscus *Phalanger permixtio* was taken often in tree traps and by casual encounter during the months June and July, and captures of some small mammals (*Pogonomys macrourus* and *Cercartetus caudatus*) peaked in July-August, and November. Most fruit bats were obtained in January and February; dwarf cassowaries were snared between August and December; and sago grubs were harvested most regularly from December to February. Among plants yams were eaten primarily during July and August while both lowland pitpit and fruit pandanus were available in quantity from only December to April. Of this list, fruit pandanus was most important in terms of amount eaten and provision of energy-rich oils. In some cases, the times these foods were eaten and the necessary work done were contingent only on the scheduling of other activities. In other cases, availability of the foods was fixed, but the associated work load was diffuse. And, with two cases, both the effort required and the period of consumption were ordained by season.

Gardening tasks after June increased access to both the cuscus and the small mammals, and, similarly, availability of sago grubs was patterned by times when palms were processed. The fruit bats captured in January and February were in two large hauls located at a cave when men hunted on Haliago. These animals breed seasonally, and the hauls were made up of females with their nursing young. They may have been more vulnerable at this time, but I think their capture was fortuitous and the timing simply because people hunted more often through the pandanus season.

With lowland pitpit and fruit pandanus seasonal changes in weather determined months when inflorescences or fruit were common. The effort needed to produce both these foods was not great and not confined to particular months. Lowland pitpit was planted with other crops and, sometimes, when a garden was weeded. The many tasks needed at pandanus orchards continued through the year at an easy, rather casual pace. Indeed, the contrast is striking between the need for ongoing maintenance of an extremely seasonal food such as pandanus and the decisions to concentrate effort connected with basically aseasonal staples such as sweet potato and sago.

Timing of work associated with yams and cassowaries was fixed. Most yams were planted in special gardens late in the year, well after the daylong drizzling rain of the cloud season had abated. The area planted was less than 1 hectare or about 4 percent of the total used as gardens in twelve months. At Bobole access to cassowaries was influenced by fruiting times of certain forest trees and wild pandanus. People said that when the fruit fell the birds migrated from lower to higher altitudes where they could be snared. Although a few men spent many hours or even days tending snares, this strategy for getting meat was not widespread. Though work that produced yams and cassowaries was restricted to particular months, it was insufficient in either case to enforce timing of other activities. The same applies with lowland pitpit, fruit pandanus, and fruit bats. With the plant foods the spread of effort did not reduce options elsewhere, and with the bats it is unlikely that a minor increase in the chance of getting a large haul dictated times when people regularly hunted game mammals.

With few exceptions, timing of food-getting tasks at Bobole was free from environmental necessity. And, it seems, no substantial gains would have accrued—in terms of lightened work loads or increased yields—had one period been favored over another in the performance of a food-getting task. Nor have cases been found in which the schedule of either work or consumption was fixed and the necessary effort enough to impose temporal order on other food-getting activities. But so far the discussion has been overly atomistic. Subsistence tasks that may be analyzed as separate entities are, in fact, connected. The connections take many forms and, even putting aside questions of actual timing, could position the tasks as a fixed and repeated sequence. In the first instance connections between subsistence tasks arise from choices made by people to spread effort through time or simplify decision making by doing a lot of one sort of thing in a concentrated burst. Choices such as these are about the organization of work and are implemented within contexts of available labor and the locations where specific activities occur. There is another class of choices open to people. This is about diet itself, the combinations of foods that will be eaten together, or the circumstances and times when they are eaten. When people exert control over diet, their choices may have far-reaching effects. In what follows, I explore scheduling implications of choice in the areas of work and consumption.

Ray Kelly described ways in which people's decisions affected the order in which they performed different tasks. They chose to spread subsistence effort and because at Gabulusado animal foods were sought in the cloud season, they did not make communal gardens during this period. Again, because people did not need sago flour when the yield of sweet potato was high and guaranteed, the periods when larger gardens were made affected times when sago was processed. I have suggested that the seasonality of getting wild animals was itself based in decisions made by people. Inasmuch as those decisions had priority, they affected times when other tasks were done. Other factors influenced these patterns. Families who chose to eat relatively more sweet potato did not all participate in the communal garden but made smaller gardens on an eight-month cycle. This meant they spent more time at garden houses where access to game was enhanced but the opportunities to socialize were restricted. Defensive considerations also made connections between subsistence tasks.

At Bobole and Namosado groups of people who regularly worked together—usually, family groups—spread their effort and, through periods of varying length, directed most effort to a set of closely related tasks. They did not need to do these things. Work loads were not so severe that, for example, they could not have made smaller gardens more often, processed enough sago starch in one month to last a year, or, at Namosado, commenced a new garden at the same time and place that they worked with sago. At Bobole people could have trapped game mammals without long-term maintenance of a line of deadfalls and always hunted on single days rather than through several consecutive days. Some people did these things some of the time, but most did not. Men could have interrupted fence building or tree felling on one day to go hunting, but they seldom did. If they worked at gardens, they usually completed a discrete set of tasks before taking up a different activity. They did not work piecemeal and sometimes said they didn't have the time. Indeed, when Sailo attempted to enclose an exceptionally large garden plot and failed to attract fellow workers, the family members ran short of food because they would not temporarily change step and work with sago. The people's perceptions were that particular activities were completed in particular ways; work at lines of traps and at gardens required a sustained commitment; work at sago and hunting was, quite properly, intermittent. These perceptions made time itself orderly.

At Bobole the decision by one family to initiate a moderately large garden at a particular time or process several palms in quick succession limited times when they could accomplish other tasks. The decision to spread subsistence effort, together with a need to sustain a yield of animal protein and perform different tasks within different altitudinal zones, was additionally limiting. Because males and females usually did different work, sometimes in the same place, sometimes in different places, the composition of families also influenced the way in which tasks were ordered through time. (The role of labor in shaping connections between gardening and sago work at Namosado and Gabulusado was described in chap. 10.) The connections between these distinct facets of subsistence—choice, labor, location—predisposed families to a fixed sequence of tasks irrespective of inherent flexibility in scheduling any single task. But such entrainment did not specify actual times when particular tasks should be done or require all families within a community to conform to the same sequence or the same timetable.

When people make decisions about the sorts of foods they will eat in the same meal, these decisions can be satisfied only by planning. The decisions may have consequences for nutrition and for scheduling. If, for example, they want to eat a food that is available during only certain months with another that could be produced at any time, then timing of work associated with the second food will be fixed. If, in addition, the association of these two foods in the diet is nutritionally or even culturally sound, then most people within a community may adopt the same sort of timetable. At Bobole the consumption patterns and, hence, work regimes associated with fruit pandanus, sweet potato, and sago may have been influenced by these sorts of factors. People made no bones about the fact that they preferred sweet potato to sago starch. When the former was scarce in October and November, their complaints were many; they said they were sick of eating sago. And when new gardens at last produced sweet potato in December, they dropped sago almost entirely from the menu. They did this even though much sago flour remained in storage.

Fresh sago flour and sweet potato differ in moisture content; the sago comprises about 20 percent moisture; the sweet potato is about 70 percent moisture. People at Bobole ate sago flour dry; they did not mix it with water to make a pasty soup as do many other Papua New Guineans. An abrupt switch from sago flour to sweet potato as soon as the latter was available would have required that (all else being equal) people ate about 2.5 times as much food for the same intake of energy. But having become habituated through earlier months to a rather small though energy-sufficient quantity of sago, they would feel satiated before they had eaten enough sweet potato to satisfy needs. In physiological terms this complication would not be long lasting. Within about a week they would have reset satiation level against adequate intake; they would once more feel hungry until, in both senses, they had had enough. Etolo people, however, may not have found this solution satisfactory. In earlier years they may have had good cause to regulate carefully the quantities they ate because individuals who were thought to be greedy, in feeding habits or sexual matters, risked being named as witches. Though this was not an overt worry in 1979, I was continually impressed by the modest amounts eaten, at least in public; there remained a concern with appearances. Where social constraints of these sorts operate, then people who alternate relatively dry with wet carbohydrate staples would be well advised to plan that the changeover coincide with ready access to a food rich in oil or fat. These nutrients contain more than twice the energy per unit weight relative to dry carbohydrates. Combination of a fat-rich food with a wet carbohydrate staple will provide higher energy for less quantity than is possible from the carbohydrate alone.[6]

At Bobole the bright red sauce made from fruit pandanus was, par excellence, rich in oils, and people ate large amounts at the time they changed from sago flour to sweet potato. They said the foods went well together. If they planned to eat them at the same time, they had to plant gardens at least five months before fruit pandanus became abundant in December. Doing this might have obliged them to repair lines of traps before they turned to gardening and committed them to working with sago after this set of gardens was planted.

At Namosado and Gabulusado gardening was not scheduled so that an abundance of sweet potato coincided with availability of pandanus, but, of course, no necessity is attached to the pattern observed at Bobole. There are other ways to adjust quantity. For example, at Bobole, from September onward, the quantity of sweet potato eaten declined, and the amount of sago flour increased accordingly. The change was not abrupt and a problem of regulating quantity not apparent. Again, though at a lesser scale, there are Papua New Guineans who usually eat sago flour dry but who make sago soup if they have had the good fortune to capture a pig.[7]

The kite I have flown in the last few paragraphs is speculative. If it is near the truth, it would be implicated in both setting the sequence of food-getting tasks to particular times and encouraging synchrony among family groups. That implication gains strength from the fact that people said they used fruit pandanus as a calendar to guide scheduling decisions.

This book opened with an Etolo text written by Efala. He wrote:

First there is the red pandanus season. When red pandanus is no longer eaten, then it is time to set deadfall traps. The trapping season finishes at the onset of the next pandanus season.

And:

In December the red pandanus season is underway. It is available for eating from December until April.

And:

At the time when red pandanus commence to set small fruit, three kinds of wild pandanus and certain forest trees drop fruit that are eaten by cassowaries. Snares are set here, and cassowaries are caught when they come to feed on the fallen fruit. . . .

And again:

Sweet potato may be planted at any time, but if it is desired to eat sweet potato with red pandanus, then the former must be planted at an appropriate time.

The mood contained within Efala's text was that of a proper way in which people should organize food-getting activities. Some times were felt to be more appropriate than others to initiate tasks of particular sorts. There is a sense of communality both of action and of eating the products that derive from the action. There is the implication that communality and the cooperation that makes this possible were highly valued by Etolo. But there was more than this alone contained within the text. It was a surface expression of former days when subsistence action was perceived to be guided by the spirits. Kelly wrote: "Almost every routine event or activity which takes place in an Etoro community is foretold in advance by the spirits during the course of seances and the spirits are, in effect, involved in nearly all subsistence activity."[8] A heightened capacity to read the signs that marked forthcoming seasonal rhythms—alterations of direction in prevailing winds, the flocking of mountain pigeons, arrival of march flies, fall of forest fruits, or phases in the annual cycle of fruit pandanus—may have been a filter through which mediums and spirits communicated at seances. Valued outcomes may have been achieved when the advice of the spirits passed through this filter. The seasons did not dictate action; they provided a repeated set of opportunities to which people responded according to various social and even cosmological needs and wants.

Interestingly, Efala's text did not specify months when sago palms should be processed. His words implied only that people should often plan ahead and that the palms were of value as emergency food. He wrote, for example, that "if one wishes to eat sago with red pandanus during the pandanus season, then sago should be processed in advance," "if one is thinking of eating sago grubs, then palms should be cut to incubate grubs and to have sago ready," and, again, " . . . if other foods are scarce, then sago should be processed." Nor did his text make any reference to hunting game mammals. Despite these absences, it seems that the timing of large-scale trapping ventures and of preparing some gardens was legislated by the phenology of fruit pandanus. People used overt calendric markers to schedule these activities, so the sequence of most food-getting practices was entrained and the actions of family groups within the community were more or less coincident.

Adherence to a biologically based calendar was a perceived and substantive cause of the timing, sequence, and synchrony of work directed at subsistence among people who lived at Bobole. One question remains. Was the calendar both sufficient and necessary as an explanation of the patterns?

Calendars of any sort are ambiguous guides to action, and the Etolo fruit pandanus calendar was no exception. There are two reasons for disquiet. While calendars may aid scheduling decisions, they seldom make a necessity of them. Calendars are there to be used. They guide but do not prescribe decisions. One calendar may be manipulated by different individuals to achieve quite different ends. At Namosado and Gabulusado people did not use the calendar to ensure an abundance of sweet potato through the months when they ate lots of fruit pandanus. At Bobole there was nothing to prevent one family from setting deadfall traps at the close of the pandanus season while another family chose to do this at the outset of the season. Both families could have asserted that their actions were set by calendric markers; their selection of those markers would be post hoc. Only where ancillary constraints operate—arising, say, from environment—or where the potential benefits are great—as higher yields, preferred combinations of food, or communality per se—will calendric markers be read in the same way by all participants. At Bobole most people did read them in the same way, but they did not have to; there were neither constraints nor pragmatic benefits of sufficient force to guarantee this.

The second reason for disquiet is more serious. Fruit pandanus did not in fact provide cues that had the sharp definition seemingly attributed to them by the people. Availability of fruit varied in a quantitative, not a qualitative, way—the yield declined; it did not cease. Indeed, like good orchardists everywhere, the people manipulated the crop to sustain a yield as long as possible. There was no actual time when the pandanus season was over and deadfall traps should be set; this was a matter of judgment. Nor was there a brief period when the trees began to set fruit. With thirteen different varieties selected over many generations to be early or late fruiters, the people had stretched the interval during which the fruit was set. Quite simply, the declared calendar contained no discrete boundaries to guide action. Its cues were of an analogical sort; they were not digital and, hence, could not serve as powerful communicatory codes. When calendric markers lack sharp focus, they are unable to contain the behavior of potentially fickle actors. The close of the pandanus season could be assessed from declining yield of one variety rather than all or of one's preferred varieties over those of other people. The time when new fruit were said to have set could be assessed in many ways. With the best or the worst intentions some families might move out of phase with others; a faulty judgment in making a garden might disrupt their plans; an unexpected opportunity to sell or trade sago flour might tempt them to reorganize tasks; or an urgent obligation to give meat could have similar outcomes. The fruit pandanus calendar that people used to organize their actions does not sufficiently explain that organization. The latitude it granted in making decisions exceeded the limits of practical consensus achieved by the people.

Early in this chapter, I asked why the food-getting activities of different family groups living within one community were synchronized. Why was it that different people did much the same things in much the same places at much the same times? The question remains unanswered. The exploration of possible cues arising from the physical and biological environments within which people acted did not reveal critical constraints upon scheduling options. Nor were options restricted by seasonal variation in the effectiveness of techniques used to obtain food. Rather, because people chose to spread effort and avoided working at different sorts of tasks within one block of time, each family group acting separately was prompted to adopt a fixed sequence of tasks. And because they chose to combine certain foods and used calendric markers to guide decisions about some of the associated tasks, the sequence itself was locked into a set time frame to which all families conformed. These causes of action were proximate. They were driven by decisions that people did not have to make, and, hence, the calendar they said they used was neither necessary nor sufficient to account for their actions. The ultimate forces that motivated synchrony and contained fickle behavior must have arisen from within the community itself. Ecological pattern was legislated through social action: at Bobole, I will argue, through the act and consequences of putting pigs into gardens and declaring everyone would go hungry.

CHAPTER 12

Sugua Mai

On the evening of December 24, 1979, most residents of Bobole gathered at their small church. They came to celebrate the birth of Christ, mark their tenth anniversary as Christians and, as well, acknowledge that this year for the first time their worship was led by a native Etolo speaker. Through the day people had decorated the church with flowers and cordyline leaves; costumes were made; and those who were to perform the evening morality play rehearsed their parts. At darkness the church bell rang to beckon the congregation.

The celebration was an enactment of the tale of the first people in the garden of Eden. The church was dimly lit with several small kerosene lamps and slow-burning grass torches. Efala, as pastor, was composer, director, and, when needed, prompter. Maga took the part of Adam; his wife, Nowalia, was Eve. Hamaga, in white robes, was God, and Siagoba, costumed in brittle-dry fronds of pandanus and trailing a 2 meter tail, was an impressive, almost frightening, serpent-cum-devil. At Siagoba's entrance some children and adults whispered, "Mugabe."

The tale was given a mild twist. As is proper, Eve fell victim to Satan's persuasive speech, was tempted to eat the fruit of the tree of knowledge, and shared this experience with Adam. Through these scenes Eve and Adam wore European clothing and ate with metal knives and spoons from enamel plates. When God banished them from Eden, they lost their fine clothing and other material possessions. They were sent forth from the church and beyond Eden dressed in only the traditional bark-string clothing of Etolo. The play had told of a great loss in a distant past. For the players and audience, their participation in the congregation spoke of renewal. What once had been was concluded—people had erred and been punished—but what had been concluded could be reconnected; Christianity was the way back to Eden.

But the end of the performance was true to the text. God and Satan departed, as they had appeared, through the men's door of the church; Adam and Eve had left Eden through the women's door. Only the audience and the cherubim remained. Fuago was the cherubim, robed and standing guard at the entrance to Eden as Efala led the congregation in song.

Chapter 3, verse 24, of the Old Testament *Book of Genesis* teaches that God " . . . drove out the man; and he placed at the east of the garden of Eden Cherubims, and a flaming sword which turned every way, to keep the way of the tree of life." Those cherubim and that flaming sword—symbolized by Fuago standing silently at the women's door to the small church at Bobole— were a boundary. They separated the world that is from the world that might have been—the actual land of the Hebrews from the ideal at Eden, the material conditions of Etolo from the conditions that Etolo perceived as European. Or better, perhaps, those cherubim and that flaming sword sepa- rated the world that is from a continuum of all possible worlds and, in this way, granted both order and sanctity to the world that is. For did not the Etolo performance declare, "what happened is how we became what we are but, through God, what we were we may become once more?"

As Mircea Eliade wrote:

The threshold is the limit, the boundary, the frontier that distinguishes and opposes two worlds—and at the same time the paradoxical place where those worlds communi- cate, where the passage from the profane to the sacred world becomes possible.[1]

And again:

The threshold, the door *show* the solution of continuity in space immediately and concretely; hence their great religious importance, for they are symbols and at the same time vehicles of *passage* from the one space to the other.[2]

On Christmas Eve, 1979, the people of Bobole had re-enacted and recreated universal themes from the panhuman myth of Genesis. The myth speaks of the paradox of order in open systems and resolves the paradox by interposing boundaries where none existed before. The boundaries may be transient or durable; they facilitate the flow of information between parts of the system—they are communicative devices. The morality play was a meta- phor for the themes of the myth of Genesis. I want to extend the reach of the metaphor; the symbolism of Eden allowed me to attach meaning to the events that, at the beginning of this book, were called Sugua Mai. That it was Fuago who was both cherubim and the first to tell me that "the pigs have eaten the garden" was, I do not doubt, coincidence. But I continue to cherish the symmetry of that coincidence.

Late in June, and early in July, 1979, people released pigs into three moderately large communal gardens. They said the pigs had got into the gardens by themselves, that the gardens were ruined, and that everyone would be hungry. There could be no doubt that their mood of despondency was genuine. In mid-July and mid-August the pigs that had been allowed into gardens were killed and eaten at two feasts. Until early December people complained of having no food, expressed concern that pigs might damage other gardens, and became increasingly emphatic that they were sick of eating sago flour. At no time were the people short of food.

The acts described above were interconnected. To give form to those connections, I borrow a verbal expression from the people, *sugua mai,* "pigs ate." Whether they were complaining about the damage pigs had done to gardens or asserting everyone would go hungry, a dejected look and the utterance *sugua mai* said it all. From July people said these words to each other and to us; sometimes they rubbed their bellies for emphasis. I use Sugua Mai to represent the set of acts that linked pigs, complaints, feasts, and the availability of sweet potato and sago starch. In this chapter I interpret Sugua Mai as a message, from the people to themselves, that facilitated scheduling of major subsistence tasks. More precisely, it was the response to Sugua Mai that prompted concordance of action among the family groups who lived at Bobole. In what follows this assertion is first elaborated and then justified through analysis of the acts and of responses to them. I show the part Sugua Mai played in Etolo ecology, its contribution to a sense of community, its place and its potential in history, and how it could have come into being. This last is necessary not because origins must always be explained before a phenomenon is accepted as real but because Sugua Mai, as I witnessed it in 1979, was historically recent. The interpretations that follow are located within a theoretical frame that concerns processes of communication and change in open systems.[3]

Sugua Mai: A Message in Code

Through June, 1979, the average yield of sweet potato from gardens at Bobole was higher than in most other months. But the pattern of planting through earlier months meant that average yield must eventually fall. This is what happened from September onward. Again, by June, 1979, few people at Bobole held very much sago starch in storage; certainly, the quantities stored in mud were not sufficient to meet needs through the months when sweet potato was scarce. Thus, by July, the people faced a potential shortage of carbohydrate foods. This was a direct consequence of the way they had scheduled food-producing tasks through the preceding months. To offset this shortage they needed to process sago palms by at least September and prepare and plant new gardens by at least July. Even so, by planting sweet potato in July, they would not reverse the decline in availability of these tubers until December. To achieve these responses people needed to read the condition of their gardens before the yield had dropped noticeably. They were, of course, skilled and experienced gardeners so this should not have been complicated. Nevertheless, the gardens spoke in ambiguous ways: in June and July the yield was high, and when it did fall, the change was slow and unidirectional. The ordinary cues available to people were neither clear-cut nor necessarily interpreted in precisely the same way by everyone.

My reading of Sugua Mai is that it recoded the essentially analogical processes under way at sweet potato gardens into digital form; it acted to transform the potential ambiguity of a pending and progressive reduction in yield to an unambiguous message of presence/absence. It did this for all the people in the community. Sugua Mai was a message, created by the people, and sent to themselves, that elicited two categories of response. If people had not already initiated new gardens, they responded by doing so; if they had commenced a new round of gardening, they accelerated the rate of work. And, also, they responded by committing more time to processing sago palms so as to have flour on hand through the period when old gardens were failing and before new ones flourished. By these means Sugua Mai contained fickle behavior; it did so by resynchronizing behavior directed at producing food and, in this way, maintained a theme of sameness in the food-producing system—it imposed stability upon the form of that system. Under this reading, there is no requirement that Sugua Mai happened every year or even at frequent and regular intervals. Nor is there any assertion that Sugua Mai was necessary to synchronize the actions of people; synchrony was contingent upon the ways people chose to order tasks and combine foods and upon their adherence to a biological calendar.

The single crucial act that constituted Sugua Mai as the digitally encoded message "there is no sweet potato" was to place pigs deliberately into a garden. Alone, however, this was not enough; there were sweet potato tubers at other gardens; there were people who did not participate in this particular garden; and there were other occasions when pigs entered gardens of their own volition and were forcibly removed. To gain strength, the message had to be repeated. If the information out of which it was made was to organize people to respond as and when needed, then the message had to be heard and seen within the public domain—it had to spread through the community. Sugua Mai achieved these qualities and effects through redundancy. The host of different acts reinforced each other; they repeated the originating information or contained ancillary messages that by building upon earlier ones served to reconstitute the primary message over and over again. Through redundancy the message was made public. At the feasts it was made visible.

I turn now to an analysis of the acts that comprised Sugua Mai and of the responses that followed.

It was not rare that pigs entered flourishing gardens at Bobole. They usually did so of their own accord by finding or making a gap in a fence or a place where they could easily scramble across. On these occasions the response from people was rapid and often dramatic. The pigs were removed and might be physically punished. The fence was repaired as needed, with other people volunteering help to the injured party. The owner of the garden protested vigorously and publicly, seeking compensation as money, pork, or future produce from the person whose pig was at fault. But the drama of these events was always short-lived; the necessary work was done; compensation claims were settled; and life returned to a more gentle pace.

There were four exceptions to the above scenario. These were times when people allowed pigs into gardens and said the pigs were at fault. In one case Gago encouraged a pig of his own to enter a garden, immediately declared it a renegade, had it killed with bow and arrows, and added the carcass to an impromptu feast. That feast had been initiated the day before when the dogs of visiting Huli men bailed up another renegade boar. The other three cases were connected with Sugua Mai. In each, the sweet potato garden was communal, with participants from two or three longhouses. With the first garden the perimeter fence remained intact and people reacted to the presence of pigs by complaining but adding others. With the other two gardens a portion of fence was removed, and I do not know whether pigs were herded through the gaps or made their own way into the areas. The second garden had pigs within one week of the first; the third, within at least four weeks of the first. Again, in each case, the garden was still producing good tubers and, without pigs, could have continued doing so for a month or more; tiny plots of taro and scattered banana trees were carefully protected from the pigs.

There can be no doubt that when people deliberately allowed pigs into these three gardens, the significance of their actions was deeper than the untruth they then promulgated. They said the pigs had got into the gardens by themselves. This was false. But their immediate response—the words they said to each other, their despondent mood, and their capacity to spread both the words and the mood rapidly through the community—located the significance of their actions as a concern with availability of food. "The pigs have ruined the garden." "There is no food." "We shall all be hungry." In the frame of what had happened these utterances conveyed meaning about the availability of sweet potato coded in the digital form: "there is no sweet potato." The statements were not explicitly about the availability of sago flour, but there was one act, at the moment when pigs were first placed in a garden, that may have been telling in this regard. Gago was responsible for this initiating act. When he had done it, he and his family left the village immediately; they went to trade for sago, and everyone knew that this was so.

Theater and Social Existence

Pigs that had been allowed into gardens were clubbed to death and eaten at two feasts, one in mid-July, the other in mid-August. All pigs from the first garden were killed, but I cannot be sure this was so with the other gardens. At the first and second gardens other pigs were allowed free rein after the feasts, but at the third the garden was closed to pigs, and people continued harvesting rather inferior tubers. In a variety of ways the feasts connected with Sugua Mai reinforced, enlarged, and dramatized the meanings already current within the community and the digital form in which those meanings were coded.

Each feast was a two-day event, and on each day, food was cooked in large ovens outside the longhouse of the hosts. Not one sweet potato was placed into any of the ovens. Indeed, there were few tubers of any sort cooked at the feasts; those few were yams, one an exceptionally large specimen that a girl of about twelve or thirteen years put onto the mound of food shortly before one of the ovens was sealed. The absence of sweet potato at the feasts contrasted starkly with the reality that sweet potato was the primary carbohydrate food eaten through both July and August. Indeed, at the second feast, when guests were invited to shelter in the longhouse during a rainstorm, people ate and casually shared sweet potato while they waited for the oven to be opened. In addition to pork, people who attended the feasts ate ferns soaked in grease and quantities of sago flour they had mixed with vegetables and wrapped in special packages. They ate sago flour at a time when this commodity was relatively scarce. Some people collected flour that had been stored in mud months before; others traveled to the west and purchased sago; and a few families felled and processed a palm in the weeks before the feasts.

The choice of one food rather than another was not because propriety required that sweet potato was not eaten with pork while sago was permissible. Nor do the reasons people offered for holding feasts show why particular foods were chosen. The first Sugua Mai feast farewelled a Huli pastor and his family; here some game mammals were included with the pigs, and sago flour, but not sweet potato, was eaten. The second Sugua Mai feast was held because pigs had damaged gardens and, people said, might damage others and now the only meat was pork. A feast in March, 1980, welcomed a visiting church group; game mammals and pig were cooked together, but I do not know what carbohydrates were chosen. In April, 1980, there were two feasts. The first was the impromptu event that followed the killing of two renegade pigs. Packages of sago flour and vegetables, together with many sweet potato tubers, were cooked with pig, and everyone ate both kinds of carbohydrate. The second April feast was to farewell us; the menu included

100 game mammals and a spectacular display of tubers, red pandanus, and greens. There was no sago. The basis of acceptance or rejection of different carbohydrate staples at the two feasts connected with Sugua Mai was to contrast the foods through artifice: the feasts provided a means to oppose sago flour and sweet potato as alternative staples. Where, in fact, the contribution these foods made to diet varied through time in quantitative ways, the statements about them that were encoded at the feasts were about a qualitative difference: "sweet potato is absent; sago flour is present."

As a participant and observer at the Sugua Mai feasts, I enjoyed the active and noisy sense of community, the smells from burning wood, singed pigs, and greasy fern fronds, and the tastes and textures of new foods. I was impressed, too, by the theater of the occasions. At both feasts, through the sometimes frenetic bustle, there seemed to be a common script, one that drew out and highlighted numerous contrasts from the social life of the people. The roles of male and female were sharply defined: men killed the animals and butchered the carcasses as women gathered fern fronds and washed entrails; men laid the meat within the ovens, retrieved it when it was cooked, divided it further, and distributed it while women prepared packages of sago flour and vegetables, arranged these in the ovens, and shared this food with others when it was ready. Only the oldest men sometimes helped in the work of women. There were public prestations of raw meat to unmarried and married youths and men, and of cooked meat to married men only. Males hosts gave small portions of the cooked carcasses to each guest in turn—a distribution of fat and a separate distribution of meat—placing the morsels directly into their mouths. Each person or family group received a large share from the hosts, and in turn, each gave to all others present by contributing first fat and then meat to the bowls from which individual portions were served. As they received their shares, guests were told that some of the food was to be eaten now in the company of all others and that the rest was for later, in the privacy of family or longhouse groups. As though to reinforce this, on the first day of each feast privacy took precedence over community with many guests departing early carrying their food away while, on the next day, everyone stayed, sitting and eating as family groups who were bonded by proximity and the gifts of food they were constantly exchanging.

As the people participated in this theater of oppositions—of male vs. female, old vs. young, married vs. unmarried, cooked vs. raw, meat vs. fat, hosts vs. guests, giving vs. receiving, community vs. family—I wondered briefly whether Claude Lévi-Strauss was the author of the script! There is a class of anthropologists (they often pay homage to Lévi-Strauss) that seeks out oppositions and finds in them the deep underpinnings of social existence. The contrasts they discover are shown to combine and recombine in multiple ways and are interpreted as fundamental codes from, or upon, which social form is constructed. Perhaps, I thought, the truth of Etolo social form, even humanity, was contained in the form of those feasts; perhaps it was in the script. I have concluded this cannot be so, that far from being a statement about what lay at the core of being, the form of the feasts caricatured the core and did so with a particular end (unconsciously) in mind.

As participants in life individual persons grow, mature, age, and eventually die. They assume different roles and, at different times, change status by becoming baptized, initiated, married, parents, separated, widowed, and so forth. In the world where they actually live and work and interact with others who are near them, these processes are gradual: puberty takes time and so does dying; the relationships that bind people to others are progressively transformed; the shape of the society that contains them remains the same as different individuals within it alter their relative positions. In egalitarian societies, where the subsistence tasks performed by males and females may be only quantitatively different, where work parties often cross-cut family ties as individuals repay help they received on earlier occasions, and where children are taught gently how to be adults, a perception of continuity, of the ebb and flow of process, must be the abiding reality of all. But this can be an ambiguous reality because, in extreme form, it is without boundaries, and no one can live there.[4] It is a reality that declares to all that the quantitative differences that separate them, by roles or by status, are entirely arbitrary. If this impasse is to be resolved, it is necessary that at suitable times and places the actuality of continuous process be recoded and expressed as qualitative difference. It is only through theater that this may be accomplished. Theater condones license. In the play the arbitrary divisions and differences in life may be briefly caricatured as necessary truths. Boundaries may be affirmed, lending credence to the roles and statuses that must be assumed when the performance is done. To take the form in which the play is written as the mainstay of being is to mistake a transient product for the process from which it arises—a rigid taxonomy for the frailty of the classificatory process. Binary oppositions are not the stuff of human sociality; they are coded caricatures that validate the arbitrariness of existence.[5]

The statements about social existence encoded in the Sugua Mai feasts gave visible expression to relational boundaries that ordered people's lives. The feasts abstracted from the relative and necessary informality, arbitrariness, and flux of day-to-day living, and declared, to all who watched and listened: this is what we are, though we could have been otherwise. At the feasts the people, as both sources and receivers of information, participated in an intense act of communication with themselves. Briefly, through theater, the boundaries that ordered their existence were made to seem concrete by depiction in digital form. The feasts effectively sanctified the routines of life;

they did so by affirming that the necessary quantitative differences separating individual persons were founded in quite proper qualitative distinctions. But the affirmation was contrived: its power was in the analytical precision of the code in which the acts of communication were written.

I attended two other feasts at Bobole. At each, there were theatrical moments, and some of the contrasts drawn at the earlier Sugua Mai feasts were again evident. But these were not stated as forcefully as I had seen them before; they were undercurrents that did not dominate the mood. Nor were they piled one upon another as successive statements connecting different features of a single theme. The Sugua Mai feasts were different. They encoded information from many facets of social existence and dramatized them to a point where the code itself was all but tangibly present. They declared that it was not merely messages about social existence that held significance: the code itself and, thus, *all* messages in that code had meaning. When people spoke to themselves about themselves through the theater of the feasts, they learned with equal force, as an integral component of the same play: sweet potato is absent: sago flour is present. The form in which messages about the social were conveyed was itself the vehicle that ameliorated ambiguity within the primary message of those feasts.

Responses and Problems

The connotations of Sugua Mai, from its inception when Gago placed pigs into a garden to the conclusion of the second feast, were about the availability of sweet potato and sago flour. The message seemed to say that the former was absent and the latter was present, but the context within which the message arose was quite different. At the time Sugua Mai was initiated, sweet potato was abundant and sago flour was relatively scarce. Within two months sweet potato would be less abundant, and thereafter the yield would decline progressively. The manner in which people responded to Sugua Mai was twofold: first, they affirmed the presence of sago flour by displaying it at feasts and, more importantly, starting to process new palms to obtain starch for the period when sweet potato would be scarce; second, they acknowledged an absence of sweet potato by excluding it from the feasts and by implementing procedures that would eventually create new tubers—they made gardens and planted fresh runners.

These assertions about responses to Sugua Mai are strong and are not literally correct. Many families prepared new gardens and a few processed palms before pigs were placed into older gardens. But after this happened, they increased their effort; families that had not yet made new gardens now did so and many more days were allocated to sago work. In the six-week period before Sugua Mai was initiated, approximately 1 hectare was planted with sweet potato. In the next six weeks, up to the time of the second feast, 3 hectares were planted, and, in the six weeks following this feast, more than 4 hectares were planted. Thereafter, work at gardens decreased markedly.[6] Again, in the two four-week periods before the first feast and between the two feasts only 114 and 44 workdays, respectively, were spent processing sago palms. After this the pace accelerated with 289, 242, and 442 workdays, respectively, in the next three four-week periods. By the last of these periods sweet potato was becoming scarce. (Fig. 25 displays these statistics and relates them to the timing of crucial components of Sugua Mai.) The consequence of these quantitative responses was to narrow the temporal spread of both gardening and sago work. In this, Sugua Mai promoted concordance of action among different family groups; groups that otherwise may have been tardy in initiating work programs were stimulated to conform. Sugua Mai served to resynchronize behavior and contain potential idiosyncrasy.

After the second Sugua Mai feast people did not cease to complain. They were now busy attending to their increasing need for sago flour and their future need for sweet potato. But for a time they still maintained the fiction that there was no food. As the months went by the words changed and so did the mood. They asked what they would now eat, complained that they were hungry, and, when sweet potato was truly scarce, bemoaned their diet and—this was heartfelt—said they were sick of eating sago. Until, and especially at, the feasts, Sugua Mai as a message that called for response was frequently and powerfully reinforced. To have concluded the second feast and then acknowledged that there was, in fact, plenty of sweet potato would have exposed Sugua Mai as fraud. This outcome was hardly politic. By maintaining the fiction, the people made that fiction eventually approach truth as the yield of sweet potato fell. By changing the words and the mood, the people progressively decoded the precise form in which the message had been first relayed and received until, finally, what was said—"we are sick of sago"—was the condition that obtained. The message that was Sugua Mai commenced abruptly, and its immediate impact was great, then it faded slowly away to merge with the reality of people's lives. In this way Sugua Mai was never exposed as an untruth.[7]

If Sugua Mai was all that I have argued, then it is fair to ask why there were two feasts. Would not one feast have done? An easy reply would be to assert that two feasts increased the impact by contributing redundancy to the message. They may have done so, but I think this answer would be insufficient. It is possible that there were two feasts because, quite fortuitously, the Huli pastor Damule and his family were to leave. They had lived among the people for four years, teaching Christianity and contributing when they could to matters of health. For several weeks their departure had been rumored, but the final announcement was sudden: Damule's dismissal as pastor

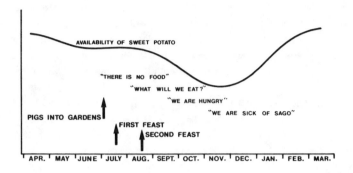

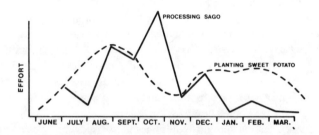

Fig. 25. Sugua Mai: events and consequences. Data shown on figures 5, 7, and 11 are summarized here.

was not a fait accompli until at least July 2, 1979—three days after the first pigs had been allowed into a garden. The need to mark his departure publicly may have advanced the time at which the first Sugua Mai feast was held. There is one clue that may support this opinion. The overt messages encoded in the Sugua Mai feasts spoke of the social and domestic spheres of people's lives. They had nothing to say of the wild domain. The pigs were clubbed to death as domestic animals should be. Despite their declared invasion of gardens they were not called renegades and shot like wild animals with bows and arrows. Yet at Damule's feast, specifically to honor him and his family, there were carcasses of game mammals that men and youths had hunted during a few days before the feast. In the frame of all I have written their inclusion seemed out of character.

At the two Sugua Mai feasts five and twelve pigs, respectively, were butchered, displayed, and arranged in large ovens, together with many packages containing sago flour and vegetables. The appearance—the visual impact—was that these were times of conspicuous consumption. They were not, of course, because the people were never voracious. Lots of the food was carried away and eaten later, at leisure, over several days. But the appearance was there and was in conflict with the attitude that people should not be seen to be greedy. Greed and witches were strongly connected. The declaration that some pigs threatened the livelihood of people lent credence to the need that they be killed. The act of placing pigs into gardens rationalized feasts at which the people seemed to eat more than was usual. Alone, however, this is not a sufficient explanation of Sugua Mai. It does not accommodate the messages about availability of food; it does not tell us why sago was present and sweet potato was absent from the feasts, why messages about these foods continued long after the feasts were over, or why people responded by working as they did. The pigs had to be killed and, therefore, had to be eaten, but this rationalization was secondary to the purpose of Sugua Mai.

Important and complex questions have lain dormant through the preceding discussion. The analysis of Sugua Mai commenced with the moment when Gago placed pigs into a garden. Yet this is not sufficient. Gago's action would not have arisen de novo. What motivated that action, why was it Gago rather than someone else, and why did people promulgate and accept an explanation that was not true? Stated crudely the questions are: what, if anything, did Gago have to gain? and—if personal gain was in the offing— why were other people compliant?

These questions are difficult to come to grips with. I was not aware that Gago was about to act as he did and, for many months, did not appreciate the far-reaching consequences of his act. To use the language of empiricists, there are no data that bear directly on the questions: I have no record or memory of anyone saying or doing anything that, in retrospect, could be linked to Gago's dramatic action. I can ask only how Etolo politics and ethos may aid understanding; I can wonder only how Gago's personality or standing within the community helps me rationalize his behavior after the fact.

Through the highlands of Papua New Guinea pigs and politics are often inextricably connected.[8] Men manipulate other men, jockey for power, achieve status, and assert they control the exchange of women through first increasing the size of pig herds and subsequently, ostentatiously, killing animals and distributing pork. Societies vie with one another and make and break alliances through hosting spectacular feasts and engaging in years-long rounds of ceremonial exchange of pork. But obligations must be *seen* to be fulfilled or established. Often it is the number of pigs killed or the amount of pork distributed that is persuasive; how else can intentions be judged? To facilitate this persistent political maneuvering, people commit many hours to growing tubers that are fed directly to pigs.

Away from the highlands, on the Great Papuan Plateau, there was no strong link between pigs and the politics of Etolo. Corporate rights to hunting and gardening land, and inherited rights to sago palms, allowed groups or individuals to gain prestige and establish obligations through generosity.

They could give what they did not need or exchange access to one class of resources for another. They could enhance their own rights through manipulating residential or marital alignments.[9] Ownership of pigs did not offer Etolo the same opportunities. Pigs were the property of family groups, not corporate groups, and their relatively short life span meant their value as potentially heritable resources was not long lasting. Certainly, their inclusion as part of the payment for a bride could result in long-term benefits to those who provided the pigs and thereby gained access to other resources connected with the woman. But these potential outcomes were diffused because both "bride-receivers" and "bride-givers" had preexisting or newly established obligations that they were now beholden to meet. With one possible exception, ownership of pigs and the transactions that included pork did not facilitate acquisition of wealth, status, or power. The exception was the recent institution of markets at which cooked pork was sold for cash. Here, there was the possibility that some individuals might enhance their standing at the expense of others. But, in 1979, so much ambivalence attached to this new practice that the possibility was no more than latent. Pig politics does not inform us why Gago acted as he did.

Etolo ethos was characterized by reserve; they were modest people who refrained from expressions of greed or self-aggrandizement. These traits were seen in many contexts. People seldom declared an intention to hunt; they said, instead, that they were "walking about" with no particular intention in mind. Successful hunters often attributed their catch to the dog that accompanied them, and people who owned few pigs might tell me they had none. Euphemisms were commonplace. People did not copulate, they "went to the forest." Neither women nor pigs gave birth, the former "went to the grass house," and the latter simply "put." No one peered into the string bag of another person or asked what was being carried, and a request—for salt, perhaps—could be deflected by replying "I do not have a large amount." Though everyone gossiped and sought information, they accepted cryptic replies as meaning the topic was closed. Often I was asked who it was that had delivered a game mammal to the house; the smell, tuft of fur, or skull was evidence of someone's success. The interrogation could be stalled by saying "I do not know the names of all the children," "it was dark when the person came," or "I was busy writing in my notebook." Ambiguity was acceptable; lying was not. Indeed, the word for *lie* translated literally as "What! (in the sense of "repeat what you said; I did not hear properly")— True" (with the connotation of "say it again; I cannot believe my ears").

Within a climate of reserve, action that was potentially self-interested might have to appear self-effacing or, at least, ambiguous. Gago's action had the outcome that a feast was held at which he was the primary host. It was Gago who called the major distributions of meat. Perhaps, from the outset, it was Gago's intention to sponsor that feast. If so, we may speculate that it was inappropriate to do so openly and that, by placing pigs into a garden and leaving the village, Gago provided an opportunity for others to accede by adding pigs or frustrate his intention by removing his pigs. At a later date, in different circumstances, Gago contributed a pig to a feast in a manner that allowed everyone to assert the pig was at fault—that Gago had no choice in the matter. If the cosmological status of pigs was unresolved or ambiguous— in earlier times it was possible that they were manifestations of the heinous spirit people *segesebe*—it might be easy to assert their culpability as despoil- ers of gardens even where people had abetted the behavior.[10] This might allow more ready acceptance of the fiction—after all, no person would wan- tonly destroy crops!—and encourage a community-wide perception that the initiating human actor was not grandstanding. If others imitated that action, the thought that one person sought personal gain might be allayed. (This argument may be relevant also to the fact that there were two feasts.) Gago's possible intention could have been frustrated without public insult to him; he provided that opportunity when he left the village. By blaming pigs for what had happened and by introducing more pigs to more gardens, people could accede to his intention as they shifted the locus of responsibility or credit away from him.

But why was it Gago and not someone else, and why were other people compliant? The easy response is to link the questions and assert that the mood of the community—a tension I had not detected—was such that some- one would have acted and, by chance, Gago was first. The awkward response is to admit that the questions are probably unanswerable. Perhaps it is rele- vant that in 1979 only Gago's family did not process a sago palm of their own; when they needed flour, they obtained it by purchase or trade. Further, his family grew much sweet potato and had less need than anyone else to be anxious about falling yields. Gago rarely hunted. He shared a line of deadfall traps with the family of the senior male, Ololo, of the longhouse where they all resided. His access to gardening land had been acquired through Ololo's generosity and through marriage with Heaga; he himself held no inherited rights near Bobole. We may wonder whether his perception of his standing was tinged with ambivalence and whether he sought to secure his position. But since he had lived at Bobole for two decades, the thought seems tenuous. We may wonder whether he was impetuous and more inclined than others to take up opportunities for personal gain. To answer this would require that I dissected his personality by spelling out peculiarities of behavior that were not common to others. There were, of course, peculiarities, though the same could be said of nearly everyone at Bobole. To rationalize Gago's action by highlighting features of *his* personality as I perceived it would be the worst form of sophistry. It seems to me that Gago's action might be understood within a frame of Etolo ethos, but the question "why Gago?" must remain open.[11]

One more comment is needed. The analysis of the acts and consequences of Sugua Mai focused upon the perceptions and responses of the community at large. In the following section I discuss the part Sugua Mai played in Etolo ecology, and, again, the focus remains with the community. The preceding speculations about Gago's behavior acknowledge that community-wide responses and collective goals always take root from the actions—however motivated—of individual persons. I do not think Gago foresaw the consequences of his action or, in some way, planned the events that followed. At most he wanted to sponsor a feast. The community acquiesced because the mood was right. Out of the continual interplay of personalities and politics that were necessarily embedded in Etolo ethos, community action emerged and unspoken, even unrecognized, goals were attained.

Ecological Form and the Sense of Community

Within small subsistence communities concordance of action can bestow many benefits. Some are ecological, others are social, but the two categories are not separable. At Bobole synchrony facilitated cooperation. People from different family groups or longhouses could more readily work together at a variety of tasks. This increased opportunities to make communal gardens, which saved work building fences and allowed individuals to spread risk by taking up small plots at several different gardens. It meant that families could travel together to sago camps, share one shelter, and give or receive assistance if the work fell behind or an unforeseen event threatened success. It meant that women could more easily combine their efforts in the chore of weeding and that men and youths could organize larger hunting parties. Having someone to help at an arduous task might encourage persistence, and camping in the forest with others could, through example, enhance hunting skills and increase individual effort.

Benefits of pooling labor in ventures such as weeding and hunting are not only ecological. Scheduling arrangements at Bobole increased the chance that several people or families were in similar places, engaged in similar tasks at similar times. Their locations in space and time made it easier to contact kinsfolk, care for other people's children, fulfill obligations, or establish them. It made it easier to gossip, plan future cooperative ventures (a hunting excursion or trading party), and bring the plans to fruition. Opportunities of these kinds were regularly taken up. Weeding was often a social occasion or a time when sisters who did not reside together shared each other's company for a day. Plans to hunt together were made when men felled trees; work parties formed to build fences and celebrated afterwards at small feasts.

When people worked together, they frequently ate together and their bonds were greater because of this. When moderately large parties of men, women, and children—kin from several longhouses—camped in the forest early in the pandanus season, their holiday outings, fishing, hunting, and eating fruit pandanus together were possible only because they had worked hard at similar tasks and could now relax. Indeed, everyone at Bobole was released from time-demanding tasks—only hunting excepted, though this was not felt to be a task—through the months January to March when the weather was likely to be pleasant, new gardens were flourishing, and fruit pandanus was abundant. Through these months trading, visiting, and communal eating peaked.

There is no compelling reason that all that flows from synchrony be beneficial. The ecological advantages I have identified were all short term. Through time, their cumulative effects might be different. Already, at Bobole, the concentration of people and their decade-long gardening activities had modified the landscape. The forest was in retreat. A permanent island of grass and inferior second-growth forest was expanding outward from the village. Some species of animals were less easy to obtain than they once had been, and new weeds had appeared that increased work loads. Fallow periods were sometimes shorter than desirable, and there was more chance that crops might be ruined because the soil slipped. Impacts of all these kinds would eventually intrude upon ways in which people behaved. Again, where people are bonded because they do similar things, in similar places and at similar times, there is, perhaps, as much opportunity that interactions are unfriendly as that they are friendly. Proximity, after all, can be irritating. Suspicions, anger, and jealousies were by no means negated at Bobole simply because people synchronized activities. When these emotions surfaced, their potential divisive effects did not always recede quickly.[12]

Sugua Mai resynchronized the activities of the people who lived at Bobole. The shape of Etolo ecology—the form of the system—was legislated ultimately through social artifice. That the system worked, that energy and protein flowed to people at adequate rates, was, however, neither a necessary nor an inevitable end point of Sugua Mai. Either open systems are suited to circumstances or they face extinction. Within existing constraints they have room to maneuver, to respond to impacts that may be either beneficial or detrimental. Sugua Mai had certain consequences for the form of Etolo ecology. But it did not arise to serve these effects. To locate forces that motivated the emergence of Sugua Mai, we must turn to the social domain. Synchronization bonded people, not merely as a particular structured array of individuals or through its effects upon scheduling, but at the levels of temperament, psyche, and, above all, community.

Among Etolo, working and eating together were deeply valued. Participation was an ideal. To fail in this could provoke censure or ostracism. The imperatives of existence—time, place, and rain—were shared by all. Companionship alleviated the risk that witches might threaten. An ethos of community was central to people's lives, to their understanding and appreciation of proper conduct. No one neglected to greet another at every encounter. Everyone *should* have attended church—though not everyone did. Yet, at Bobole, with 109 residents, the realization of this ethos was jeopardized by the mere fact that people were dispersed among four separate longhouses. In this context coresidence could not, of itself, bring about the ideal to which people aspired. There were too many others who, by their presence nearby, were tempting distractors. A new level of integration was needed, one that dissolved the separateness of longhouse groupings, that brought people together as a single congregation and focused their lives, collectively, upon a seemingly shared outcome. This was the achievement of Sugua Mai. It pushed the ideal of community to a new level that, for the people, was neither more nor less than the ideal they had always valued: that harmonious relations should prevail among people who resided together. That Sugua Mai had profound impacts upon the form of Etolo ecology was immaterial to the people whose lives it shaped. What was important was that people's relations to one another and to the environment were reaffirmed.

Scheduling arrangements at Bobole were not necessitated by environment. Ecologically the system worked though it was the sort of system that is prone to drift. It was not bound by the impact of climate on the growing regimes of plants or availability of game. It was contingent upon choices made by individuals, choices that were not in any way imperatives. This meant that idiosyncratic behavior of particular family groups had the potential to erode the collective synchrony. A change could even have been ecologically beneficial to the instigators. If there were costs, they would be social, arising from the threat they posed to the ideal of community. These might not accrue immediately to the idiosyncratic group though their impact might be felt by all other families. Sailo's attempt to make a garden that was much larger than the norm (chap. 3) offers a useful case study.

Had Sailo's actions achieved what he wanted by encouraging others to join the project, then his prestige within the community would surely have been enhanced. In this event we may speculate that other men would have subsequently imitated his actions resulting in a shift to larger gardens with more participants. (I know of no environmental constraints to prevent this; gardens at Bobole could have been larger than they were.) In turn, larger gardens would require the formation of larger than usual working parties and the availability of sufficient sweet potato runners and seed stock of other crops to plant the larger than usual areas. These new demands would then affect the performance of other tasks, causing scheduling regimes to drift to a different form. But Sailo's intentions were not realized because other people did not associate with the project until it was too late. This made food-producing arrangements awkward for his family, and eventually he conformed without disruption to patterns of cooperation among others. (Sailo commenced his garden early in July, 1979, and it was several weeks before his intention to enclose a huge area was apparent. Thus, his work may have been in response to Sugua Mai but, in that year, was not causally associated with its occurrence.)

Sailo's overt attempt to gain prestige could have altered scheduling arrangements. This was prevented by ignoring the project. Less substantial or calculated alterations to the ways in which, or the times when, people made gardens or processed sago palms could not be easily prevented by ignoring them and, if they accumulated, would similarly alter the architecture of subsistence. Indeed, Sailo's garden may still have had this effect. Though people made it clear they would not join his project, they eventually helped complete the fence enclosing the 5 hectare plot. By May, 1980, when we left Bobole, four of those hectares remained unfelled—nearly as much land as residents from House IV, where Sailo lived, had planted in twelve months—but some people had begun to plant small plots. If the rate of planting within this now conveniently fenced area increased, then the cycle of sweet potato production for those who participated would not have been as I saw it in 1979. If the alteration disrupted social bonds within the community, its effects would need to be contained. Sugua Mai provided a means to contain the actions of people who, by accepting options when and where they arose, might otherwise drift apart; it acted to maintain a status quo by containing actual or potential fickle behavior of individual actors.

The people who lived at Bobole were connected to each other and to an environment within which they produced food through a complex of exchanges. These had both social and ecological dimensions. They were repeated sufficiently often that an intruder such as I had little difficulty depicting their form. Yet, under analysis, the immediate connections, the plausible links, were diffuse. They did not have to be as they were. The form of the system was intrinsically vulnerable because the people who comprised it, and their actions that made it, were not so constrained that perpetuation of form was guaranteed.

There are other reported cases where the ultimate forces shaping relations between people and their environments have major social dimensions, although the usual interpretations of these may need to be partially upended. Sometimes the associated rituals have been regarded as celebrations of past ecological successes or symbolic acts intended to rejuvenate sources of food: the rituals give thanks to or seek blessings from mysterious forces that ultimately govern the destiny of people. Here, it is commonly implied that the rituals merely rationalize the inevitable. But, irrespective of what people say or believe they do, it is what they actually do that shapes their ecological destiny. We need to ask, therefore, whether and how the information contained in the rituals may organize people toward the end of satisfying subsistence needs. In other cases the associated rituals have been interpreted as homeostatic mechanisms that adjust the numbers of people and their relations with neighboring people to the availability of resources where the latter is considered an objective property of the environment. What the people say or believe they do is located within a religious sphere, but, it is suggested, their acts contribute to ecological well-being. However, availability of resources is rarely environmentally given but is contingent upon belief. What people eat and how they choose to produce it are ultimately dependent upon their perceptions of the environment. We need to ask, therefore, whether and how the information contained in the rituals acts to substantiate preexistent perceptions and whether, for these reasons, the system stays the same. Under these modified interpretations the rituals concerned may be seen as acting, like Sugua Mai, as powerful conservative forces in the food-producing system. But perceptions are extraordinarily fickle; they combine in new ways; and, hence, the intent to stay the same is always embedded in a frame of change. Change is the concluding theme of this chapter. It is necessary to show that my interpretation of Sugua Mai does not reduce Etolo ecology to a condition of empty stasis. But a digression is needed: connections between ritual and ecology among Umeda and Maring people of Papua New Guinea inform my understanding of the context from which, and the processes through which, Sugua Mai emerged.

Ida and *Kaiko:* Ritual and Ecology in Papua New Guinea

Umeda people lived at altitudes around 250 meters in the West Sepik Province of Papua New Guinea. Sago flour was their primary source of carbohydrate though this was supplemented by some taro and yams from small gardens. The people cultivated breadfruit trees and coconut palms, collected bamboo shoots, fruit of various kinds, fungi, grubs, fish, and the eggs of jungle fowl, and they hunted wild pigs and, less often, cassowaries. Alfred Gell described the *Ida* fertility ritual of Umeda.[13] This was initiated when wooden flutes were played in October or November, before the wet season began, and culminated eight to ten months later as spectacular, colorful theater. Through two nights and days women and men danced—the latter decorated as cassowaries, fish, sago palms, firewood, termites, ogres, ogresses, and bowmen—to recreate their world by dramatizing its transformation from a wild state to one that was accessible to and comprehensible by people. The play was over when the bowmen, painted red to symbolize that they were new men, shot arrows from the cleared dance ground at the center of the village, across the houses and into the forest. As new men they rejuvenated the forest, and all people were, once again, in control of their own destinies.

Ida was not an annual event. It was held when life was relaxed and everyone agreed the time had come. In less settled years, when sickness was rife or important people had died, the ritual was forgone, and, through these adverse periods, many people abandoned the village and dispersed to small gardens and sago groves through the forest where, for subsistence purposes, they acted as independent family units. The announcement that *Ida* was pending refocused their activities. During the following months most subsistence work was to satisfy their own needs, but these now included the accumulation of surpluses of sago flour, garden produce, and dried meat to meet requirements of the forthcoming performance. Gell wrote:

It is no empty truism to say that the prospect of the eventual performance of the ritual gave meaning and direction to the productive activity of the people, even if it is also true that for the most part the work went towards basic necessities of subsistence, and no very spectacular surpluses were accumulated. *Ida* placed day-to-day subsistence activity within the context of a larger purpose, and gave the productive units a role to play in a project which embraced the entire society.[14]

At *Ida* everyone came together, united as social beings and reunited in the themes and timing of subsistence tasks. When the flutes were played, groups of people who, for a time, perhaps several years, had acted separately now acted with a common purpose. Each group acting alone fulfilled subsistence needs; all groups together recreated both the ecosystemic relations that had long prevailed, and of which they were a part, and their collective perception of those relations. Gell continued by writing: *"Ida* and the productive activity which preceded it were very much part of a unity. . . ."* We could insert also: and the productive activity that *followed* it. The acts of communication connecting people with their environment were recursive: through *Ida* people re-created the system that contained them, and thus it remained the same.

In the Madang Province, until the time of European colonization, connections among Tsembaga people, their neighbors, and environment were ordered through performance of a *kaiko*. This was a year-long sequence of rituals, initiated by uprooting cordyline shrubs that marked territorial borders, punctuated by pig feasts where alliances were established and by a period of warfare at which a few people were killed, and terminated by replanting the shrubs. Roy Rappaport lived among Tsembaga during the early 1960s.[15] The people were horticulturalists—sweet potato was the primary carbohydrate—and pig husbanders living at altitudes between about 1,000 and 2,000 meters. Rappaport argued that after a run of ten to twenty favorable years pig herds might increase to a size where the animals were both difficult to maintain—much of their food was grown by people—and environmentally destructive. The *kaiko* was implemented at these times. Although the rituals performed were understood by the people in entirely religious terms, they had far-reaching ecological effects. A drastic reduction in the pig population released pressure on land needed for gardens, allowed long fallow periods, and conserved resources of the forest. Rearrangements of territorial borders through warfare adjusted human populations to available land.

The conclusion that *kaiko* established or affirmed many connections between people and environment does not require that it acted to fix those connections through time or nicely match demands people placed upon environment to the capacity of environment to satisfy those demands. In any case, the first conclusion would be unwarranted because Tsembaga society and ecology must have changed frequently, perhaps continually, through past centuries; what Rappaport witnessed was merely an historical moment. There is an easier interpretation that allows for change while constraining it. A growing pig population, increased pressure on land, and difficulties with neighbors who are perceived as enemies are the sorts of events that might encourage vast transformations within a society. It is possible to reshape the connections between people and environment, to modify, invent, or borrow alternative manipulative modes and to extract more energy and matter from the same area of ground. This has happened many times to many societies through human history. But such changes are not inevitable. They require, at base, that people perceive themselves, their neighbors, and their environment in thoroughly new ways. Inasmuch as their perceptions of an apparently extrinsic world are bound by their own understanding of the cosmological, so transformation may be inconceivable. Thus, my interpretation of the *kaiko* is that, above all, it was protective of people's perceptions. The *kaiko* was instituted once every decade or so as people's perceptions became out of kilter. When it had run its course, the connections between Tsembaga, their neighbors, and their environment were reaffirmed: those connections need not be as they had once been, though the people would imagine this to be the case. Each turn of the ritual cycle may have had a different outcome. Indeed, each performance of the *kaiko* may have differed from the last. Perceptions that had combined in new ways through the preceding years would be contained within and by the most recent outcome.

Although *Ida, kaiko,* and Sugua Mai took vastly different forms, each acted to reestablish connections among people—and between people and environment—that reaffirmed the people's perceptions of themselves as social beings and of the proper way in which things were done. In each case the performance was required only at intervals; with *Ida* as an affirmation that all was well; with *kaiko* to subvert the possibility of sweeping change; and with Sugua Mai, the least spectacular of the three, to promote a sense of community and quietly contain fickleness. And, with each, the ecological spin-off was great: the intent to stage the performance, the performance itself, or both, carried the information that organized people to work according to modes or schedules that they imagined had always prevailed.

It is not possible to know when *Ida* and the *kaiko* originated or what they may have looked like when they were first performed. Probably, had we witnessed early performances, we would not have grasped the potential that, by the times of Gell and Rappaport, had been already realized. Through time, *Ida* and *kaiko* must have taken shape by combining and recombining older modes of expression to give new meanings, by assembling preexisting ritual elements from disparate domains in new ways, and by incorporating newly imagined insights into what seemed, to the actors, a repeat performance.[16] There is no necessity either that the preliminary drafts of *Ida* and the *kaiko* were strongly connected with perpetuation of environmental relations. This could have come later, as the developing ideologies that underwrote the rituals were wedded to what people did as they attended to their day-to-day secular concerns. But, inasmuch as the marriages of sacred and secular were convenient, reestablishing ecosystemic links through bestowal of grace, *Ida* and *kaiko* would have emerged as inseparable parts of the ecology of people. Through them, more than through any other medium, people would have perceived their proper connections with environment and understood the proper responses to it.

Gell and Rappaport described ritual events of great importance that may have been vanishing as they were recorded. The impact of the modern, the intrusion of Europeans, missionaries, national and provincial governments, and multinational corporations are altering forever the ways of life of all Papua New Guineans.

Change as History

Change is inevitable. Our descriptions of form—organic or cultural, social or symbolic—are embedded in change. They are timeless constellations that we abstract from the flux of existence. Our knowledge of Etolo is of two privileged glimpses, two moments from a trajectory with unknown beginnings and an indeterminant end. Ray Kelly, in the late 1960s, lived with people who had barely come to terms with momentous events whose impact and interpretation could be only cosmological: the brief appearance of Europeans, their later return, recurring epidemics, the collapse of population. Their world—that of the mind—had assumed a different shape. Ten years later my own momentary glimpse was of a people transformed. On the surface, at least, the cosmological had been adapted to the new. The overt concerns were more pragmatic because now people were linked in different ways with their Etolo and Onabasulu neighbors, the numerous Huli across the mountains to the northeast, the institutions of a Christian church and the diffuse though far-reaching powers of a national government. Their aspirations were locked within the material frame offered by these connections: the knowledge that revengeful raiding had ceased, the hope that witchcraft no longer threatened, and the promises of health, literacy, and increased access to a more inclusive economic sphere.

At Bobole, in the late 1970s, 109 people lived at the one location. They had done so for the better part of a decade. In the recent past communities had been smaller; to resolve tensions, people had parted company, and new groupings had emerged. The connections between people and landscape had been fluid. Consolidation of Bobole as a geographically fixed village had major effects. Rights to garden on land near at hand or to capture animals in the forest had to be reassessed. Old rules of propriety had to be relaxed. Codes of giving and sharing that had suited smaller groups had the potential to generate ambiguity or tension in the context of the larger population. Increasingly, the ethos of community was itself challenged. It was not practical that all families participated in the one venture, yet where relatives from different longhouses joined in a project, this might disrupt the cohesion otherwise possible among coresidents. In small groups a sense of community may arise directly from the mutuality of participation and sharing. Disgruntled individuals may always move on. In a larger group where sharing is more awkward and not everyone can connect with the ventures of everyone else, an ideal of community may be less easy to sustain unless it is given tangible, institutional, form. Sugua Mai, I suggest, was such an institution.

In 1979 people who lived at Bobole were expanding their global perspective and involvement in both political and economic spheres. Often, the immediate impact upon their lives and their model of a different future arose out of their interactions with highlanders. At the provincial elections of 1980, people of the Great Papuan Plateau successfully joined forces to ensure a win by a plateau-born man who had stood against several Huli candidates. People actively championed the opinion that although, within their electorate, they were outnumbered by Huli, the latter were likely to split the vote according to various group loyalties. In the economic sphere people perceived a new dependence upon Huli shop owners for access to clothing, cooking utensils, axes, and other items of modern manufacture. Because these and other items seemed easily accessible to Huli, trade goods that Etolo controlled were correspondingly devalued. Now they traded raw materials to Huli where once they had provided finished products; string instead of net bags, bow blanks instead of bows. But not all economic change was similarly influenced. Two men had each purchased a few shares in a government-sponsored issue of bonds. Live pigs were included in bride wealth payments, and there were markets at which pork was sold for cash. These latter changes mimicked Huli practices but were not dependent upon them. In them there seems potential for Etolo to shift progressively the place of pigs to a more overtly politico-economic plane and, perhaps, link themselves more completely with Huli institutional forms. It may be significant also that many Huli attended the second Sugua Mai feast and that both Huli and Etolo pigs were cooked and eaten at that feast. Changes that increasingly connected pigs, politics, and economics could lead Etolo toward eventual incorporation within the extensive networks of exchange that characterize highland Papua New Guinea. Sugua Mai could act as a springboard for changes of these sorts.

Through the 1940s and 1950s the cosmos of Etolo was subject to impacts of extraordinary kinds. Through the next decade, as people recovered from these events, colonial administrators arrived to encourage new practices and demand new conformity. Simultaneously, the people were exposed to a model espoused by fundamentalist Christians. The two could be wedded. To accept the promises and guidance of the new religion was, of itself, consistent with the dictates of foreign, powerful administrators. A new way of living was required; a new religion offered a path that might lead there. The combination widened economic horizons. Much was to change. The forest spirits would fade and witches go into retreat. Participation at seances had to be represented as membership of a different congregation. Mortuary rites, initiation, and dance were seemingly set aside. But the changes were not absolute. From the outset the lay preachers were young Etolo men and, finally, so was the pastor.[17] Advice was still sought from outside, but control and, thus, interpretation were increasingly internalized. In accommodating to the new, customary Etolo practice and belief were reshaped: the process was syncretic. The world of spirits was organized in different ways. The codes that had underlain ritual were given different expression. Sugua Mai, I shall argue, contained an expression of sacred codes within a secular domain. Whatever its eventual fate, the achievement of Sugua Mai was to make possible an old ideal of community within a new context. It guided and legitimized a collective response to the seasons.

But history alone is not enough: a chain of forms, of dates and momentous events, forms and events interpreted within broader contexts, a catalog of impacts to which form responded, the terrible temptation to translate response as necessity. The pictures are too easy. Identified stages, lines of connection, a jigsaw assembly that, despite its intricacies, remains a static product. History transfers past events onto a canvas that is ever-present. The dynamics that drove them, that made them what they were, is not revealed.

It is lost in the act of building, of reconstructing, the past. My concern is not with history but with process—with the dynamics of change in open systems, with their seeming stability and inherent vulnerability, their recursive properties, their capacities to disassemble old components as they reconstruct new forms. Change in open systems occurs as they consolidate and replicate sameness. It was this that was implied in my accounts of both *Ida* and *kaiko*. What then of the process through which Sugua Mai was manifest?

Sugua Mai: The Re-creation of Form

Among the societies of the Great Papuan Plateau and of the Strickland Plain to the west, there was a commonality of ritual form in which people from two or more longhouses joined in "an all-night dance and songfest."[18] At these events the arrival of visitors was marked by ritualized hostility, anger, or, at least, coolness in the relations between visitors and hosts, though finally this gave way to a deeply felt, communal experience. Socializing and the public exchange of food were facilitated, and dancing, by one or more men, elaborately costumed to represent Raggiana birds of paradise, accompanied by singing, gave a nightlong aesthetic focus to the ritual. As Bruce Knauft wrote: "Throughout the Strickland-Bosavi area, this basic ritual is a major form of aesthetic expression as well as being the primary peaceful setting for neighboring settlements to coalesce, irrespective of kinship."[19]

Between societies of this region there were striking variations within the common themes summarized above. The Kaluli *gisaro* ritual was described by Edward Schieffelin.[20] Here, songs composed and sung by visiting dancers referred, metaphorically, to past tragedies experienced by hosts who, when their grief became extreme, wept and burned the dancers with resin torches. Schieffelin's analysis of *gisaro* was as a theatrical expression of "forming and resolving oppositions" that were "the major mode of forward motion in Kaluli society."[21] The logic of ritual expression was contrastive; the communal experience that it facilitated was of an analogical kind. Weddings at which pigs were part of bride wealth and ceremonial prestations of pork were major occasions when Kaluli opposed each other in groups, as hosts and guests, as givers and receivers. They were also occasions when *gisaro* was likely to be performed.

The Etolo version of *gisaro* was named *gosa*. Costumed men danced and sang; people wept; and the dancers might be burned. But in the late 1970s *gosa* was no longer performed at Bobole.[22] My own direct knowledge of it extends no further than to have seen the deep nostalgia of some men as they spoke of waiting in ambush for birds of paradise and of many men as they examined photographs in Schieffelin's book *The Sorrow of the Lonely and the Burning of the Dancers*. *Gosa* had been abandoned in favor of new—

though only partially understood and not totally incorporated—ritual expressions. Acceptance of a Christian model had usurped past theatrical forms that validated social existence, but the new model lacked the color, movement, sound, and publicly expressed emotions of *gosa*. It was crude. It spoke of moral conduct, an imminent second coming, material benefits, and earthly immortality. It spoke only of the possible. It lacked tangible messages that were emotionally connected to people's actual existence, and, in this, it left a vacuum in their lives.

Yet the Christian model was itself changing. The enactment of Adam and Eve in the garden of Eden was, perhaps, a first step that connected emotional needs with the new teachings, a step that could not have been taken until the people themselves, through having one of their own as pastor, exercised some control over the form of Christian expression. Indeed, a later church performance, at Easter, 1980, went further because now almost all who attended were themselves performers. The messages were overt. In one part of the church young men played cards for money. Elsewhere, a fancily dressed, town-experienced, heavily smoking man (played by the pastor Efala) interrupted a church service to spread largesse and lure men to the good life. The community was reduced progressively to the elderly and to women and children. Finally, former residents reappeared as drunken louts, and the people rebelled, evicting those who would not mend their ways and reconsolidating around former, community-centered values. Even the structure of the church was altered to promote this outcome. The central partition that separated male and female sitting areas was removed. This partition had been installed under the guidance of Huli pastors; it incorporated Huli perceptions within the Christian model. The mere fact of its removal created a spatial configuration of males and females that accorded more precisely with the day-to-day experience of the people.

With the advent of an Etolo pastor at Bobole the potential to enlarge the Christian model by incorporating symbols that spoke directly to people's actual experience and cultural values was enhanced. This was achieved with the enactment of the Genesis tale. More than this, the mood was established whereby the status of the congregation might shift from observation to participation and of the performance itself from distanced instruction to immanent reality. In rituals of the sort represented by *gosa* and *gisaro* there is little if any separation of audience and performers. All who participate are performers. Through their interactions they share equally in constructing the reality and the meanings of the total performance. So, too, they may share in translating from those meanings to appropriate responses. Schieffelin depicted this effectively in an analysis of Kaluli seances: "theatre becomes reality, where spirits who are birds converse with men in human voices" and, again, "the structure of the performance space . . . is one of shared assumptions that everyone brings to the occasion."[23] At a Kaluli seance it was the interaction between the medium (or the spirits to whom the medium was a vehicle) and the participants that evoked reality. It was through their participation as performers, not as audience, that "the people reach fundamental symbolic understandings and arrive at solutions to their problems." Thus, Schieffelin argued, the meanings of many ritual performances are constructed during the performance itself; they are not locked into particularized symbols and symbolic structures. In this sense rituals and their meanings have historicity.

Knauft wrote: "The patterning of Strickland-Bosavi rituals appears to be one of structural permutation, in which the same elements of ritual form and structure are present in all societies, but are subject to distinctive emphases and combinations in each."[24] It is my interpretation that Sugua Mai, as witnessed at Bobole during 1979, contained and was constructed about fundamental elements from preexisting ritual forms and, like those forms, facilitated an experience of community. The context in which Sugua Mai took place was new; the relatively permanent association of four longhouse communities. It was the potential this held to damage the sense of community that promoted emergence of Sugua Mai; in the new way of living more value than ever before attached to concordance of action because only in this way might preexisting, though noninstitutionalized, modes of behavior be incorporated within a tangible expression of communality. *Gosa* and seances were abandoned; sharing was awkward; the values that accrued from residence within a single longhouse were challenged by too many near neighbors, and Christianity, as yet, was insufficient to replace the losses that these represented.

Sugua Mai was no surrogate for past ritual. There were no beautifully costumed young men, no songs or weeping, no dancing or burning of dancers as had happened at *gosa*. It neither took the place of those rituals nor satisfied people's nostalgia for them. But there was a connection. Out of elements of their own recent past people had assembled a different play that fulfilled old needs.[25] The evidence was at the feasts. Here people from several longhouses joined as a greater community, old tensions surfaced as visitors arrived and held themselves apart, and food was publicly displayed and distributed. These were common features of customary ritual forms. But Sugua Mai was built from more basic stuff. At the outset hosts and guests, givers and receivers, were contrasted, but through the performance these contrasts were dissolved. Everyone gave and all received; hosts and guests merged as a single congregation. At the feasts people had retrieved fundamental statements from now abandoned ritual forms and built them into a different setting. It was the code in which those statements were written that was all-important because this was the language that had always underlain theatrical performances that addressed social existence. The code was contrastive; its logic digital. It generated boundaries across which communication was possible. By carica- turing elements of social existence the code legitimized conventions of that existence. It obviated ambiguity and made it possible that all who partici- pated shared in constructing the performance, its reality, and its meaning. This act of communication was the necessary condition that the system, ecological and social, of which the people at Bobole were a part, maintained a semblance of order.

Sugua Mai used pigs to secular ends and theater that sanctified the sharing of pork. It re-created—even institutionalized—a sense of community in a context where this was in jeopardy. It was new in its form though old in its purposes. It was the message that declared that the act of putting pigs into gardens was itself a message. It was this that the people themselves, as performers, constructed, and it was to this that they then responded. Sugua Mai was a historically recent metamessage that came into existence as the people and the system of which they were a part—all caught in a turmoil of change—attempted to contain fresh insights within customary frameworks and remain the same. The necessary outcome and success of that attempt was that form itself had changed.

Epilogue

During our stay at Bobole we often camped in the higher-altitude forest. Our small hut at Magidobo was roofed with ginger leaves, though, eventually, it leaked very badly. But it was our place, used sometimes as a retreat from pressures of the village and, more frequently, for the pleasure of the sounds and smells of the forest itself. At times we camped alone, at others with youths and men who hunted during the daylight hours while we did different work—trapping small mammals, mapping the distribution of ant colonies, or sorting invertebrate animals from leaf litter. A few men brought their young sons and left them with us while they hunted. Minape was about nine years old and Mane about seven; they both came and were, respectively, sons to Maga and Sailo, who were skilled and enthusiastic hunters.

When Minape stayed with his father, they spent the night in a hut adjoining ours and talked for several hours. I did not understand what they said but each time Maga spoke he instructed Minape to repeat the words. When the lesson was done, they shared a Christian prayer and slept. At first light the next morning Maga, with his dog, Uguno, left to hunt, and Minape joined me to clear rat traps on a grid that I had operated for many months. There was a place where large trees had fallen in a storm several years earlier and small, wild banana trees now grew among the tangle of logs we had to cross. Minape pushed the banana trees down. He pushed all of them down and checked that they had been properly broken. *Go etolo,* "What is it?" I asked, still unable to formulate or receive satisfaction from a "why" question. "Mugabe" was Minape's only reply. He was killing the wild banana trees that a decade earlier, before he was born, sometimes harbored evil spirits that threatened the success of domestic varieties grown by people.

At a later date Mane came with Sailo and the dog Gedigi. There was no formal instruction through the night but, instead, just before dark a fearful storm broke. There were lightning, thunder, and torrential rain, and in the distance on all sides, we heard trees crashing to the ground. Sailo held Mane and, from the brink of their shelter, watched every movement of the forest. He was assessing the trees, ready to flee to the protection afforded by one huge tree if another should hurtle toward us. The forest spirits, the *segesado,* were surely beating on the walls of their houses through the fury of that storm. But it dissipated, and through the night we heard the calls of the spirit's hunting dogs. The next morning Sailo and Gedigi went hunting. I cleared traps as usual, and Mane stayed with Kristine, watching her sort through litter she had collected and marveling, perhaps, at our strange ways. The uninitiated seldom persist with leaf litter, and Mane grew distracted, attending to his own thoughts until he interrupted the work to whisper that he heard a noise, that something was coming. There was no sound except the birds, and the forest drying after the storm. Kristine asked "What is it?" and was told that Mugabe approached the hut and was getting near. "How do you know?" asked Kristine, her command of Etolo so much better than mine, "How many legs has it got?" "He has ten," Mane replied, no longer whispering . . . and collapsed in giggles, his teasing joke revealed.

Mane's small, beautiful, dangerous joke in the forest of Mt. Haliago may have been another beginning in the world where Etolo lived. Minape's experience was of the immanence of Mugabe. Mane relocated Mugabe to the imaginary place where entities abound, and through time this achievement could prove formidable.

But there is, after all, only motion. Sugua Mai, born of change, validated an experience that all remained the same when, in truth, nothing ever had . . . nothing, that is, except the rain falling on Haliago.

Appendixes

Plant Cultigens and Their Etolo Names

The following list includes the most common garden cultigens and a few other important plants. Etolo vernacular names that include several or many named subcategories are indicated by an asterisk.

Scientific Name	English Vernacular	Etolo Vernacular
Ipomoea batatas	sweet potato	*siabulu**
Colocalia esculenta	taro	*nau**
Xanthosoma sagittifolium	tannia	*ulumabi; heligei nau*
Dioscorea sp.	yam	*elebo*
Dioscorea sp.	yam	*ubula; emogafe*
Dioscorea sp.	yam	*mali**
Manihot esculenta	cassava	*i siabulu*
Arachis hypogea	peanut	*galus*
Zingiber officinale	ginger	*fogomo*
Nasturtium officinale	watercress	*nadebale*
Rungia klossi	acanth spinach	*muluwa*
Hibiscus manihot	aibika (hibiscus)	*aso**
Oenanthe javanica	Javanese dropwort	*mogome*
?	?	*sa fani*
Brassica sp.	Chinese spinach	*gola*
?	?	*sogo* (cf. tobacco leaf)
Lablab sp.	bean (short pod)	*faraga*
Phaseolus sp.	bean (long pod)	*fabalo*
Setaria palmifolia	highland pitpit	*safu**
Saccharum edule	lowland pitpit	*ote**
Saccharum officinarum	sugarcane	*baile**

Sechium edulae	choko	*sogo* (homonym of *sogo* = tobacco)
Cucumis sativus	cucumber	*mahabo*
Trichosanthes sp.	climbing cucurbit	*mahabo*
Cucurbis maxima	pumpkin	*pamigin*
Legenaria siceraria	bottle gourd	*maio*
Zea mays	corn	*goni; helepe giria*
Musa sp.	banana	*gai**
Carica papaya	pawpaw	*popo*
Pandanus conoideus	*marita* pandanus	*gaheo**
Metroxylon sp.	sago palm	*waharo**
Nicotiana tobacum	tobacco	*sogo*

Mammals and Their Etolo Names

The following list includes all mammals known to occur at Mt. Haliago. I use currently accepted scientific names of the species and provide brief English vernacular glosses for sets of related species. The taxonomy of New Guinean mammals is currently undergoing much revision; some of the names I have used will be altered by future workers. In earlier identifications I attempted to follow the recommendations of Dennis and Menzies (1979); George (1979); Kirsh and Calaby (1977); Taylor, Calaby and van Deusen (1982); and Ziegler (1982). Subsequently the cuscuses, *Phalanger,* have been extensively revised by Menzies and Pernetta (1986) and by several authors in a volume edited by Archer (1987). In this book I have usually followed the recent overview of New Guinean mammals by Flannery (1990) and, for the rodent genus *Mallomys,* Flannery, Aplin, Groves and Adams (1989). The list has benefited from the advice of Ken Aplin, University of New South Wales, Australia, who examined material I collected and himself surveyed mammals at Mt. Haliago during two months in 1985. Additions resulting from Aplin's work are acknowledged in what follows. Where names listed below differ from those used by me in earlier publications concerning Mt. Haliago, I indicate the earlier name.

Although English vernacular names have been proposed for most New Guinea mammals, I have misgivings about using these (cf. Dwyer 1983b). Indeed, at present, the names used by Etolo may lack universality but have greater stability! Etolo used the collective taxa *Oheo* and *Ebele* for larger and smaller species, respectively, of echidnas, marsupials, and rodents. In the list below *O* and *E* code these higher categories of Etolo taxonomy. Bats, pig, dog, and domestic cat were not affiliated to *Oheo* or *Ebele*. Etolo taxa with a capitalized initial letter are uninomials; those without capitalized initial letters are parts of binomials (e.g., the marsupial carnivore *Antechinus melanurus* is sufficiently specified by the name *Sole,* but the marsupial cat *Dasyurus albopunctatus* is not sufficiently specified by the name *gaietetoni.*

In the latter case *gaietetoni* must be predicated by *Awini*). I have included Etolo synonyms when these are known to me.

Scientific Nomenclature	Etolo Nomenclature

MONOTREMES (echidnas)
   Zaglossus bruijni — *O. Habomi*
   Tachyglossus aculeatus — *O. Habomi*

(Etolo said that echidnas originate by transformation from a variety of other mammalian species. They named categories within *Habomi* according to the species from which particular individuals originated; e.g., *godobo Habomi* from the bandicoot *Peroryctes raffrayanus*, *gageleso Habomi* from the tree kangaroo *Dendrolagus dorianus*, etc., Dwyer 1980*a*.)

MARSUPIALS
Carnivorous marsupials
   Antechinus melanurus — *O. Awini Sole*
   Myoictos melas — *O. Awini Sesebu (Sese)*
   Murexia longicaudata — *O. Awini*
   Dasyurus albopunctatus — *O. Awini gaietetoni*
Bandicoots
   Microperoryctes longicauda — *O. Mititolo*

(In earlier publications I named this species *Peroryctes longicauda*.)
   Peroryctes raffrayanus — *O. Godobo*
   Echymipera kalubu — *O. Mahi*
   Echymipera rufescens — *O. Mahi*

(Some small *Mahi* were said to be *Mahi go;* they were recognizable by their call.)

Pygmy possums
   Cercartetus caudatus — *E. Gusigeno*
   Distoechurus pennatus — *E. Sega*

(*D. pennatus* was sometimes placed in the category of larger mammals, *Oheo. Sega* was also the name used

for the small ring-tailed possum
Pseudocheirus mayeri.)

Gliding possum
  Petaurus breviceps   *O. Afoadola*
Striped possums
  Dactylopsila trivirgata   *O. Naialo (Awaiya, Nagelibia)*
  Dactylopsila palpator   *O. Naialo (Awaiya, Nagelibia)*
                           (Most Etolo were aware that there
are two kinds of *Naialo*. The names
Awaiya and *Nagelibia* were used
sometimes to specify *D. trivirgata*
and *D. palpator,* respectively.
Awaiya is also an Onabasulu name
for *D. trivirgata*.)

Ring-tailed possums
  Pseudocheirus mayeri   *O. Sega*
                           (*Sega* was also the name used for the
pygmy possum *Distoechurus pen-
natus*.)

  Pseudocheirus canescens   *O. Yefuliga*
  Pseudocheirus forbesi   *O. Momoleba (Simomole)*
  Pseudocheirops corinnae   *O. Bo (Bo gosavi, Gosavi Oheo)*
                           (The *o* of *Bo* is a nasalized *oa* as in
coat. Gosavi was the Etolo name for
Mt. Bosavi, and it was from this
mountain, they said, that *P. corinnae*
originated. In earlier publications I
named this species *Pseudocheirus
corinnae*.)

  Pseudocheirops cupreus   *O. Bo (Boapia, Sinagua, Hinini)*
                           (In earlier publications I named this
species *Pseudocheirus cupreus*.)

Cuscuses
  Phalanger orientalis   *O. Udumo* (females); *O. Mega*
(males)
                           (To Etolo *Udumo* and *Mega* were
separate kinds, but *Udumo* reared the
young of both kinds.)
  Phalanger permixtio   *O. Ninesida* (females); *O. Gepa*
(males)
                           (To Etolo *Ninesida* and *Gepa* were
of the same kind. *Hopeaiyae* was

apparently equivalent to *Gepa* among western Etolo speakers. People at Bobole were ambivalent regarding *Hopeaiyae*, saying that it was like *Gepa* or a subcategory of *Gepa* with either a special smell or peculiar tail scales. In earlier publications I named this species *Phalanger interpositus*.)

Phalanger carmelitae   *O. Gedigi*

Phalanger sericeus   *O. Gedigi*

(In earlier publications I named this species *Phalanger vestitus*.)

Strigocuscus gymnotis   *O. Hatagaui* (*Samegi*)

(Some small *Hatagaui* were said to be *Hatagaui galiapusano;* they were recognized by the call they gave— *goi, goi, goi*—as they ran away from hunters and climbed trees. In earlier publications I named this species *Phalanger gymnotis*.)

Spilocuscus maculatus   *O. Baiaga* (*Mibei*)

(In earlier publications I named this species *Phalanger maculatus*.)

Forest wallabies

Dorcopsulus macleayi   *O. Gauso* (*Badaba*)

(Some small *Gauso* were said to be *Gauso igulusalo*. In earlier publications I named this species *Dorcopsulus vanheurni*.)

Dorcopsis sp.   *O. Gabaiya*

(*Gabaiya* was said to occur at altitudes below 700 m. K. Aplin saw specimens of *Dorcopsis* south of Etolo territory, but *Gabaiya* could include *Thylogale*.)

Tree kangaroos

Dendrolagus goodfellowi   *O. Elesoda*

Dendrolagus dorianus   *O. Gageleso*

RODENTS

Small rodents (< 200 grams)

Rattus steini   *E. Salagomo* (*Segafi*)

	(*R. novaeguinae* may be also present up to altitudes of 700 m; K. Aplin.)
Rattus verecundus	*E. Salagomo* (*Segafi*) (In Dwyer 1984, this species was named as *R. leucopus*.)
Rattus niobe	*E. Igiebele* (Some people identified species of *Rattus* solely on the basis of the habitat in which an individual was found. If it was in houses, gardens or early regrowth, then it was named *Salagomo*; if it was from advanced secondary forest or from primary forest, then it was named *Igiebele*. At Mt. Haliago, *R. niobe* may comprise separate higher-altitude [> 1200 m] and lower-altitude [< 1200 m] species; K. Aplin)
Melomys lutillus	*E. Sasione*
Melomys levipes	*E. Ebebole*
Melomys platyops	*E. Ebele* (*Ebele fani, Ebele afate fani*)
Melomys rubex	*E. Ebele* (*Ebele fani, Ebele afate fani*) (*M. platyops* and *M. rubex* are, with only slight overlap, altitudinally separated. The listed synonyms translate, respectively, as the "true *Ebele*" and the "one true *Ebele*.")
Melomys leucogaster	*E. Golaio* (In earlier publications I named this species *Pogonomelomys bruijni*. At Mt. Haliago it was often associated with marita pandanus.)
Melomys rufescens	*E. Damaleba* (*waharo Ebele;* also *Ebele sole*, K. Aplin) (Within Papua New Guinea *M. rufescens* is probably a complex of species. In earlier publications I named this species *Pogonomelomys mayeri*. At Mt. Haliago it was often associated with sago palms.)

Chiruromys vates	*E. Yesulu*
Pogonomys macrourus	*E. Goso*
Pogonomys loriae	*E. Bulo*
Pogonomys sp.	*E. Bulo*

(*Pogonomys loriae* and *Pogonomys* sp. are altitudinally separated; the latter is a large *Pogonomys* that cannot be accommodated within the species described by Dennis and Menzies [1979] or Flannery [1988].)

Lorentzimys nouhuysi	*E. Dadigaga*
Leptomys elegans	*E. Yauwie*
Microhydromys cf. *richardsoni*	*E. Ebele mano*

(I.e., the animal was said to be a baby rat; the intention may have been that it was a baby *Melomys*.)

Pseudohydromys sp.   *E. Ebele mano* (*Yauwie mano*)

(Different people identified this animal as either a baby rat or a baby *Leptomys elegans*. The single individual captured did not fit any described forms of *Pseudohydromys*.)

Medium-sized rodents (200–1,000 grams)

Macruromys major	*O. Yelifege*
Anisomys imitator	*O. Sau*
Xenuromys barbatus	*O. abane Haniano*

(The animal is rare in Etolo territory, and the name was borrowed from Onabasulu speakers.)

Uromys caudimaculatus	*O. Fagena*
Uromys anak	*O. Worobo*
Crossomys moncktoni	*O. Emobeligei* (*ota Oheo*)

(*Ota Oheo* translates as the "water" *kapul; kapul* is pidgin for game mammal.)

Hydromys chrysogaster   *O. Migalu* (*ota Oheo*: also *Agamo,* K. Aplin)

Parahydromys asper   *O. Migalu*

(*Migalu* translates as "swollen nose." Several Bobole people said there were two kinds of *Migalu,* one with a swollen muzzle and the other with

a slender muzzle; these were, respec-
tively, *P. asper* and *H. chrysogaster*.
At Namosado the former was named
Migalu and the latter was named
Agamo; K. Aplin)

Large rodents (> 1,000 grams)
  Hyomys goliath

                                      O. Dabalidi Masiadamulo (Gome-
                                        nodamulo, Wabibi)

  Mallomys aroaensis
                                        O. Dabalidi fani (Dabalidi etefate)
                                        (*M. aroaensis* was nomenclaturally
marked by declaring it as the true—
fani—Dabalidi or the large—
etefate—Dabalidi. In earlier publications I named this species *Mallomys
rothschildi*.)

DOG
  Canis familiaris
                                          Uguno (domestic dog)
                                          ilua Uguno (wild dog)

CAT
  Felis catus
                                          Busi (pidgin term)
PIG
  Sus scrofa
                                          Sugua foi (domestic pig)
                                          Sugua Segeligi (Iliba) (wild pig)

FRUIT BATS
  Dobsonia moluccensis
                                          Dobolu
  Pteropus sp.
                                          Galugei (Momogabi)
                                        (In some years *Pteropus* sp. arrived
within Etolo territory from lower alti-
tudes; Kelly [1977] described nocturnal hunting expeditions.)

SMALL BATS
  *Syconycteris, Macroglossus Phile-
tor, Miniopterus*, etc.
                                          Utegede
  *Nyctimene, Paranyctimene, Rhi-
nolophus*, etc.
                                          Gumaiye (per K. Aplin)
                                          (*Utegede* and *Gumaiye* were distin-
guished as having long and short
noses, respectively, and, further, as
having doglike or piglike faces; K.
Aplin.)

Sugua Mai Chronology: A Diary of Events

The following diary of events is compiled from field notes. Because I did not know what was happening, or even that something was happening, until well after it had happened, these notes are less full than I would wish. They are included as support for my account of the chronology of events that I have chosen to call Sugua Mai. The codes I to IV indicate the longhouses at which various people lived.

1979

June 29: Fuago (III) stops me to report that Gago's (I) pigs have got into a garden belonging to House I, that there is no food, and that we shall all be hungry. Within the next few days I conclude that Gago had placed his pigs in the garden and learn that he had left to trade for sago. During the week more pigs appear in the garden, and several women complain that there is no food. We learn the conventional statement *sugua mai*, "pigs ate."

June 30: Fuma (IV) says that new gardens are being prepared, that yams are plentiful but sweet potato is scarce.

July 6: Fuma (IV) complains that Gago's (I) pigs are in a garden and that Gago has left Bobole to purchase sago. He reports that pigs have got into another garden belonging to House III. (Their access to this garden was facilitated by removal of part of the fence. A third garden, belonging to House IV, was treated similarly, but precise dates are not known to me.)

July 13–14: The pigs placed into the garden belonging to House I are killed and eaten at the first Sugua Mai feast. (See chap. 9 for an account of this feast.)

July 15–28: We receive many complaints that pigs are destroying crops. Women often stop us to say *sugua mai* or *mono made*, "there is no food," or they indicate hunger by gesture. Gamia (I) tells us that pigs have got into gardens.

July 31: Sailo (IV) visits us privately to say we must not leave the village for several weeks. There is to be a feast, and we are invited. Later, on the same day, Fuma (IV) and Otai (I) justify the pending feast in terms of concern that pigs may damage new gardens.

August 13–14: The pigs allowed into the gardens belonging to Houses III and IV are killed and eaten at the second Sugua Mai feast. (See chap. 9 for an account of this feast.)

August 19: Sailo (IV) links recent pig feasts to the damage they had done to gardens. They had to be killed for this reason; he says that Bauwa (IV) even killed a piglet because of concern for gardens. Yaude (IV) says gardens are destroyed, that she has no food because pigs have ruined everything.

August 25: Sailo (IV) repeats the connection between feasts and gardens.

August 26: For the first time we have difficulty in purchasing sago.

August 27: Efala (I) agrees that food is in short supply and complains (at length and in detail) that rats have been invading gardens and ruined recently planted crops. He asserts that it has never been this serious before. Later, his younger brother, Huia (I), dismisses the notion of current damage to gardens and says that only later, when the sweet potatoes are ready, will rats become a nuisance. Aubelia (I) says there is neither sweet potato nor sago to eat.

August 28: Efala (I) discusses the current food shortage and lists families that will be soon going to process sago.

August 31: We fill a shortage of sago by purchasing from Namosado and are strongly reprimanded for misdirecting our money.

September 13: Haboyado (III) says his family has no sweet potato, that their only garden was destroyed by pigs. (At this time, in fact, the family had at least one plot that was yielding sweet potato.)

September 21: Fuma (IV) complains of having no food to eat. He has to eat sago, pumpkins, and choko because pigs have ruined gardens. He is sick of eating these foods.

September 24: People from Namosado make a large gift of taro to people from House I.

November 2: We tell Sabaiya (II) in congratulatory fashion that we have visited and mapped his gardens at Walataia. He replies with a long impassioned speech saying that there is no sweet potato, that he is hungry, and he rubs his belly for emphasis.

November 3: Ilabu (I) says that he has been weeding and that though there is now "no sweet potato for eating," there will be some in the future.

November 22: Sailo (IV) tells us that there is almost no sweet potato, only some scraps from an old garden. He is reduced to eating chokos; even pumpkins are finished.

November 22: Sailo (IV) reports that people are now eating sago, pumpkins, and choko. (His mood was that of Hanrahan in the Australian ballad "'We'll all be ruined,' said Hanrahan, 'before the year is out.'") When pressed, he agrees there is some sweet potato in the garden that had previously had pigs.

December 3: Gago (I) says that he has no sweet potato.

1980

January 9: People from Namosado make a large gift of cooking bananas to House I.

January 11: Gago and Heaga (I), sharing the burden of a string bag that overflows with sweet potato gathered from a newly productive garden, complain bitterly that rats have ravished their crop. They ask me to trap rats in their garden. I interpret their comments as a mixture of inverted pride at the bountiful harvest and annoyance that some should be spoiled. The comments have nothing to do with a shortfall in food; gardens are now flourishing. No complaints are heard after this date.

February-March: On a few occasions I ask Efala for information about the times when domestic pigs were killed and eaten, trying to lead him into connecting the killing of pigs to their entry into gardens. He is always insistent that there was no connection of this kind, saying that pigs were killed when they were large enough or (his preferred response) "Pigs are eaten when they are ready for eating."

Notes

Chapter 1

1. Haliago is the name used by Etolo and neighboring Huli for the mountain shown on maps as Mt. Sisa (latitude 6°9'S, 142°45'E). Sisa is the Kaluli name for the same mountain.

2. Early in 1980, people who lived at Namosado, several kilometers south of Bobole, built a new longhouse. At the insistence of women the design was altered to eliminate the cramped corridors used traditionally as sleeping quarters by married women. The women said the places were uncomfortable and the new house included a larger than usual communal section.

3. Demographic pyramids based on estimated ages are shown below for the period March, 1979, through April, 1980; births and deaths during this period are indicated.

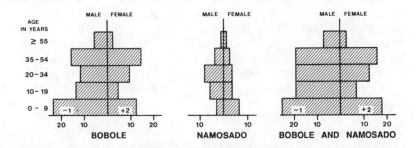

4. Beek 1987; Ernst 1978, 1984; Feld 1982; Kelly 1977, 1988; Schieffelin 1977, 1982; and Sørum 1980 are major ethnographic sources about people of the Great Papuan Plateau and their neighbors to the west. From April, 1968, to July, 1969, Ray Kelly lived with approximately twenty-five people who resided at Kaburusato (Gabulusado) longhouse. Gabulusado was located 11 kilometers southwest of Bobole at an altitude of 775 meters near the western boundary of Etolo territory. The two communities differed in that Gabulusado people often interacted and sometimes intermarried with Bedamini to their west while Bobole people often interacted and sometimes intermarried with Onabasulu to their south. Indeed, a longhouse community at Namosado, five kilometers south of Bobole, was identified as Etolo but was strongly connected with Onabasulu through frequent visiting, intermarriage, and, in 1979, land dispute. Members of this community sometimes gave both Etolo and Onabasulu names

217

to particular species of animal and said they did not know which name was associated with which language. Kelly lived in a monolingual situation and, though his 1977 book focused on social structure, provided a detailed statement of Etolo subsistence. Ten years later I lived in the deceptively advantageous circumstance that most men had some competence in pidgin, and it was this language that served as my lingua franca. My work had an ecological focus and at times yielded observations seemingly at variance with those reported by Kelly. It is important to make clear how these differences are treated in this book. Their potential bases are fivefold: (1) the different skills and biases of the observers, (2) the different social and historical alignments of western and eastern Etolo communities, (3) the difference of 325 meters that separated Gabulusado and Bobole, (4) the difference of size between the communities, and (5) the lapse of ten years between the two studies. I have detected no basis from which to judge the first as a significant influence upon any differences between Kelly's and my accounts. The second factor was reflected, however, in some details of mythology, spirit-belief, and language that intrude occasionally in the present book. (Note, for example, that I use *Etolo* where Kelly used *Etoro,* and I use *segesado,* not *sigisato,* to name the forest spirits.) With regard to ecological concerns, differing alignments had little impact. Indeed, perhaps the needed caution is that differences of ecology should not be too readily rationalized in these terms. By contrast, groups of people who normally live at different altitudes may be expected to differ ecologically despite the facts that they speak one language and are culturally united (cf. Ernst's 1984 study of Onabasulu). Altitude had major effects upon the suitability and availability of plant and animal foods at Mt. Haliago and, sometimes, on the manner in which these could be exploited. Much that separated ecological practice at Bobole in 1979 from that at Gabulusado in 1968 is directly attributable to altitudinal effects. These differences, then, are not sources of embarrassment, and I have not always spelled out the details. Where I have described a situation at Bobole and failed to comment on, or footnote, Kelly's somewhat different reading, it is because I have accepted both as faithful reports. The fourth and fifth factors listed here are connected. The relatively large size of the community at Bobole was itself a result of recent change. Change, in all its guises, was an important component of the differences between Gabulusado and Bobole, but it is one that is always difficult to come to grips with. Indeed, missioniza-tion and contact with Europeans and their goods was under way somewhat earlier among eastern than western Etolo speakers. Because part of my argument concerns change, I must avoid prejudicial judgments that favor my case, and because manifesta-tions of change may be subtle, their recognition requires a high order of confidence in the observational and reporting skills of different observers. In this area, therefore, I have chosen to tread carefully, unwillingly to interpret hastily differences between the two accounts in terms of change but willing, I trust, to give history its due. After all, the people and societies of Papua New Guinea are enmeshed in change. One way in which I acknowledge that change is pervasive is by writing in the past tense: I have avoided the ethnographic present. The theoretical orientation of the present study requires a sharp focus upon events at Bobole during 1979–80. Only when the matter is important to either methodology or argument do I assess possible discrepancies between Kelly's work and mine in detail. Methodological concerns are taken up in chap. 8 and relevant ecological comparisons appear in chaps. 10 and 11.

5. Bateson 1979; Wilden 1972.

Chapter 2

1. The myth of "the place where the earthworm was eaten" was told in pidgin by Efala. The words *wafule molulu fi salia* are in the Onabasulu language and translate literally as "earthworm, eaten, in the beginning, stops." Animals and plants mentioned in the myth were given Etolo names; *dabaia* is the name for earthworms. In Efala's version of the myth, he specified both Onabasulu and eastern Etolo groups that had dispersed from the site of the feast.

2. The account of customary hunting practices was told by Efala and supplemented by some other men.

3. The account of the spirit world combines information I obtained with material from Kelly (1976, 1977). Kelly (1977:41) wrote that the *segesado* (*sigisato*) "are nonancestral but are associated with particular lineages through co-ownership of territory." They validated a person's ownership of land. Two notable differences between western and eastern Etolo cosmology are the lack of connection between pigs and forest spirits and the apparent lack of *segesebe* among the former. In these cosmological features eastern Etolo bear comparison with Kaluli (Schieffelin 1977).

4. The mythological-historical account of Waisado origins was told by Efala, who traced the wanderings of Amasulu and Mahia on the first topographical map he had seen. The torrent Hesau, mentioned in the myth, is located west of the Giwa River (fig. 1); it is the stream shown as Hesi by Kelly (1977:12). The myth reinforces connections between eastern Etolo and Onabasulu but, more important, weakens the connection between eastern and western Etolo by declaring their relationship to be one of fosterage rather than common descent.

5. Additional information about early Europeans on the Great Papuan Plateau and about the impact of Christianity on plateau peoples is available in Hides 1936 and Schieffelin 1977, 1981.

6. The "story of the game mammals" was told in Etolo by Efala and translated, with his guidance, via pidgin. Schieffelin (1980:516) briefly noted a similar Kaluli myth.

7. Some animals mentioned in this chapter by vernacular names only may be identified more precisely: cassowary (dwarf cassowary) = *Casuarius bennetti;* mountain pigeon (D'Albertis's mountain pigeon) = *Gymnophaps albertisii;* koel = *Eudynamis scolopacea;* hornbill (Papuan hornbill) = *Aceros plicatus;* Raggiana bird of paradise = *Paradisaea raggiana;* striped possum = *Dactylopsila palpator.*

8. At altitudes lower than Bobole, *marita* or fruit pandanus bear fruit from about October. At these altitudes there may be little ambiguity concerning the transition from cloud season to pandanus season. This would be consistent with Kelly's (1977) observations. The word *mugi*, reported by Kelly, is an alternative to *gene* to denote mist and cloud; at Bobole people strongly favored the latter word when referring to the cloud season.

Chapter 3

1. Watercress (*Nasturtium officinale*) was an important and popular vegetable at Bobole. It was grown in convenient places within gardens and was also managed separately in small plots, within or near creeks, that could be easily protected from pigs. Sometimes special arrangements were made to direct a flow of water across the growing plants.

2. App. 1 lists English and Etolo vernacular names, together with scientific names, of important plant cultigens used by Etolo.

3. Kelly (1977) gave a detailed account of gardening procedures at the Etolo community of Gabulusado. Schieffelin (1975) discussed the common Great Papuan Plateau practice of felling trees after the crop had been planted. Several features of my account reflect recent change in Etolo practice. Mounding of sweet potato was in imitation of Huli procedures and was encouraged by early government agricultural officers and Huli pastors. At Bobole, most mounded sweet potato was located within the village domain; it provided a rapidly maturing, handy source of food on occasions when people had been caught short. The careful management of felled trees within garden areas to provide firewood was probably a response to the amalgamation of several longhouse communities and their relative permanence at Bobole. Also, my observations indicate a great reduction in the use and growing of tobacco; ten years earlier tobacco had been important as a trade item. The species of bird that had colonized the vicinity of Bobole within the past decade were the willie wagtail (*Rhipidura leucophrys*) and the sacred kingfisher (*Halcyon sancta*). There were no Etolo names for these species.

4. A few comments are in order about nondomesticated plants that were eaten by people at Bobole. Various species of fungi were available and eaten throughout the year; for the most part these were treated as snacks and were cooked and eaten during the day away from the longhouse. The fronds of certain tree ferns were eaten, either when people cooked game mammals in the forest or, particularly, when pork was available. In the latter case the ferns were gathered from areas of regrowth. At high altitudes of Haliago the nuts of wild pandanus were available in quantity in some years; in 1979 an August expedition by two men and three youths revealed a poor crop and no one else made the arduous journey. Small quantities of cultivated pandanus nuts reached Bobole as gifts or by stealth from groves of pandanus that were maintained by Huli. But, apart from fungi, ferns, and pandanus nuts, the forest was seldom used as a source of plant foods. The hearts of palms were eaten if the palms had been felled for some other purpose and, rather rarely, leaves of sandpaper figs were used as a green. The fruits of many plants such as wild raspberry and species of fig and of *Syzygium* were declared to be edible but seldom collected. Acorns and wild yams were regarded as pig food and as unfit for people. Relative to their availability, potential plant foods of the forest were underexploited.

Chapter 4

1. Some comments are needed regarding the quantitative data summarized in this chapter. Between March and May, 1979, records were kept about age, cover, crops,

etc., at a few gardens where I was surveying populations of rats. In the first week of June, I commenced detailed recording at one, newly started, small garden. My aim was to learn how a garden was made. Early in July the extent of felling trees and fencing new garden sites increased greatly and, by August, I appreciated that complaints about a shortage of food were not, in fact, true. From this time I attempted to locate, regularly visit, and map all gardens made in a twelve-month period. In some cases it was necessary to estimate the times of fencing, felling, or planting from the condition of the garden when it was first visited. Forty-one gardens were prepared from May, 1979, to April, 1980; thirty-four of these, amounting to 20.2 hectares, were mapped with compass and tape. A combination of pacing and guessing accounts for an additional 0.6 hectares of sweet potato garden, 0.8 hectares of taro garden, and 0.45 hectares of yam garden. One large taro garden was estimated to be 1.15 hectares by running a tape through the middle, controlling the orientation of this by compass, and pacing or judging distances from the transect to the perimeter. Records for April-May, 1980, combine known information from the first two weeks of the four-week period with expectations of felling and planting in the second two weeks. With large gardens I usually knew who the participants were but often did not know either the details of sharing or the sequence in which participants took up their options on plots. In the latter cases I apportioned areas on the basis of family sizes and assumed all participants worked synchronously. The latter assumption will seldom be true and will affect analyses for 2.2 hectares. In general, the accuracy of records analyzed in this chapter will diminish, first, as the data are broken down from the village, through longhouses to families and, second, from House I, through Houses III and IV to House II.

2. In this and subsequent chapters data have been sorted into consecutive four-week periods with the first period starting March 25, 1979. Thus, all relevant figures show thirteen points distributed across twelve months.

3. Areas cultivated per year by Tsembaga Maring (Madang Province, Papua New Guinea) were estimated at 0.06 to 0.09 hectares per person (Rappaport 1968). The high value was during a period when much sweet potato was fed directly to a large population of domestic pigs. These values are less than half the average value recorded at Bobole, yet the Tsembaga Maring did not use sago as a source of carbohydrate. See also Waddell 1972. Kelly (1977:51) estimated that people at Gabulusado each used between 0.3 and 0.4 acres (0.12–0.16 hectares) as garden per year. Sweet potato gardens comprised 80 percent of the total. My estimates for Houses II and IV at Bobole are close to his.

4. The index to availability of sweet potato was calculated as follows: for an area A, planted in the interval one-to-four weeks, availability is 0.5A in the interval nineteen-to-twenty-two weeks; 1.0A in each of the three four-week intervals from twenty-three to thirty-four weeks; 0.75A in the interval thirty-five-to-thirty-eight weeks; and 0.5A in the interval thirty-nine-to-forty-two weeks. With 3.7 hectares I did not know whether planting had preceded or followed felling and attributed half the area to each category.

5. Presumably yield per hectare varied among garden sites at Bobole. My analyses assume this variation canceled out between longhouse communities. If short fallow

periods reduced yields, then House II was disadvantaged because 38 percent of the area used as sweet potato gardens by residents of this longhouse was cut from relatively young regrowth.

Chapter 5

1. Bride prices at Bobole in 1979 were different from those recorded by Kelly ten years earlier at Gabulusado. My records for never-married women are: (*a*) five pigs plus 140 kina, (*b*) seven pigs plus 150 kina, and (*c*) seven pigs, one ax, one bush knife plus 70 kina. (One kina was equivalent to approximately one Australian dollar.) In both b and c, the two largest pigs were killed and eaten on the day of the marriage (part of one pig was sold) and the five smaller pigs were transferred live into the care of those who "gave" the bride. In 1969 the standard price was one pig (killed and eaten at the marriage), four mother-of-pearl shell ornaments (each worth approximately one pig), and additional minor valuables. Kelly (1977:215–16) reported both inflation and change in composition of bride wealth through the decade or so before he lived at Gabulusado.

2. Kelly (1988) provided a detailed account of pig husbandry and of the social importance of pigs at Gabulusado in 1968–69. He compared his data with the situation I observed at Bobole and considered implications of Etolo practice for theoretical accounts of exchange that use data from the Papua New Guinea highlands. At Bobole the failure to castrate all male pigs, the extent to which pigs were confined by using old gardens as enclosures, and the provision of shelters where sows gave birth differed from the situation at Gabulusado. The first of these differences was a direct consequence of the scarcity of wild pigs at the altitude of Bobole. The second and third were connected to the concern people had that their domestic pigs might run wild, though, additionally, fertilization of oestrus sows may have been facilitated by placing a boar in the same enclosure. Incorporation of live pigs into bride wealth and the exchange of pigs for money were instances of change; the ambivalence associated with the latter transactions may well have been heightened by amalgamation of four longhouse communities as a single village. During the period I lived at Bobole no instance of affinal exchange of pork came to my attention.

3. The index of sago-processing activity based on families was calculated as follows: a score of 1.0 was given to each family, or working party thereof, that left Bobole to process sago for one week (five days); a score of 0.25 was added for any nonfamily person who went as an assistant during that time. Estimates of the number of person-days of work processing the palms include persons over the age of ten years. The quality of data about sago work improves to about August or September and should be consistent thereafter.

4. The estimate of 25 person-days of work to process one sago palm raises the specter of the taro garden that Awabi, of House IV, may or may not have had in the area he and his family visited to process palms (see chap. 4). The record of four palms processed in 152 person-days (averaging 38 person-days each) was from Awabi's family and was well outside records from eight other palms. Those records averaged 18.4 person-days of work per palm with a range from 15 to 27 person-days. It is

possible that Awabi's family spent some of their time on other activities. The fact that this record was for October hints that taro gardening might have been the other activity. If true, then I have underestimated the number of sago palms processed in one year; the figure is more likely to have approached 75.

5. Estimates of the relative contributions of tubers and sago starch to the diet may be expressed in terms of weight or calories. The value I have provided was obtained by first indexing minimal shortfall in the supply of sweet potato. From figure 8 (chap. 4), it was assumed that the maximal yield of sweet potato in any four-week period was the minimal value needed to satisfy carbohydrate requirements from sweet potato alone. (This value was provided by the yield data from House III.) Yield values lower than this represented shortfall; for the 109 people at Bobole these values summed to a minimal annual shortfall of 41 percent. This value assumes that supplementary starch foods are equivalent to sweet potato in caloric content. Taro and yams are similar to sweet potato but, per unit weight, the caloric content of sago starch is roughly 2.5 times that of the tubers; the difference results from the lower moisture content of sago. Taro and yam gardens comprised 15 percent of garden area at Bobole. Assuming a yield like that of sweet potato gardens, one sees that taro and yams would reduce the shortfall by 8.9 percent; i.e., $(100 - 41) \times 0.15 = 8.9$. Sago starch was available to fill out the remaining 32.1 percent expressed as calories or 12.8 percent expressed as weight. The quality of available information does not warrant more detailed analyses; thus, some sweet potato was fed to pigs, reliance upon taro and yams varied among longhouses, and a component of the effort committed to processing sago was to obtain starch for trade to Huli. More embarrassing is the fact that these estimates ignore fruit pandanus. This food is very rich in calories and, at Bobole, was eaten in quantity during months when sweet potato dominated sago in the diet. Thus, I may have underestimated the minimal value needed to satisfy carbohydrate requirements from sweet potato alone. Because the yield profile derived from the sweet potato gardens of House I (fig. 8; chap. 4) peaked at a time when pandanus was seldom eaten, and the peak value matched that from House III, the procedures I have used gain some support.

Chapter 6

1. Some species of bird listed by vernacular names can be identified more precisely: magnificent ground pigeon (pheasant pigeon) = *Otidiphaps nobilis;* wren warbler (black and white wren warbler) = *Malurus alboscapulatus;* peltops (mountain peltops flycatcher) = *Peltops montanus;* barefaced crow (gray crow) = *Gymnocorvus tristis* (see also n. 7, chap. 2). Throughout this book I have used "jungle fowl" in reference to three species of mound-building megapodes; i.e., scrub fowl *Megapodius freycinet;* brush turkey *Talegalla* sp.; and wattled brush turkey *Aepypodius arfakianus* (see Dwyer 1981).

2. App. 2 lists Etolo vernacular names, together with scientific names, of all mammals recorded from the Mt. Haliago area.

3. Detailed descriptions and illustrations of traps and snares used by Etolo, together with an Etolo classification of the equipment, are reported in Dwyer 1989.

4. Four-week capture tallies of all species of game mammal are tabulated in Dwyer 1982.

5. Statistical analyses of the seasonal switch in composition of the catch of game mammals are available in Dwyer 1982.

Chapter 7

1. Some of the quantitative data summarized in this chapter have appeared in greater detail in Dwyer 1982, 1983a, 1985a, and 1985b. The 1982 paper discussed temporal patterns of trapping and hunting. The 1983 paper analyzed hunting returns according to the age of hunters and in cost-benefit (energy) terms. Indeed, the account of hunting in this chapter glosses some awkward matters that were covered in detail in the earlier report; in particular, records of hunting returns were obtained in several different ways—from one-day and more-than-one-day hunts, and from occasions when I camped in the forest with the hunters and others when I was based at the village. Diagrammatic summaries that appear in this chapter collapse different categories of data in ways that are statistically unwarranted. The conclusions are not altered, but cautious readers are directed to the detailed analyses. Dwyer 1985a provided a list of small mammals captured by people at Bobole and some quantitative records of nonmammalian wildlife. The second 1985 paper analyzed differences in trapping and hunting performances of the four longhouse communities. One other qualification is needed. In earlier papers and in chap. 6, I used strict criteria to assign game mammals to the various categories of technique of capture. Thus, the category "casual encounter" combined animals that had been taken casually with others when, although they had been hunted, I was not told that the person responsible had gone hunting. Further, there was a category called "technique not known" that received animals about which I had been told few details. Circumstances connected with these returns allow me, retrospectively, to assert fairly confidently that the animals had in fact been trapped or hunted even though I was not told this was so. In this chapter I have taken the liberty of reassigning the relevant capture records. The following tabulation shows what I have done:

Technique	Number	Adjusted Number
Trapped by		
lines of deadfalls	501	573
single deadfalls	52	52
tree traps	95	95
snares	1	1
not specified	28	—
Hunted	653	790
Casual encounter	331	260
Stolen from dog	31	31
Technique not known	110	—

2. Kelly (1977:143) wrote that "of all resources to which the lineage lays claim, rights over game animals are the most jealously guarded. The corporate descent group maintains hunting and trapping rights over all the animal products of its territory." He commented that for nonagnatic residents of a community, "specific permission is still required in every instance for the hunting or trapping of wild pigs, cassowaries, marsupials, fish and eels, and the collection of woodgrubs." At Bobole only five of fifteen functioning traplines were located within the lineage territory of the male operator of that trapline; in one of these cases a co-operator did not share similar rights. In seven cases the operator of the trapline acquired rights through kin (as near as deceased husband, as distant as wife's sister's husband). In the remaining four cases rights to trap within specified areas had been granted to the operator of the trapline by nonkin. One man who no longer operated a trapline said that this was inconveniently located within his own lineage territory west of Bobole, though, in fact, he might have sought local access through his wife's father. This flexibility of access to faunal resources near Bobole was, presumably, influenced by the long-term association of formerly separate longhouse communities. Access to game mammals by persons lacking inherited rights or rights conferred by kinship had been sometimes exchanged for rights to sago palms at lower altitudes.

3. Five hundred and ninety-two game mammals were captured on hunts during an estimated 2,899.6 hours (Dwyer 1983a). Another 198 game mammals are known, or thought, to have been taken by hunting. I estimated the effort required to capture these latter animals by first assigning them to the relevant longhouse and four-week period and subsequently using average return rates (i.e., hours per mammal) from that longhouse. The additional period amounted to 1,007.3 hours to give an aggregate of 3,907 hours spent hunting.

4. Dwyer and Plowman (1981) reported that parasitic nematodes and cestodes from marsupials were eaten by Etolo. Flannery (1985) has recorded Mianmin of the Western Province eating cestodes; and Bulmer and Tyler (1968:345) noted that Kalam, Madang Province, ate leeches that had parasitized frogs; the people regarded the animals as delicacies. Some people of my acquaintance have reacted to these morsels of culinary news with abhorrence. It is worth saying that no harm can come of the practices, and since the parasites were probably gravid, they would have been more like caviar than anything else.

Chapter 8

1. Aspects of Etolo classificatory procedures are discussed in Dwyer 1980a, 1980b, 1983b, and 1984/85. See also Dwyer and Hyndman 1983 and app. 2.

2. The discussion of the capture of animals at Gabulusado is based on Kelly 1987, n.d., and additional information provided by Ray Kelly.

3. Etolo were proficient at, and enthusiastic about, counting. Indeed, counting was the first language skill we Europeans acquired; people counted all our possessions, especially the mammal traps. The base of the counting system was 17 with each number indicated by a particular body part, starting with the little finger, climbing the

arm, and ending at the nose. Numbers greater than 17 were denoted by saying, in effect, "the one (or the two, or the three . . .) belonging to the one lot of 17 that has gone" for 18, 19, 20, etc. Here, however, a different set of words marked the first five lots of 17; that is, Etolo used one set of terms (from one to five) to indicate objects or persons that were actually present and used a different set (from one to five) to indicate number in the abstract. Thus, to ask "how many people came yesterday?" would elicit, if the count was five or less, a term from the latter set, but to ask "how many people are standing here?" would elicit a term from the former set. Above five the two sets converged. "Some" or "a few" was denoted by modifying the term for three from the abstract set. In 1979 people were consciously, and simultaneously, adapting their base-17 system to the base-15 system of neighboring Huli and to the base-10 system of modern money. They were doing this not by adopting the Huli or pidgin terms for numbers but by modifying their own terms; they either deleted two body parts prior to arriving at the nose to conform with the Huli system or they stopped at the upper arm to adjust to the decimal system. (When Etolo did count in pidgin, they declined to use the suffix *pela* after *wan, tu, tri,* etc.) Many people could translate among these three different bases with far more ease than I ever accomplished. When engaged in trade with Huli and, early on, when negotiating with me, people discussed prospects among themselves by using various Etolo words in a metaphorical way to denote different denominations of money. Another set of terms was used to specify the number of days, up to four in either direction, from the present day. Direction (i.e., before or after today) was indicated by tense or context. Some ethnographers have stated that certain Papua New Guineans fail to distinguish yesterday from tomorrow; they have written that the people used the same word for both. It is probable that, like Etolo, the people were counting off days from the present and marking direction in other ways.

Chapter 9

1. Schieffelin (1977) and Feld (1982) have described the ceremonial life, and the connections between birds, song, belief, and people, in the life of Kaluli who lived south of Etolo on the Great Papuan Plateau.

2. Kelly (1977:41–45) discussed restrictions upon eating animals that obtained at Gabulusado in the late 1960s. These related to both the life phase of individuals and the activities they engaged in at particular times. I was not satisfied with the little that was said about past practices at Bobole. I did not understand whether people did not want to talk about the subject, had forgotten much detail, or failed to articulate a coherent account of what had been an ever-varying (with age, sex, status, and current activity) set of restrictions. It seemed likely also that people of different lineage affiliations spoke of restrictions that had applied to them or their parents, and that it was I who could not detect pattern within the variation. At Bobole, in 1979–80, people ate large black grasshoppers that lived among the fronds of sago palms, and they ate rats of the genus *Rattus* when these were captured in gardens. They said that these items had formerly been taboo to everyone. Rats from houses remained prohibited as food, but this was based on the recommendations of pastors. Some people said that

the lower-altitude tree kangaroo *Dendrolagus goodfellowi* also had been forbidden as food and asserted that if an animal had been killed by a dog or trapped accidentally, then it was buried or placed high in a tree. Other people said this species was eaten in the past.

3. A widespread, customary practice across the Great Papuan Plateau was the preservation of meat by smoke drying (Kelly 1977, Schieffelin 1977). The carcasses of game mammals were treated in this way when they were needed in numbers for intercommunity prestations. In 1979–80 smoke drying of meat did not occur at Bobole. When game mammals were held for later eating, they were intensely singed over a fire and placed on a rack in the forest. Animals used in prestations beyond Bobole were also singed. Carcasses that had been treated in this way were never stored for more than a week.

4. Kelly 1977:42, 62, concerning connections between sharing pork, cassowaries, and forest spirits. The elaborate network of giving that followed one hunt on Haliago, and the motives underlying that hunt, are analyzed in Dwyer 1985*c*.

5. Estimation of protein content of an animal from the weight of its carcass or, worse, from dimensions of its skull is fraught with difficulty. The procedures I used are presented in Dwyer 1980*c*, 1983*a*, and 1985*a* and Dwyer and Reichelt n.d. Dwyer 1985*a* contains details of the contribution pigs and nondomesticated animals made to protein in the diet of people at Bobole, Namosado, and, using Kelly's (1977:34) data, Gabulusado. Kelly stressed that his data were not suited to quantifying dietary intake. Nevertheless, his estimate of 550 pounds live weight of pork from domestic pigs eaten by 25.5 people in one year is roughly equivalent to 2.5 grams of protein per person per day. This is comparable with the estimate from Bobole. (Protein content of pork is approximately 13 grams per 100 grams of edible weight and, with pigs, edible weight is approximately 65 percent of live weight. See Dwyer 1983*a* for further details.) I did not weigh any pigs. Etolo used several terms to indicate size; they accompanied these with gestures that implied bulk. The usual sequence of terms from large to small was *etefate, honobo etefate, honobo,* and *nefani. Honobo* could be replaced by *honobo nefani.* To me, as listener, there was often ambiguity in the middle range. Piglets were never *nefani,* they were *mano,* "child." I was guided by Etolo judgments of size in assigning weights to pigs that were killed. I added a "very large" category to receive one wild boar and one four-year renegade and have guessed median weights as follows: very large, 80 kg; large, 65 kg; medium-large, 50 kg; medium, 35 kg; small, 20 kg; piglet, 5 kg. With one exception I apportioned weights among residents of Bobole and visitors in proportion to their numbers; the exception was when a few Huli received about one-quarter of a renegade pig.

6. Kelly (personal communication) observed leg injuries that resulted from arrows shot by men who had been denied compensation when they angrily confronted an accused witch and his kin.

Chapter 10

1. A detailed analysis of the influences of choice and constraint upon subsistence options at Bobole is available in Dwyer 1985*b*.

2. The account of subsistence activities at Namosado, especially of gardening and sago-processing regimes, should be regarded with caution. In large part, it is impressionistic. My visits were few; a week each in May, 1979; September, 1979; and March, 1980. During the last two visits I noted the current phase of gardening and sago work and made inferences about past activity, but I did not obtain quantitative data. Information about the use of nondomesticated animals is of better quality, and details are available in Dwyer 1985*a*. The account of the building program at Namosado is based on my observations supplemented by much enthusiastic gossip.

3. One other project was undertaken near Namosado early in 1980. It was initiated by people from Bobole, and the work was done during 2.5 long working days by twenty-two men and youths from Bobole and Namosado. People at Bobole asserted that Etolo territory lay at the center of a great triangle, the vertices of which were the airstrips at Mogulu (Bedamini territory), Bosavi (Kaluli territory), and Komo (Huli territory). They felt disadvantaged relative to their neighbors and were rankled by rumors of a second airstrip planned at the Bosavi area. They wanted to forestall the plan and sought advice from the government and the mission. The former seemed uncooperative. The latter agreed to inspect any site recommended by the people. They would do so from the air but needed to see the site in its entirety . . . cleared! My 30–meter tape was recalibrated to the base-17 counting system used by Etolo; the airstrip within Huli territory was measured; and late in February, 1980, nearly 2 hectares of forest located a few kilometers west of Namosado were felled. The long sweep of fallen trees was dotted with untouched clumps of sago palms. For their efforts the workers were rewarded with one cuscus (*Phalanger orientalis*), one bandicoot (*Peroryctes raffrayanus*), one tree rat (*Uromys caudimaculatus*), and a few pygmy possums (*Distoechurus pennatus*). From the air the mission pilot wisely assessed the sloping, swampy clearing as too hazardous. Had it been otherwise, there were major plans afoot. The people of Bobole contemplated moving to the vicinity of their own airstrip. They reasoned that with this as focus and with increasing population, the government might cease to argue that they were too few and too dispersed to warrant either a school or a medical orderly. (In 1985 the population of Bobole still numbered about 100 people; K. Aplin, personal communication.)

4. Kelly 1977:32–64.

5. Scheduling patterns recorded by Kelly at Gabulusado in 1968–69 appeared less tightly synchronized than at Namosado and Bobole in 1979. Kelly reported that some families operated gardens on an eight-month cycle where most conformed to a twelve-month cycle. He wrote: "The articulation of these two cycles makes it possible for individual families to easily move from one to another, switching over from eight-month to twelve-month planting intervals when the two cycles converge in October and thus participating in large communal gardens" (1977:48). The move to a new longhouse could have provided a stimulus for such community-wide convergence.

6. Kelly 1977:52.

7. Kelly 1977:47.

8. Three species of jungle fowl in the Mt. Karimui area are the same as those found at Mt. Haliago. Hide (1984:360–61) provided data on availability of eggs from November, 1980, to December, 1982. Most eggs were collected through the months

September to March, though at least *Talegalla* provided some eggs in the intervening months. Differences in availability of eggs were evident between years.

9. A reconstructed account of the lengthy initiation rituals among Kaluli, Onabasulu, and Etolo of the Great Papuan Plateau is provided by Schieffelin 1982.

Chapter 11

1. Some data about the ecology of small rats at Mt. Haliago are available in Dwyer 1984.

2. Williams 1976.

3. Weiner 1988 (the quotations are from page 39).

4. Hide, Pernetta, and Senabe 1984.

5. In the West Sepik Province many smaller streams dry out during drier months of the year. These streams are often the places where sago palms grow, and, consequently, it is not easy to process palms during the dry season. Gell (1975:164) wrote of Umeda people as follows: "With the onset of the wet season, an intensive period of sago working begins. At this time all the little creeks and streams in the bush become full of water, facilitating the processing of stands of sago in areas which, at other times, are too waterless to make this possible." In most years, rainfall patterns at Haliago would not impose constraints of this sort.

6. The comparative discussion of the merits of sago flour and sweet potato concerns only their relative value as sources of calories; it has nothing to say of nutrient contents. The former food is nutrient poor with little by way of protein or vitamins; sweet potato is richer in these nutrients. Recognition of this fact raises a related matter. Studies at various localities through Papua New Guinea indicate that caloric yields per unit of effort are notably higher with sago-processing ventures than with gardening. But this need not mean that where choice is possible, processing sago should be the preferred strategy. The cost of reliance upon sago is that essential nutrients must be obtained from other foods that may be located at other places. An extensive strategy may be imposed. An advantage of using sweet potato as a staple is that the gardens where it is grown may be used simultaneously to produce numerous crops that are rich in vitamins, minerals, and even protein. An intensive strategy may be possible. That people at Bobole were adamant that they preferred sweet potato over sago starch may have been underlain by other considerations. In particular, the balance of nutrients obtained from gardens may have been more favorable, and thus more satisfying, than that received when sago flour was the primary carbohydrate food. It is possible, too, that the assertion contained a forward glance to the time when pandanus would be abundant.

7. Townsend 1974.

8. Kelly 1977:63.

Chapter 12

1. Eliade 1959:25.

2. Eliade 1959:25.

3. Bateson (1979) and Wilden (1972) have been major influences in the development of my understanding of processes of communication and change in open systems.

4. The impossibility of living at a place where there are no boundaries is described by Douglas (1972); the experience of trying to do so is vividly portrayed in Colin Turnbull's *The Mountain People* and Doris Lessing's novel *The Memoirs of a Survivor*.

5. Turner (1974) analyzed many "rituals of reversal" in which the arbitrariness of existence was validated through theater. The *naven* ceremony of the Iatmul people of the East Sepik Province, Papua New Guinea, may be understood in similar ways (Bateson 1936). In a somewhat different context, Harrison (1985:413) showed that "ritual does not 'reflect' social reality but temporarily alters it" among Manambu, East Sepik Province.

6. I have discussed responses to Sugua Mai in terms of planting sweet potato and not in terms of fence building or tree felling. This is because it is only planting that will create more tubers and because some fence making and tree felling before July was associated with taro gardens.

7. That Sugua Mai was initiated as fiction may be of theoretical moment. "The paradigm of the paradoxical injunction is the Cretan paradox 'I am lying' . . ." (Wilden 1972:122). A lie generates ambiguity, which is the condition of boundaries that, themselves, are necessary if communication is to happen.

8. For earlier and more recent discussion of the role of pigs in highland politics, see Glasse and Meggitt 1969 and Strathern 1982 and references therein. Kelly (1988) provided a detailed account of the significance of pigs to Etolo. See Morren 1977 for an ecological perspective on these matters.

9. Kelly (1977:137–44) discussed ways in which residence, inheritance, and generosity influenced access to sago palms, garden land, and hunting areas at Gabulusado.

10. Kelly (1988:123) did not detect any connection between pigs and forest spirits among western Etolo speakers. He wrote that witches, but not *segesado*, were symbolically equated with pigs and that in this sense pigs had a rather negative value. My opinion that the cosmological status of pigs among residents of Bobole was, at least, ambiguous is based upon statements that implied *segesado* could appear as pigs and, particularly, on one story that seemed to concern the behavior of *segesebe*. The story was told by Efala, who had heard it directly from an old man, Dugai, who lived at Namosado in 1979. Dugai recalled a terrible night of thunder when he had been young. "Everyone in the longhouse had awakened. They were frightened by the noise of the storm. A gigantic eel had fallen from the sky and crashed through the roof. A huge man appeared at the doorway. People ran outside, but the longhouse was surrounded by huge men who advanced upon them. The people got their bows and arrows and shot at the intruders. Everything was confused in the darkness. There were lightning and thunder. The people killed some of the huge men, and when the others fled, the people returned to the house and slept. In the morning they found the ground strewn with dead pigs and cassowaries. Each dead animal had an arrow projecting from it. There were banana trees growing near the longhouse that also had arrows in them. Seeing these things, the people understood that the huge men that had come during the

storm were not real men. They were *segesado,* perhaps *segesebe,* and in death they had changed to pigs, cassowaries, and banana trees. It had been a night of fear, but the people had been strong; they had killed and dispersed the angry spirits." This story has very strong parallels among Onabasulu and Kaluli to the south of Bobole; the traditional abode of *segesebe* was southwest of Namosado on the boundary of Onabasulu territory.

11. App. 3 provides a brief diary of events connected with Sugua Mai.

12. The divisive potential of angry dispute at Bobole was detailed in one case study in Dwyer 1985c.

13. Gell 1975. The *Ida* ritual is depicted in the film *The Red Bowmen.*

14. Gell 1975:168.

15. Rappaport 1968.

16. Barth (1975) described ways in which the initiation rituals of Baktaman, Western Province, Papua New Guinea, may alter through time. His description influenced my general comments about the process of change.

17. Efala was inaugurated as the first Etolo-born pastor in 1979. By 1985 three Bobole men, one based at Bobole and two outside Etolo territory, were pastors (K. Aplin, personal communication).

18. Knauft 1985:323.

19. Knauft 1985:324.

20. Schieffelin 1977; see also Feld 1982.

21. Schieffelin 1977:114.

22. Ray Kelly did not observe a strong connection between weddings or affinal exchange and the performance of *gosa* or between the performance and the killing of pigs (Kelly 1988). One of six *gosa* recorded by Kelly took place in association with a wedding and at this ceremony the one pig included in the bride price was killed and eaten. No pigs were killed and no pork was distributed at other *gosa* performances. At the *gosa* performance held at Gabulusado sago flour was the main food eaten even though, at that time, in July, sweet potato production was high. When people discussed preparations for the ceremony they focused on the need to accumulate sago starch to feed guests. Although no *gosa* took place at Bobole during the period I lived there, it is possible that a performance was staged at Namosado. Two Namosado men, one in his forties, the other in his fifties, attended the first Sugua Mai feast at Bobole with raw, weeping wounds across the shoulders. The wounds were consistent with burns. The older of these men had contributed one pig to the feast. Young men from Namosado, but not from Bobole, sometimes participated as costumed dancers and singers at cross-cultural public performances sponsored within the territory of Huli. Participation by Etolo dancers as part of rituals of fertility held by Huli was a traditional practice (Goldman 1983).

23. Schieffelin 1985:713.

24. Knauft 1985:326.

25. An excellent example of a new form of ritual expression, constructed from old elements, is the women's savings and exchange system, *wok meri,* of the Eastern Highlands Province, Papua New Guinea (Sexton 1982).

Bibliography

Archer, M., ed. 1987. *Possums and Opossums: Studies in Evolution*. Sydney: Surrey Beatty and Sons and the Royal Zoological Society of New South Wales.

Barth, F. 1975. *Ritual and Knowledge among the Baktaman of New Guinea*. New Haven: Yale University Press.

Bateson, G. 1936. *Naven*. London: Cambridge University Press.

———. 1979. *Mind and Nature: A Necessary Unity*. New York: E. P. Dutton.

Beek, A. G. van. 1987. The way of all flesh: hunting and ideology of the Bedamuni of the Great Papuan Plateau (Papua New Guinea). Ph.D. diss., University of Leiden.

Bulmer, R. N. H., and M. J. Tyler. 1968. Karam classification of frogs. *Journal of the Polynesian Society* 77:333–85.

Douglas, M. 1972. Environments at risk. In *Ecology, the Shaping Enquiry*, ed. J. Benthall, 129–45. London: Longman.

Dennis, E., and J. I. Menzies. 1979. A chromosomal and morphometric study of Papuan tree rats, *Pogonomys* and *Chiruromys* (Rodentia, Muridae). *Journal of Zoology* 189:315–32.

Dwyer, P. D. 1980a. *Habomi ae etolo:* a footnote to monotreme taxonomy. *Mankind* 12:348–50.

———. 1980b. The ignorant silvereye: names is power, is problems. *Occasional Papers in Anthropology*, no. 10, 221–28; Anthropology Museum, University of Queensland.

———. 1980c. Edible-waste ratios for some New Guinea mammals. *Science in New Guinea* 7 (3):109–16.

———. 1981. Two species of megapode laying in the one mound. *The Emu* 81:173–74.

———. 1982. Prey switching: a case study from New Guinea. *Journal of Animal Ecology* 51:529–42.

———. 1983a. Etolo hunting performance and energetics. *Human Ecology* 11:143–72.

———. 1983b. Naming mammals in Papua New Guinea: a plea for inconsistency. *Science in New Guinea* 10:78–88.

———. 1984. From garden to forest: small rodents and plant succession in Papua New Guinea. *Australian Mammalogy* 7:29–36.

———. 1984/85. Other people's animals: two examples from New Guinea. *Search* 15:321–27.

———. 1985a. The contribution of non-domesticated animals to the diet of Etolo,

Southern Highlands Province, Papua New Guinea. *Ecology of Food and Nutrition* 17:101–15.

———. 1985*b*. Choice and constraint in a Papua New Guinean food quest. *Human Ecology* 13:49–70.

———. 1985*c*. A hunt in New Guinea: some difficulties for optimal foraging theory. *Man*, n.s., 20:243–53.

———. 1989. Etolo traps: techniques and classification. *Memoirs of the Queensland Museum* 27:275–87.

Dwyer, P. D., and D. C. Hyndman. 1983. "Frog" and "Lizard": additional life-forms from Papua New Guinea. *American Anthropologist* 85:890–96.

Dwyer, P. D., and K. P. Plowman. 1981. Edible internal parasites from Papua New Guinea. *Search* 12:409.

Dwyer, P. D., and R. E. Reichelt. N.d. Estimating the weight of some New Guinea mammals. Manuscript.

Eliade, M. 1959. *The Sacred and the Profane: the Nature of Religion*. New York: Harcourt, Brace and World.

Ernst, T. M. 1978. Aspects of meaning and exchange of items among the Onabasulu of the Great Papuan Plateau. *Mankind* 11:187–97.

———. 1984. Onabasulu Local Organization. Ph.D. diss., University of Michigan.

Feld, S. 1982. *Sound and Sentiment: Birds, Weeping, Poetics, and Song in Kaluli Expression*. Philadelphia: University of Pennsylvania Press.

Flannery, T. F. 1985. Losing our way. *Australian Natural History* 21:430–31.

———. 1988. *Pogonomys championi* n.sp., a new murid (Rodentia) from montane western Papua New Guinea. *Records of the Australian Museum* 40:331–41.

———. 1990. *The Mammals of New Guinea*. Australia: E. J. Brill.

Flannery, T. F., K. Aplin, C. P. Groves, and M. Adams. 1989. Revision of the New Guinean genus *Mallomys* (Muridae:Rodentia), with descriptions of two new species from subalpine habitats. *Records of the Australian Museum* 41:83–105.

Gell, A. 1975. *Metamorphosis of the Cassowaries: Umeda Society, Language and Ritual*. London School of Economics, Monographs on Social Anthropology, No. 51. University of London: Athlone Press.

George, G. G. 1979. The status of endangered Papua New Guinea mammals. In *The Status of Endangered Australian Wildlife*, ed. M. J. Tyler, 93–100. Proceedings of the Centenary Symposium, Royal Society of South Australia, Adelaide.

Glasse, R. M., and M. J. Meggitt, eds. 1969. *Pigs, Pearlshells and Women*. Englewood Cliffs: Prentice Hall.

Goldman, L. 1983. *Talk Never Dies: The Language of Huli Disputes*. London: Tavistock Publications.

Harrison, S. J. 1985. Ritual hierarchy and secular equality in a Sepik River village. *American Ethnologist* 12:413–26.

Hide, R. L., Pernetta, J. C., and T. Senabe. 1984. Exploitation of wild animals. In *South Simbu: Studies in Demography, Nutrition, and Subsistence*, ed. R. L. Hide, Simbu Land Use Project. VI:291–379. Boroko: Institute of Applied Social and Economic Research.

Hides, J. 1936. *Papuan Wonderland*. London: Blackie and Son Ltd.

Kelly, R. C. 1976. Witchcraft and sexual relations: an exploration in the social and semantic implications of the structure of belief. In *Man and Woman in the New Guinea Highlands*, eds. P. Brown and G. Buchbinder, 36–53. Special Publication No. 8, American Anthropological Association.

———. 1977. *Etoro Social Structure: A Study in Structural Contradiction*. Ann Arbor: University of Michigan Press.

———. 1988. Etoro suidology: a reassessment of the pig's role in the prehistory and comparative ethnology of New Guinea. In *Mountain Papuans: Historical and Comparative Perspectives from New Guinea Fringe Highlands Societies*, ed. J. F. Weiner, 111–86. Ann Arbor: University of Michigan Press.

———. N.d. The Social Relations of Etoro Food Production, Distribution and Consumption in Comparative Perspective. Manuscript.

Kirsh, J. A. W., and J. H. Calaby. 1977. The species of living marsupials: an annotated list. In *The Biology of Marsupials*, eds. B. Stonehouse and D. Gilmour, 9–26. Baltimore: University Park Press.

Knauft, B. M. 1985. Ritual form and permutation in New Guinea: implications of symbolic process for socio-political evolution. *American Ethnologist* 12:321–40.

Lessing, D. 1976. *The Memoirs of a Survivor*. London: Picador.

Menzies, J. I., and J. C. Pernetta. 1986. A taxonomic revision of cuscuses allied to *Phalanger orientalis* (Marsupialia: Phalangeridae). *Journal of Zoology*, London (B) 1:551–618.

Morren, G. E. B. 1977. From hunting to herding: pigs and the control of energy in montane New Guinea. In *Subsistence and Survival: Rural Ecology in the Pacific*, eds. T. P. Bayliss-Smith and R. G. Feachem, 273–315. London: Academic Press.

Rappaport, R. A. 1968. *Pigs for the Ancestors: Ritual in the Ecology of a New Guinea People*. New Haven: Yale University Press.

Schieffelin, E. L. 1975. Felling the trees on top of the crop: European contact and the subsistence ecology of the Great Papuan Plateau. *Oceania* 46:25–39.

———. 1977. *The Sorrow of the Lonely and the Burning of the Dancers*. St. Lucia: University of Queensland Press.

———. 1980. Reciprocity and the construction of reality on the Papuan Plateau. *Man*, n.s., 15:150–56.

———. 1981. Evangelical rhetoric and the transformation of traditional culture in Papua New Guinea. *Comparative Studies in Society and History* 23:150–56.

———. 1982. The *Bau a* ceremonial hunting lodge: an alternative to initiation. In *Rituals of Manhood: Male Initiation in Papua New Guinea*, ed. G. H. Herdt, 155–200. Berkeley: University of California Press.

———. 1985. Performance and the cultural construction of reality. *American Ethnologist* 12:707–24.

Sexton, L. D. 1982. *Wok meri:* A women's savings and exchange system in highland Papua New Guinea. *Oceania* 52:167–98.

Sørum, A. 1980. In search of the lost soul: Bedamini spirit seances and curing rites. *Oceania* 50:273–96.

Strathern, A. J., ed. 1982. *Inequality in New Guinea Highland Societies*. Cambridge: Cambridge University Press.

Taylor, J. M., Calaby, J. H., and H. M. van Deusen. 1982. A revision of the genus *Rattus* (Rodentia, Muridae) in the New Guinea region. *Bulletin of the American Museum of Natural History* 173:177–336.

Townsend, P. K. 1974. Sago production in a New Guinea economy. *Human Ecology* 2:217–36.

Turnbull, C. M. 1974. *The Mountain People.* London: Picador.

Turner, V. W. 1974. *The Ritual Process.* Gretna, La: Pelican Books.

Waddell, E. 1972. *The Mound Builders: Agricultural Practices, Environment and Society in the Central Highlands of New Guinea.* Seattle: University of Washington Press.

Weiner, J. F. 1988. *The Heart of the Pearlshell: The Mythological Dimension of Foi Sociality.* Berkeley: University of California Press.

Wilden, A. 1972. *System and Structure: Essays in Communication and Exchange.* London: Tavistock Publications.

Williams, F. E. 1976. Natives of Lake Kutubu, Papua, Part I. In *F. E. Williams: The Vailala Madness and other Essays,* ed. E. Schwimmer, 161–203. St. Lucia: University of Queensland Press.

Ziegler, A. C. 1982. An ecological check list of New Guinea recent mammals. In *Biogeography and Ecology in New Guinea,* ed. J. L. Gressitt, Monographiae Biologicae 42:863–93. The Hague: Junk Publishers.

Index

Adams, M., 205
Airstrip, construction of, 228 n.3
Animal foods: altitudinal availability of, 113; as exchange items, 127–28; preferred types of, 122–23. *See also* Animals; Birds; Fish; Frogs; History; Invertebrate animals as food; Mammals; Pigs; Protein; Reptiles
Animals, variety of, 70–71. *See also* Animal foods
Aplin, K., 205, 209, 210, 211, 228 n.4, 231 n.17
Archer, M., 205

Baktaman people, 231 n.16
Barth, F., 231 n.16
Bateson, G., 9, 219 n.5, 230 n.3
Bats, captures of, 100, 152, 162. *See also* Animals
Bedamini people, 2, 68, 217 n.4, 228 n.3
Beek, A. G. van, 217 n.4
Birds: capture of, 100; ritual connections of, 195; species mentioned, 19 n.7, 220 n.3, 223 n.1; variety of, 70. *See also* Animals; Cassowaries; Ethnoclassification; Jungle fowl; Spirits
Bridewealth, 56, 183, 194, 195, 222 n.1
Bulmer, R. N. H., 225 n.4

Calaby, J. H., 205
Calendar, 165–69
Cassowaries, 133, 189; capture of, 99–100, 143, 154, 163, 167; spirit connections of, 15, 20, 127
Christianity, 231 n.17; Genesis myth, 171–72; Huli pastors, 130, 176, 181–

82, 196; influence of, 18–20, 21, 116; syncretism, 20–21, 196. *See also* History
Climate, 22–24. *See also* Seasons
Counting system, 225–26 n.3, 228 n.3
Crops: list of cultigens, 203–4; management of watercress, 220 n.1; planting locations of, 28, 29, 35–36; variety of, 34–36. *See also* Gardening; Gardens

Demography, 5–6, 217 n.3. *See also* Division of labor
Dennis, E., 205, 210
Division of labor: complementary roles in, 142–43; demographic influence on, 149–50
Dogs: hunting with, 75, 79, 92, 93, 96, 135; killing piglets by, 55–56; mammals stolen from, 73, 76, 124; prohibition on eating of, 122. *See also* Wild dogs
Douglas, M., 230 n.4
Duguba people, 2
Dwyer. P. D., 205, 206, 209, 223 nn.1, 3, 224 nn. 4, 5, 224 n.1, 225 nn. 3, 4, 225 n.1, 227 n.5, 227 n.1, 229 n.1, 232 n.12

Echidnas, 109; captures of, 79, 81–82
Eliade, M., 172, 229 nn.1, 2
Ernst, T. M., 217–18 n.4
Ethnoclassification, 121–22; Etolo names of cultigens, 203– 4; Etolo names of mammals, 205–11. *See also* Mammals

In **The Pigs That Ate the Garden,**
Peter D. Dwyer examines the subsistence ecology of 109 Etolo people who
live on the wet, forested mountain
slopes of Papua New Guinea. Dwyer
describes the community's practice of
deliberately placing pigs in gardens so
that the pigs depredate the vegetation
there. He shows how this practice is
actually the community's method of
sending a message to itself that serves
to resynchronize a switch from sweet
potato gardening to sago starch processing. The interrelationships of the
different food-producing activities of the
Etolo — gardening, hunting, tree-crop
cultivation, etc. — are shown to have
seasonal rhythms, and these rhythms
maximize the Etolo's use of food resources at appropriate times and areas.
Dwyer argues that the "shape" of Etolo
ecology is ultimately driven by socio-
cultural, rather than environmental,
forces, and is set within a theoretical
frame concerning processes of communication and change in open systems.

Peter D. Dwyer is Professor of Zoology
at the University of Queensland.